SAS South Georgia Boating Club

SAS South Georgia Boating Club

An SAS Trooper's Memoir and Falklands War Diary

With a foreword by Mark Palios,
Chairman Tranmere Rovers Football Club

TRANMERE ROVERS
FOOTBALL CLUB

Tony Shaw

Pen & Sword
MILITARY

First published in Great Britain in 2022 by
Pen & Sword Military
An imprint of
Pen & Sword Books Ltd
Yorkshire – Philadelphia

ISBN 978 1 39908 776 6

A CIP catalogue record for this book is
available from the British Library.

Typeset by Mac Style
Printed and bound in the UK by CPI Group (UK) Ltd,
Croydon, CR0 4YY.

Pen & Sword Books Limited incorporates the imprints of Atlas,
Archaeology, Aviation, Discovery, Family History, Fiction, History,
Maritime, Military, Military Classics, Politics, Select, Transport,
True Crime, Air World, Frontline Publishing, Leo Cooper, Remember
When, Seaforth Publishing, The Praetorian Press, Wharncliffe
Local History, Wharncliffe Transport, Wharncliffe True Crime
and White Owl.

For a complete list of Pen & Sword titles please contact

PEN & SWORD BOOKS LIMITED
47 Church Street, Barnsley, South Yorkshire, S70 2AS, England
E-mail: enquiries@pen-and-sword.co.uk
Website: www.pen-and-sword.co.uk

Or

PEN AND SWORD BOOKS
1950 Lawrence Rd, Havertown, PA 19083, USA
E-mail: Uspen-and-sword@casematepublishers.com
Website: www.penandswordbooks.com

Contents

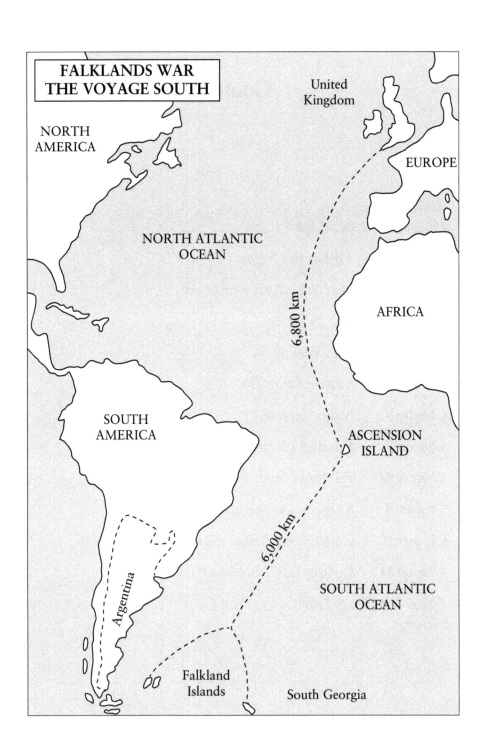

**FALKLANDS WAR
THE VOYAGE SOUTH**

NORTH
AMERICA

United
Kingdom

EUROPE

NORTH ATLANTIC
OCEAN

6,800 km

AFRICA

SOUTH
AMERICA

ASCENSION
ISLAND

6,000 km

Argentina

SOUTH ATLANTIC
OCEAN

Falkland
Islands

South Georgia

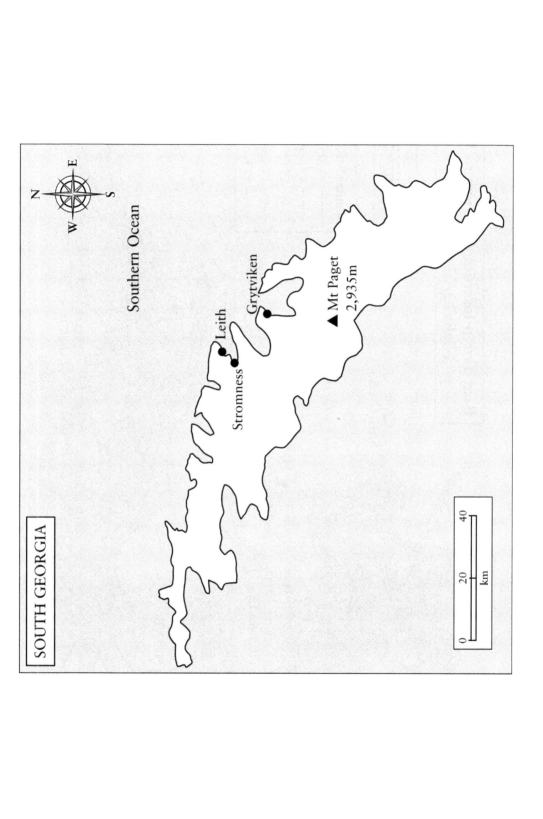

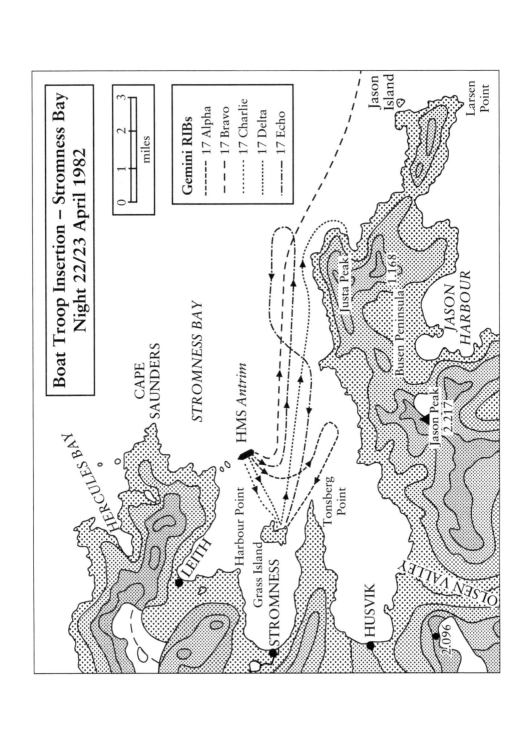

**Boat Troop Insertion – Stromness Bay
Night 22/23 April 1982**

Gemini RIBs

—·—·— 17 Alpha
— — — 17 Bravo
·········· 17 Charlie
············ 17 Delta
——— 17 Echo

0   1   2   3
miles

HERCULES BAY

CAPE SAUNDERS

STROMNESS BAY

HMS *Antrim*

LEITH

Harbour Point

Grass Island

STROMNESS

Tonsberg Point

HUSVIK

OLSEN VALLEY

2,096

Jason Peak 2,217

JASON HARBOUR

Busen Peninsula 1,168

Justa Peak

Jason Island

Larsen Point

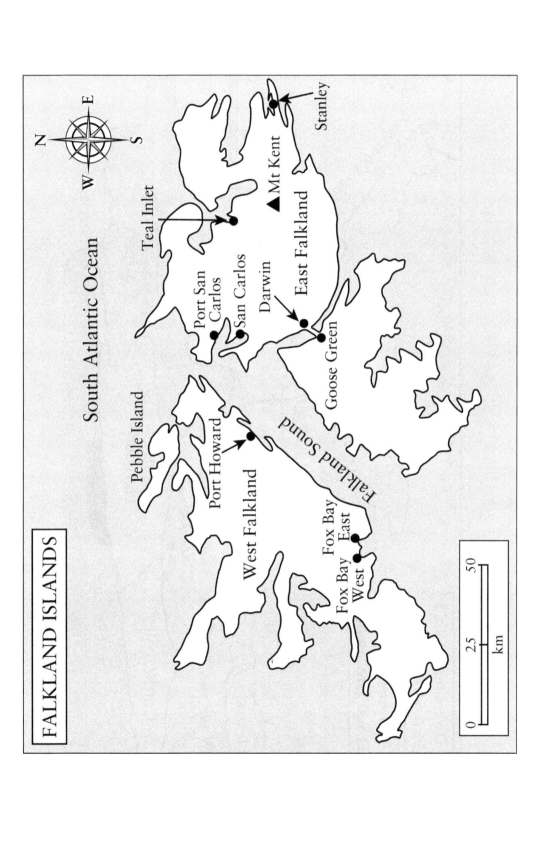

FALKLAND ISLANDS

South Atlantic Ocean

N E S W

Teal Inlet

Port San Carlos

San Carlos

Darwin

East Falkland

Mt Kent

Goose Green

Stanley

Pebble Island

Port Howard

West Falkland

Fox Bay East

Fox Bay West

Falkland Sound

0   25   50

km

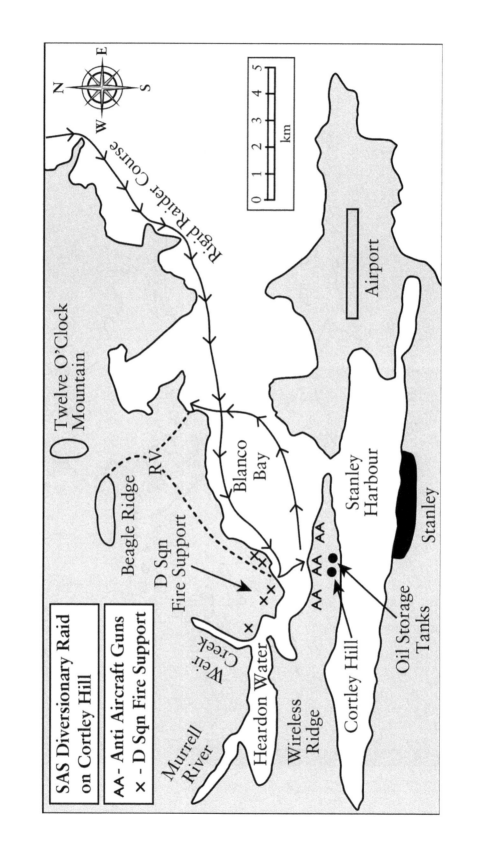

SAS Diversionary Raid on Cortley Hill

AA - Anti Aircraft Guns
x - D Sqn Fire Support

Twelve O'Clock Mountain

Rigid Raider Course

Beagle Ridge

RV

D Sqn Fire Support

Blanco Bay

Murrell River

Weir Creek

Heardon Water

Wireless Ridge

AA AA AA

Cortley Hill

Oil Storage Tanks

Stanley Harbour

Stanley

Airport

km
0 1 2 3 4 5

N W E S

Foreword

When Tony asked me to write the foreword to his book, I was surprised and flattered in equal measure. Tony is a Tranmere Rovers fan who, like me, is an old boy of St Anselm's College. Again like me, he'd started out in post-war Birkenhead and led an interesting life that eventually brought him home to Birkenhead. We both started out in that rugby-playing school, and while it led to the playing fields and football pitches across the country for me, it led to the battlefield that was the Falkland Islands for Tony, as well as a more than full career after completing his army service. Like me he took up cross-country running at school, something which St Anselm's were and are very good at. Starting life in the tough background that was post-war Merseyside, coupled with an endurance sport, undoubtedly provided Tony with the mental and physical resilience underpinning his military career which included making the grade as a trooper in the world-renowned Special Air Service Regiment of the British Army.

This book, without sensationalizing, portrays a man who served his country in some of the most demanding situations you can experience and which, thankfully, most of us will never experience. Following his career in the British Army and Special Forces, Tony carved out a career providing specialist security services in some of the hotspots across the globe. While Tony left St Anselm's at 15 years old, he later in life continued with his education, picking up various academic and vocational qualifications as diverse as telecommunications, business management, quality assurance and close protection. Throughout, Tony carried with him the impossible love of his local professional football club, Tranmere Rovers.

I enjoyed reading Tony's book and would recommend *SAS South Georgia Boating Club* to anyone who's interested in understanding what it takes to pass selection for the SAS while staying sane supporting a club which doesn't play in the rarefied atmosphere of the English Premier League. Or simply anyone who just wants to be inspired by an ordinary guy from an ordinary background who has led an extraordinary life.

Mark Palios
Chairman Tranmere Rovers Football Club

Acknowledgements

I wish to offer my grateful thanks to all those who have encouraged and supported me in my endeavours. There are too many to name, but the following deserve a special mention: My family, including sister Barbara and brothers Tom and Mike. Also, my children, Tracey-Anne, Elizabeth, Anthony and Pauline. My brothers-in-arms from the SAS, especially those former members of 17 (Boat) Troop, D Squadron, 22 SAS. Much of my story is also your story and I thank you all for your lifelong support and friendship. Likewise, my friends from 264 (SAS) Signal Squadron and all the other Royal Signals units that I have served with in a career spanning over thirty years. A particular debt of gratitude goes to those who have contributed photos to enhance the book and to 'Don' for suggesting the book title and allowing me to adapt his sketch map of Stromness Bay. The names of my former SAS comrades have been changed to keep them safe, although I have not changed the names of the deceased or those already in the public domain.

I am very lucky to have the full support of Irene. She is the love of my life and encourages me in all that I strive to achieve.

Thank you also to Mark Palios who has written the foreword. Thanks Mark, I feel privileged to have your support.

Finally, thanks to all at Pen & Sword. Without their advice and encouragement, I doubt this book would ever have been published.

When writing about events that took place many years ago it is inevitable that some memories will have faded. If I have made errors, they are mine alone. I can only state that I have worked diligently to keep the story as accurate as possible without any attempt to exaggerate what actually happened.

The army took a boy and made him a man…

Prologue: That Special Spark

This book is a work of non-fiction and is based on actual characters and events. The story describes my personal experience in the Falklands War as a trooper in 17 (Boat) Troop, D Squadron, 22 Special Air Service Regiment. I had only served two years in the Regiment before the Falklands War. I kept a diary from the moment we were tasked to fly south to the day we arrived back home over eighty days later. At the end of the Falklands War, I spent a week copying the war diary from its notebook into a folder which has formed the nucleus of four chapters. However, the story would not be complete without knowing about my background and life story. This approach, I trust, will give you an insight into my personal circumstances and upbringing which I strongly believe gave me the physical fitness, mental toughness, and courage to serve in the elite special forces regiment that is 22 SAS.

The story begins with me as a child in Birkenhead and chronicles my journey to make a success of life. It covers the early years and also my enduring support for Tranmere Rovers, the local football team. The book continues through my thirty years in the army, including service in the SAS and afterwards on commissioning as a Royal Signals officer. The book goes on to describe what I have done since leaving the army and also gives an insight into life as a security consultant in various Middle East terrorist hotspots.

When writing this book I was conscious of not revealing any current *modus operandi* of United Kingdom Special Forces (UKSF). I therefore submitted the original manuscript to the MOD Disclosure Committee for Express Prior Authority in Writing (EPAW) before publishing. This process required me to consider safeguarding the tactics, techniques and procedures (TTP) of UKSF, together with national security, operational capability, intelligence matters and personal security. The EPAW process required a few redactions, but I believe this was achieved without spoiling the continuity of the book.

If you are expecting to read about my heroics you will be disappointed. I was nothing more than an average SAS trooper, but then again there is nothing average about an SAS trooper...

Chapter 1

My Journey Begins

Falklands War Diary – SAS Diversionary Raid – Diary Entry Monday 14 June 1982

Deciding we could still get away with it, Ted our Troop Boss, told me to radio the three rigid raider boats to come and pick us up. The boats arrived within ten minutes as they had been loitering waiting for our call. Leaving three men from Boat Troop on this 'safe beach' we now had three patrols, one of these from the SBS, making a total of eighteen men. Each rigid raider also had its Royal Marine coxswain who all proved to be great guys who you could rely upon in a difficult situation as we were soon to find out. Our mission was to create a diversion at the eastern end of Wireless Ridge in an area known as Cortley Hill. This was at the far end of Wireless Ridge and looked directly on to Stanley Harbour. There were two large, diesel fuel storage tanks there at a distance of about 600m from where we intended to land. If we didn't encounter enemy forces, we were to blow these tanks to create the diversion. This meant some members of Boat Troop were carrying demolition charges. As always, I was part of callsign 17 Alpha and we were on the Squadron VHF radio net. We started our journey via a circuitous route to avoid the hospital ship. When we were half-way across the bay, Ted gave the signal for our 81mm and 60mm mortars to begin firing. They fell short at first and then exploded harmlessly in the peat above our selected landing point. With 300m to go our MILAN team from 23 Troop, G Squadron, fired a missile to our right at a target that they had identified with their night sights. It was actually an Argie gun position and they scored a direct hit. As we were making our final run in to the beach the remainder of D Squadron opened up with several GPMG machine guns in the sustained fire role. Immediately, several enemy machine guns and anti-aircraft guns firing on a horizontal trajectory returned fire and the sky lit up with tracer, some of it passing directly over our heads. Incredibly we still hadn't been spotted in the boats and were able to land unopposed a short distance away from the nest of enemy machine guns that were firing away.

We formed up in three patrols with a slight gap between each patrol. I was lead scout and took up point position with Tommy immediately behind me and then Ted, the Boat Troop Boss. I started advancing cautiously up the hill with most of the firing 200m to our right meaning we still hadn't been seen. I came across a wire, stretched taut at knee-height and beckoned Tommy to come and check it out with me. We agreed it marked the edge of a minefield, probably immediately in front of the Argie defensive positions. We turned right and followed the wire for about 50m, before it made a sharp turn uphill. Again, we followed the wire hoping to make our way around the edge. The wire turned right again and was going directly in front of the enemy machine guns which were still firing sporadically across the bay at the remainder of D Squadron. Ted came up to me and Tommy and suggested we might like to cross over the wire and the rest of Boat Troop would follow in our footsteps through the mined area. Now this was not what I wanted to hear, but if that's what the Boss wanted, who was I to argue?

I was born in Birkenhead, a large town on the Wirral Peninsula. It lies on the south bank of the River Mersey, opposite Liverpool. Shipbuilding was the main industry in the town. The largest ship ever built at Cammell Laird was the aircraft carrier HMS *Ark Royal*, launched in 1950. Cammell Laird remained the largest employer in Birkenhead until their closure in 1993. Subsequently, the shipyard reopened as a ship-repairer, until in 2012 the company won an order to build two car ferries.

I was born in a small, terraced house, the youngest of four siblings. My father had contracted TB before my birth. Due to his ongoing poor health, he only worked the occasional day in the summer as a coach driver and our family survived on sickness benefits. Dad was a Roman Catholic while my mum was Church of England. That was quite unusual in those days as sectarianism thrived on Merseyside. My paternal grandfather, Thomas, married Mary, an Irish Romany gypsy, and they moved to Birkenhead in 1910.

I don't remember having many toys during childhood. I do however recall a photo being taken on my third birthday. The photo shows me with a bus conductor's hat, a doll and a kitten. The hat was almost certainly left behind by a child on a coach excursion to Blackpool. My father would have been the coach driver and brought the hat home for me. The doll belonged to a girl called Judy who lived next door and was the same age as me.

My father took the decision to send us all to Catholic primary schools, but I was the only one in the family to regularly attend church. From when I was 7, my mother would walk me to the Catholic church every Sunday to attend Mass. She always waited outside the church, never setting foot inside.

I had a Protestant friend, Alan, who lived on our street. When I was 11, Alan suggested we join the local company of the Boys Brigade, which boasted a fine marching band. The Boys Brigade had strong connections with the Orange Lodge, a Protestant fraternity. The company commander welcomed both of us and quickly agreed that we could learn how to play the bugle and wear their uniform. He then gave us joining forms to complete. Alan handed over his form first and the company commander smiled when he saw that Alan attended 'The Woodlands C of E Primary School'. Then he saw that I had written 'St Werburgh's RC Primary School'. He went ballistic, telling Alan to get the fuck out of his sight and take his 'Fenian' friend with him!

I did well at primary school and passed my 'eleven-plus'. I was awarded a scholarship at St Anselm's College, a Catholic grammar school for boys. This was, and still is, a prestigious school with an outstanding reputation for excellence. Each year, six boys from Birkenhead were awarded one of these scholarships while the remainder of the boys were fee-paying. I looked smart in my new uniform, which my mother had obtained using a council clothing voucher. I found the transition to grammar school very difficult, as most of the boys had attended preparatory school together since the age of 7.

As I was growing up, I thought about supporting Everton or Liverpool. Eventually, having listened to the roar of the fans on a Friday evening, which was when Tranmere played most of their home games in those days, I decided to support the Super White Army. It wasn't until 1966 that I managed to visit Prenton Park. Tranmere will always be close to my heart and I am proud to be a long-suffering fan.

When I was 12, Alan and I started part-time jobs at the local chippy. The owner, Ralph, was paranoid that the local authority would discover he was employing underage boys. He made a cubby hole for us behind sacks of potatoes and instructed us to hide there if anyone entered the yard. Ralph had been brought up on a plantation in Uruguay. Ralph's wife was a Jewish refugee who had managed to evade the Nazis and emigrate to Uruguay just before the Second World War. The two met in Montevideo and married, before moving to England. Twenty years later, they bought the fish and chip shop. The work at the chippy was tiring as we peeled and then 'eyed' the potatoes, before putting the processed potatoes into a tank of diluted bleaching agent. Our hands were always sore, with cracked skin. We worked in the shed until 10 pm each evening and it was often cold.

Ralph always brought us mugs of tea at 8 pm and stayed to talk about his past life. I looked forward to Ralph's stories and found them a gateway to another world. Ralph had moved to Montevideo in his mid-20s and found work in the port. He remembered seeing the badly damaged German battleship *Admiral Graf Spee* tied up alongside at this neutral port in December 1939, the day after a battle with HMS *Exeter*, *Ajax* and *Achilles*. The German captain was informed by the Uruguayan authorities that his stay could not be extended beyond seventy-two hours and the ship was scuttled rather than face the Royal Navy waiting on the high seas.

I joined the Boy Scouts at the age of 12. There wasn't any money to buy a uniform, but I scrounged second-hand items. I normally walked the three miles home as I seldom had the bus fare. I was walking home one evening when three youths grabbed me. They held me down and demanded money which I didn't have. I managed to throw a few punches and escaped their clutches, but I still had a black eye to explain to my mum. As always, my dad didn't show much interest, looking up from his newspaper to suggest that I should find a different route to walk home in the dark!

I started going to 'The Vikings Youth Club' in Rock Ferry where I played five-a-side football every Thursday. George Yardley, Tranmere Rover's centre-forward, gave up his spare time to train us. I was in complete awe of George and when he told me I had played well one evening I couldn't stop smiling! After playing football, we always went to the clubroom upstairs. I was shy, but eventually started to speak to the teenage girls there. I still had to keep it a secret that I went to a 'posh' school, as Rock Ferry was a rundown part of town and it wasn't wise to be different. As part of my double life, I spent ages perfecting my scouse accent for use at the youth club, but would get the leather strap at school from the Christian Brothers for dropping my aitches! Quite a few of the Brothers had a perversion for corporal punishment and we would hide when one of the 'mad monks' was on the warpath!

I was an enthusiastic Tranmere Rovers fan by this time, although could rarely afford the entrance fee. The Rock Ferry boys would climb over the wall at Prenton Park, but we were often caught and ejected from the ground. I did however pay to watch Tranmere beat Coventry City 2–0 in a replay with an attendance of almost 24,000 at Prenton Park during an excellent FA Cup run in the 1967/68 season, finally losing 2–0 to Everton in March 1968 (61,982 was the official attendance figure at Goodison Park). It took until January 2001 before Tranmere beat Everton in the FA Cup. The final score was Everton 0–3 Tranmere, in front of a crowd of 39,207 with Steve Yates scoring two goals and Jason Koumas the other. Victory was sweeter after waiting all those years.

My exam results at St Anselm's were always poor. I was still going to the youth club and getting to know the girls there. All this left no time for homework. When I was 13, I came bottom of the class. From that day, I resolved to work harder and gradually improved. I had left it too late with my French studies though and the French tutor wrote in my school report that I would never be able to speak a foreign language. How wrong he was! By the end of my time in the SAS I had learnt five languages (German, Greek, Italian, Arabic and Spanish) at colloquial level. I also learnt quite a few phrases in Swahili and Malay, adding to my versatility as an SAS linguist.

I joined the Army Cadet Force (ACF) aged 14 and attended two drill nights a week. The detachment was affiliated to the Cheshire Regiment. We went shooting on the indoor range and I discovered that I was a good shot. I soon confided in the detachment commander that I wanted to make a career in the army and he advised me to improve my school grades. I took his advice, and by the time I left school I had good grades for all subjects, except maths, where I still struggled.

One drill night, a recruiting sergeant visited us. When he discovered I wanted to join the army and attended a grammar school, he tried to persuade me to wait until I was 18 years old with two GCE A-levels before joining as an officer. I wasn't interested in this proposal and the sergeant eventually conceded that I could join under the junior entrant scheme.

Soon after, I visited the local Army careers office to enlist. After filling in some forms, I was sent to Liverpool for an army medical. Within a few weeks I attended the Army Youth Selection Centre. The test centre was co-located with Army Apprentice College (AAC) Harrogate, a military academy for the Royal Corps of Signals. At the end of the selection test an officer informed me my scores were excellent, with the exception of maths which was borderline for a technical trade. When I told the officer that my preference was either the Cheshire Regiment or the Parachute Regiment, he explained that my scores were too good. We eventually agreed that I would join as a Royal Signals radio technician, but he cautioned that my maths must improve. Choosing to become a radio technician meant I would return to Harrogate in September to begin my apprenticeship.

Before leaving the army cadets, I went to the Cheshire County ACF summer camp at Dering Lines in the town of Brecon in Wales. Nowadays, Dering Lines is home to the Infantry Battle School, but in those days it was a battle school run exclusively by the Parachute Regiment for their own NCO cadres. We had a demonstration one day of all the kit that a paratrooper would carry into battle, including a main and reserve parachute. The para corporal showed us how the main chute would deploy by means of a static line. It was a windy day and immediately the canopy filled with air, before he demonstrated the correct technique for collapsing the chute on the ground. I was transfixed and vowed that one day I would learn how to parachute.

While at summer camp, we had an orienteering exercise. I was wearing canvas shoes, shorts and a T-shirt. I knew nothing about orienteering and set off alone up the nearest mountain on a compass bearing. As I crested the summit, I heard gunfire and spotted a red warning flag. I had inadvertently stumbled into the wrong end of the firing ranges above Cwm Gwdi Camp. I was soon spotted and firing ceased. A Land Rover set off up the track to apprehend me. The range officer, an ACF lieutenant, jumped out of the vehicle screaming at me, 'You stupid cunt! What the fuck are you doing up here?' When I explained I was orienteering and my strategy was to go in a straight line he laughed in disbelief and said

I would have to stay with them and get a lift back at the end of the day. The firers were all ACF sergeants on a cadre course using Lee-Enfield rifles. They also had some Bren machine guns. After a mug of tea, the lieutenant asked me if I wanted to fire a rifle. I was given a couple of magazines and fired off twenty rounds. I was also allowed to fire sixty rounds in short bursts with the Bren. When we arrived back at Dering Lines, I discovered that I hadn't even been missed!

On returning from summer camp, I reported to the Army careers office in Birkenhead to formally enlist into the army. I had a pleasant surprise as I was paid a day's wages together with a travel warrant with instructions to report to Harrogate the following week. Seven days later, I boarded the train to start my new life. At the age of 15, I was now a junior soldier.

At Harrogate railway station, two sergeants in their best uniforms with peaked hats, white belts, red sashes and pace sticks directed us to an army truck. The journey took about twenty minutes and I quickly realized that Harrogate was a lovely place in contrast to my hometown. On arrival we were issued bedding and other essential items. Once we had made our beds, it was time to grab a meal. But we weren't finished yet as, without exception, we had to have a haircut.

The next day, we were issued uniforms, including two pairs of ammo boots with leather soles and heels. While ammo boots were excellent for foot drill, they were useless for any other purpose. The following day, we were taken on a four-mile run to break in our boots before starting to bull them all over as best boots.

Each day began at 5.30 am and was crammed full of activities. Trade-training started the following Monday. I discovered that a group of six potential radio technicians, including me, were to receive additional maths classes every evening on account of our comparatively poor scores during the selection test.

AAC Harrogate ran a common core trade-training syllabus. This meant in addition to the technical subjects, I was expected to learn touch-typing and Morse code. The radio technicians' course also included metalwork which was a new skill for me.

Not only was I now following a military training programme and a trade training apprenticeship, we also had to cram education, sport and hobbies into the week. Every Saturday morning started with RSM's parade, when all 1,500 junior soldiers marched onto the parade ground behind the College Band. We marched to church every Sunday morning in our best uniforms. The first few Sundays I went to the Roman Catholic Mass which took just over an hour, before switching to the Anglican service as this only lasted fifty-five minutes. By doing this, I moved up the NAAFI queue for tea and cake by more than a hundred places. Within months, I no longer considered myself a Roman Catholic and felt equally comfortable in both churches. This was a useful experience when I started to work undercover with the SAS in Northern Ireland.

We were encouraged to take part in various pursuits and I chose gliding. Every Sunday after church we were driven to a nearby RAF airfield. Once there, we had to sweep the entire hangar with yard brooms before our flight in an open-cockpit glider. The take-off began with a gut-wrenching pull from the towing cable and then we were in the air after being dragged 500 metres along the ground. Up we surged until the instructor pilot released the cable. We slowly glided back to earth after a brief circuit from a maximum altitude of one thousand feet. I only stuck at it for three months, spending most of my time being used as free labour by the club manager, an RAF flight sergeant. It wasn't a complete waste of time though, as I completed fifteen flights and learnt how to drive a tractor.

After six weeks we had to pass a test requiring us to wear our best uniform and march up to an officer and salute. We were then presented with our Royal Signals cap badge and permitted to go into town in best uniform on Saturday afternoons. We had to repeat the marching and saluting pantomime on pay-day every Thursday. After halting and saluting, we had to shout out to the young subaltern: 'Pay and pay-book correct Sir!' while saluting him yet again and doing a smart about turn and marching off. The boredom of waiting to be paid was relieved one week when a recruit failed to halt on the highly polished corridor floor in his hob-nailed ammo boots and sent the table, money and officer flying in all directions!

After a few months, Recruit Squadron participated in the Lyke Wake Walk, a forty-mile crossing of the North Yorkshire Moors. This was a tough challenge and we hadn't undertaken any special training. We set off wearing green combat kit, berets and ammo boots. It started raining after a few hours and then it started to snow. Our clothing wasn't waterproof and we were absolutely frozen. Eventually my small group reached the twenty-five-mile checkpoint just before midnight. I was very tired, but still keen to continue to the finish. We each received a mug of coffee and were informed that this was a compulsory rest stop. We were then instructed to get into small tents and sleep, not that we had any sleeping bags. The drink warmed me up for a few minutes before I started shivering. Being an absolute novice, I stupidly removed my boots and socks and left them outside the tent. I stuck my bare feet inside my haversack, but it was far too cold to sleep. When we were roused a few hours later my boots and socks had frozen solid! It was grim walking in frozen boots without any socks and soon my feet were raw and bleeding. I managed to get to the thirty-mile checkpoint, but was pulled out as I could hardly walk. I learnt many valuable lessons that day and discovered that I was mentally tough.

My parents came to the pass-off parade at the end of my first term. I was disappointed that I hadn't been promoted to junior lance corporal. My dad in his normal monotone just said, 'Don't worry son, you're a late developer and will overtake all these smug arseholes in a few years.'

At the start of the second term, I reported to the Chief Instructor to be informed I had failed analogue electronics, a mathematics-based exam, the previous term. I was given a choice, either change trade to radio telegraphist or start the whole of the first term again. The next day I had made my decision and moved all my personal kit to Scott Squadron.

I enjoyed training to be a radio telegraphist, excelling in Morse code and keyboard skills. As a radio telegraphist, I also learnt how to service generators, including two-stroke petrol engines, a skill that proved vital working with problematic outboard motors during the Falklands War.

Gliding in an open cockpit in the winter months didn't appeal to me so I switched to amateur radio. I was soon able to send and receive speeds in excess of 25wpm. This made the trade-training exam, requiring me to send and receive Morse code at 18wpm, something of an irrelevance.

The education programme wasn't aligned to the GCE 'O' level curriculum but the Army Certificate of Education (ACE). By the end of the first year I had passed all five different ACE subjects. Only then was I allowed to commence GCE 'O' Level studies in English Language and Mathematics. Nine months later, I passed English Language, but failed 'O' Level Maths.

When I joined the army in 1969, 'The Troubles' were flaring up in Northern Ireland. The civil rights marches staged by Catholics demanding fair treatment regarding jobs and housing quickly escalated into violence when loyalists sparked counter-protests and rioting ensued. The situation was exploited by the Irish Republican Army (IRA). The Royal Ulster Constabulary then responded by calling in their reserve force of police officers known as the B-Specials. This force was overwhelmingly Protestant and Unionist and had many links to the emerging loyalist paramilitary groups which grew into the Ulster Defence Association and formed a counter-force to the IRA. In August 1969, the government of Northern Ireland in Stormont requested direct support from the British Army. This led to decades of intervention by the British Army against the IRA and other terrorist groups on both sides of the sectarian divide.

Senior Term was a busy period for me. We managed to fit in a comms exercise where I was deployed to Scotland. Next up was a battle camp at Strensall Training Camp. This was where I had my one and only experience of a mobile shower unit. It comprised a couple of wheeled containers towed behind army trucks. We stripped off outside in a screened area in the rain and stood there freezing our balls off until it was our turn. The Territorial Army (TA) sergeant in charge advised us that the water would be switched on for exactly ten seconds to get completely wet. Then we had one minute with the water switched off while we lathered our bodies with soap. Finally, we would get another thirty seconds to rinse the suds off. With a curt word of command, he told us to each stand under a shower-head. He turned on the water and we screamed in unison that the water was freezing cold! The big, fat twat ignored our cries and after ten seconds switched off the supply. We lathered ourselves up in a frenzy and then he turned the water back on again to our screams for mercy. After twenty-five seconds or so the water started to warm up, but already our time was up and he bundled us back out into the rain.

Soon it was my last day at the Apprentices College. My parents came to the graduation parade. I had graduated in the top five of more than ninety telegraphists. After some leave, I was posted to 30 Signal Regiment, based at Blandford in Dorset.

During the Second World War, Blandford Camp was the site of several US general hospitals constructed to treat American soldiers evacuated as casualties after D-Day. As instructed, I reported to the Regimental Sergeant Major (RSM) who welcomed me to the regiment. I was allocated the only spare bed-space in a twelve-man hut. The hut contained twelve tubular steel beds, twelve steel lockers and twelve bedside tables, all painted a drab grey colour. Everything, including the ablutions block, was in a state of disrepair. The only bright spot in these drab surroundings was each bed-space had a window, above which a plywood pelmet was positioned with a wooden shield fixed to the centre point. On each shield was painted a scantily clad beauty, for example Marilyn Monroe, in the same style that you used to see on American aircraft. I was told my hut had formerly been occupied by male nurses manning the US general hospitals and one of them must have painted the artwork. After one month we moved into our new accommodation block. I wish I had removed a couple of the shields to keep as souvenirs, but I had left it too late and the huts were soon demolished.

On arrival in Blandford Garrison, I was taught how to operate the PRC 316 radio. This lightweight radio was already in service with the SAS as their patrol radio. My first deployment took me to the Army Air Corps (AAC) base at Middle Wallop. I was tasked to man a control station communicating with several helicopters on training missions. I deployed straight after this on another comms exercise on Dartmoor operating an HF radio rear link back to Blandford as part of a three-man detachment. On return to Blandford, my troop was deployed to Northern Ireland (NI). The army had just introduced a rule that you must be at least 18 years old to deploy to NI. This meant that instead of going to NI, I was sent on a six-month attachment to the United Nations Forces in Cyprus (UNFICYP).

My new unit, 644 (UNFICYP) Signal Troop was based at Airport Camp, across the road from Nicosia International Airport. The troop was a joint British and Canadian unit. For the first few days I kept posing in front of a mirror to admire my sky-blue UN beret!

We went drinking on my first weekend in down-town Nicosia. Regardless of nationality, all UN troops were required to wear uniform when off duty. We were soon parted from our money by the smooth-talking beauties in high heels and miniskirts we called whisky dollies. Their technique was simple. They would come and sit next to you and ask you your name. Then with crossed legs touching your thigh they would purr into your ear, 'I really like you honey; will you buy me a whisky?' Few soldiers could refuse this request and the equivalent of forty pence for a watered-down whisky would be added to your bar tab. That doesn't sound much at today's prices but a pint bottle of Keo Lager sold for fifteen pence in the bars at that time. All the UN troops had a midnight curfew. At 11 pm we would go to the nearby Greek Cypriot takeaway for a *pita souvlaki*, known as a *doner kebab* in the Turkish Cypriot sector, before returning to Airport Camp.

Just before Christmas I was reassigned to the 'Force Rebro' (radio-rebroadcast) station on top of Mount Troodos. This was to provide a short-term replacement for a signaller who had been admitted to the military field hospital in Nicosia. I stayed on the mountain for three weeks. The detachment commander was a Canadian corporal, together with a British lance corporal, a Canadian signaller and me. Radio rebros receive a call on frequency A and then automatically retransmit the call on frequency B to greatly extend the range. The higher the rebro station, the further the range will be extended, which was why we were on top of the highest mountain in Cyprus. After dinner, we always played cards and drank.

The detachment members were much older than me and exploited my naïveté to get me to man the radio room for seventy-two hours non-stop over the New Year period with the promise of a three-day skiing course as my reward. I worked non-stop over this period with only a few hours' sleep on a camp bed beside the banks of radios. Meanwhile the other three members of the detachment drank themselves silly! The following week I spent three days at RAF Troodos on an introductory skiing course. RAF Troodos was a major comms site with their own ski slope three kilometres from our rebro shack.

On return to Nicosia, I started work in the communications centre (commcen) sending teleprinter (teletype) messages via the major relay station at Episkopi, which linked into the worldwide Defence Communication Network. I hated working in the commcen, so volunteered as an antenna rigger. The selection test was straightforward enough. After putting on a climbing belt, I was instructed to free climb to the top of a 120ft lattice mast. I was then told to attach myself by the belt to the mast, lean back and place my hands behind my head while turning my gaze to look at the ground far below. That was it. I had passed the course and was now a fully qualified rigger! Every day we would drive to UN police stations in different parts of the island to carry out maintenance on the comms masts situated there. The work was easy: perhaps bolt on another antenna, or paint a mast section. Afterwards we usually stayed overnight and went drinking with the UN policemen. I learnt to drink *ouzo* in shot glasses and still kept fit by climbing the masts each day.

It was on 5 February 1972 that Tranmere Rovers had an all-time record attendance figure of 24,424. This was a fourth-round FA Cup match against Stoke City which resulted in a 2–2 draw. I leapt in the air when I heard the score on the BBC World Service.

Early in 1972, we had a medal parade to receive the 'United Nations Medal for Peacekeeping in Cyprus'. Lieutenant General Prem Chand, an Indian Army officer, was the inspecting officer in his role as Commander UN Forces in Cyprus. He spoke a few words to each of us individually, but stopped abruptly when he stood in front of my friend John. Now John was Maltese, and with darker skin than most of us. General Chand asked John about his time in the army. John replied that he was 28 years old and had already served nine years in the rank of signalman, with a clean conduct sheet. The general asked the same question to the white lance corporal standing next to John and the response was 22 years old, served four years and promoted the previous year. After the parade the general was our guest of honour for a curry lunch. The troop OC and the general were in deep conversation and we were all speculating why the troop boss was looking flustered. Suddenly, the troop staff sergeant ushered John out of the door and he disappeared for thirty minutes. When John returned, he was wearing a lance corporal's stripe!

My job as a rigger took me to many UN police stations in Turkish and Greek Cypriot villages all over the island. Everyone was friendly to us, although it was clear there were underlying tensions and it came as no surprise when Turkey invaded in 1974, the ensuing ceasefire creating the divided island we have today.

In August 1972, I was at the Blandford Garrison Open Day which featured static display stands from most Royal Signals units. I spent the day inside a D11 radio cabin communicating in Morse to HMS *Ark Royal*. When I had a break, I took the opportunity to look around the various stands.

One stand entitled '**264 (SAS) Signals Squadron**' had me intrigued. The stand comprised a pink Land Rover under a desert camouflage net manned by four Royal Signals soldiers. They wore SAS smocks, olive-green shirts and trousers, sand-coloured army pullovers and desert boots together with SAS beige berets and Royal Signals cap-badge. All of them had an air of confidence, but no badges of rank which was puzzling. The range of equipment on display was impressive. I recognized the PRC 316 patrol radio but nothing else. Their weapons included Armalite AR-15 and Kalashnikov AK-47 assault rifles. They informed me that they were based in Hereford, spent a lot of time on operations in the Middle East and were parachute-trained which attracted extra pay. Their role was to provide comms support to 22 SAS worldwide. They had vacancies for radio telegraphists, but explained that I should wait until I was 21 as it was unusual for the squadron to accept volunteers below that age. This was all fascinating news to me as an 18-year-old and I was left thinking, 'If these guys are just the attached arms, the SAS must be super-troopers!'

In January of 1973, I was informed that I was to deploy to Kenya with 53 Field Squadron RE as part of a three-man detachment providing comms support as the sappers undertook a major road-building task. We were allocated one VC-10 passenger aircraft and two transport aircraft. The plan called for the transport planes to land in Kenya the day after our passenger aircraft so that we could be there to unload the airfreight straight onto trucks.

We flew to Kenya via an epic journey from RAF Brize Norton to Nairobi with refuelling stops at Cyprus, Dubai and Masirah. Now in those days Dubai Airport was not one of the world's busiest international airports that it is today. There was only one runway, and after we landed we taxied over to a large hut where the RAF Liaison Officer (LO) was based. The LO walked out to the steps of the VC-10 accompanied by a labourer pushing a hand-cart. The locally-employed lackey then proceeded to hand each of us a stale sandwich and a bottle of warm lemonade! We took off again as soon as the aircraft was refuelled.

We next flew a short leg to RAF Masirah located off the coast of Oman to drop off some passengers. While sitting outside the terminal to enjoy the sun, one of the RAF baggage handlers came across for a chat. I asked him why there were two HF radio receiver sites and then further away towards the end of the runway two HF radio transmitter sites with their larger antenna arrays set back from the runway. He looked at me suspiciously, obviously wondering why I would ask him such a thing. I explained that I was a signaller and knew all about long-haul HF radio and there was no need for two transmitter and two receiver sites. He came up close and quietly told me the second set of comms sites were manned by SAS 'scaleys' (signallers) in support of military operations in the Dhofar region of Oman. He went on to tell me about the SAS in Oman and how they were supported by BAC Strikemaster jets, Shorts Skyvan transport aircraft and UH-1 'Huey' helicopters. He added that there was another airfield closer to the action at a place called Salalah, which was often mortared at night. Up until this moment, I had no idea that the SAS were fighting a secret war in Oman. I logged this information away in the back of my head until it was time to volunteer for 264. Soon we boarded the VC-10 for the final leg of the journey.

After landing at Nairobi, we were driven to Kahawa, home to the British Army Training and Liaison Staff Kenya. They had a warehouse containing all the items necessary to establish a tented camp. The next day, we unloaded the airfreight and sorted everything into truck-loads before departing up-country.

The engineering task was to construct a graded road, including bridges and culverts, across 30km of rough terrain near Kisii Town. Squadron Headquarters (SHQ) was located about 40km from Lake Victoria. The road trip up-country took us west of the Rift Valley, past the tea plantations at Kericho, and Lake Naivasha, famous for its pink flamingos. The last hour or so we engaged four-wheel drive and drove at a crawl (demonstrating the need for a road in this area). We set up camp on arrival, including large marquee tents for SHQ and the cook-tent.

Meanwhile, the signals detachment installed radios inside the SHQ tent and erected antennas. One of the TA signallers controlled the forward radio net while the others acted as driver/operators in Land Rovers travelling up and down the road sending SITREPs. This left the Royal Signals detachment to provide the rear link to the UK using Morse via a relay station in Cyprus, working daily radio 'skeds' (schedules).

The security at this forward base was enhanced by employing Maasai warriors equipped with bows and arrows to patrol the barbed wire coils that made up the perimeter fence. One night a Maasai guard shot an arrow through the thigh of a villager who was trying to steal tools out of a truck-cab. The highlight of the trip was a farewell party to which the Maasai warriors were invited. After some tuition from the Maasai, the squadron were let loose with bows and arrows and then had a spear throwing competition. I remember one of the sappers stuck some toilet paper up his arse which he lit before performing the 'Dance of the Flaming Arsehole' while we all sang 'Hurl them down, you Zulu Warrior! Hurl them down you Zulu Chief, Chief, Chief!' This was a well-known drinking song sung by the British Army for many years. The Maasai warriors really enjoyed our rendition! A few days later, we began the long journey back to the UK.

On my return to the UK, I was sent on attachment to HMS *Bristol*, a guided-missile destroyer, which introduced me to navy terminology. A few weeks later, we deployed on battle camp to Garelochhead Training Camp in Scotland. The battle camp was a great learning experience for a 19-year-old.

Soon after arrival back in Blandford I was informed that I had been recommended for promotion to lance corporal, but as there were no vacancies I was to be posted to 604 Signal Troop in Germany and could expect to be promoted soon after arrival. The next month, I arrived at Portsmouth Barracks in Münster, Nordrhein-Westfalen, the home of 8 Regiment Royal Corps of Transport (RCT) and also 604 Signal Troop. I reported to work only to be told by the Troop OC that there weren't any prospects for promotion. So much for promises! I was assigned to a three-man detachment manning a D11 HF radio station mounted on a Bedford truck.

The move to Germany coincided with the second round of the League Cup where Tranmere played away against Arsenal. In typical giant killer tradition, Tranmere had a great game and won by the only goal, which was scored by striker Eddie Loyden. Arsenal had some great players in their team, including the England international Alan Ball. The victorious Tranmere team included Ron Yeats, Ronnie Moore, Ray Mathias and Mark Palios. Although I couldn't be there in person, I read in the Liverpool Echo that the Highbury crowd of 20,337 gave the Tranmere players a standing ovation at the end of the game.

Our role in 604 Signal Troop was to provide comms support to 8 Regiment RCT. The regiment was responsible for the transport of tactical nuclear warheads from NATO Atomic Supply Points, manned by 570 US Army Artillery Group. The warheads were then moved to Weapon Handling Areas to hand over to the Royal Artillery to fire at the Soviet troops we expected to encounter in a nuclear conflict. In reality we only ever transported empty missile containers up and down the Main Supply Routes. I would tap away on a Morse key while we created massive traffic jams as our convoy slowly drove along the autobahn. We were escorted by a mechanized infantry company in tracked armoured fighting vehicles Type 432 (AFV-432). When we arrived at our next hide location, we had to camouflage our truck and then 'stag-on' radio watch twenty-four hours a day.

While at 604, I became a member of 8 Regiment RCT tug-of-war team. We were brigade champions in 1974 and then division runners-up, losing to the champions, 32 (Heavy) Regiment Royal Artillery. I also played squash, volleyball and five-a-side football. I soon passed my heavy goods vehicle driving test. In my second year I attended a Colloquial German course. I also went skiing, kayaking, and free-fall parachuting, logging thirty free-fall parachute jumps.

It was about this time that I went on leave to Birkenhead. I managed to go to a match at Prenton Park and enjoyed watching the players, including Mark Palios who went to school at St Anselm's in the year above me. Mark was a midfielder and played for Tranmere for nine years. He became a successful chartered accountant and later a senior partner at PricewaterhouseCoopers. Mark became the Football Association's Chief Executive in 2003, where he used his business skills in the field of sports governance. Subsequently, Mark worked as a consultant specializing in turning around failing businesses. In August 2014, Mark and his wife, Nicola, took a controlling interest in Tranmere Rovers Football Club.

I attained Developed Vetting in 1974, a lengthy process that looks into your background, including family, friends and associates to ascertain if you should be entrusted with the nation's secrets. Developed Vetting status was necessary because of my role handling signal messages regarding potential nuclear release. In early 1975, I completed the Radio Telegraphist Class 1 course at 8 Signal Regiment in Catterick Garrison. I finished as top student and was promoted to lance corporal on my return to Germany.

I often went training with a 40lb bergen along the canal towpath near the barracks. One evening I was running along the towpath towards the end of a 15km tab. An elderly gentleman out walking his dog in the heavy rain shouted to me: *'Das, ist aber schwer, nicht wahr?'* (That's really difficult, isn't it?) and my reply: *'Doch! Man kann das wohl sagen!'* (Yes, you can say that again!). It was quite lonely training by myself, but that actually toughens you up even more.

One day I was cleaning my truck prior to an inspection when an army ambulance pulled alongside. They were shouting my name and once they confirmed that I had B-negative blood I was put in the back of the ambulance. We drove at high speed, with blue lights flashing, to Münster British Military Hospital. On arrival I donated a pint of blood to a British woman who was on the operating table and had lost a lot of blood. Afterwards I asked the nurse why all the fuss? She informed me that B-negative blood was very rare and only four soldiers in the entire garrison had my blood group.

Soon after this my application to join 264 (SAS) Signal Squadron was approved. I was instructed to report to Hereford in July 1976.

Chapter 2

Hereford – A Culture Shock

The first thing I noticed about the SAS base at Bradbury Lines was the armed MOD police manning the main gate. A helpful MOD policeman pointed out the Signal Squadron accommodation. The accommodation at that time was in Second World War huts, similar to those in Blandford five years earlier. There were six huts linked together with an ablution block at the centre and each hut was called a 'basha'. To the SAS, wherever you lay your head is your basha!

I found a spare bed-space and unpacked my kit. Later a friend already serving in 264 arrived to show me around the camp. First we went to see the SAS clock tower. The names of SAS members who have died on duty are inscribed on the clock tower. They are said to have 'failed to beat the clock'.

We were welcomed to the 264 (SAS) Signal Squadron probationary course by the Squadron Sergeant Major (SSM), Mick, who was SAS-badged, as were most senior posts in the Signal Squadron. Mick surprised all of us when he insisted that we call him by his first name. This use of first-name terms is common across the SAS and attached arms. The officers are called 'Boss' rather than 'Sir' and it is a close-knit brotherhood. It is not over-familiarity as many outside the regiment believe, but rather a sign of mutual respect while maintaining high standards of self-discipline. The course lasted three weeks and comprised a physical training session every morning, followed by trade-training for the remainder of the morning and then weapon training and map reading until 4 pm. We ended each day with either a run or a tab over the nearby hills carrying a 30lb bergen. It was fine running on the flat, but I found it very hard going once we started to go uphill. The SAS use the acronym 'tab' for marching over the hills carrying a bergen. The word came from the Parachute Regiment and is derived from the phrase 'Tactical Advance to Battle'. It took me a while before I felt comfortable tabbing on the uphill stretches, but it was a valuable lesson for when I started training for SAS Selection a few years later.

We went for a couple of tabs over the Brecon Beacons and each time stopped for an hour to establish comms back to the Hereford base on the PRC 316 patrol radio. Our final exercise was again on the Brecon Beacons and we did a fair bit of tabbing, but this time with heavier bergens. Late in the afternoon, each patrol member would set up his basha by stretching a waterproof 'basha' sheet over his sleeping bag. For the final exercise, we used the new 'Clansman' PRC 320 HF manpack radio, which was issued to the SAS ahead of any other unit. The PRC 320, which I went on to use during the Falklands War, was more powerful than the PRC 316, giving greater range, but it was three times as heavy as the older radio. The batteries were also heavy and we had to carry spare batteries that were distributed throughout the patrol.

At the end of the course, ten of us were successful and we were told our probationary period would continue for a full twelve months before we would be permitted to wear the SAS beige beret with Royal Signals cap-badge. All the radio telegraphists on the course were allocated to signal troops embedded in the SAS 'Sabre Squadrons', whereas the technicians and data telegraphists remained in 264 SHQ. I was attached to D Squadron and worked shifts in 'Receivers' until their return from an operational tour.

Adjacent to the Regimental Headquarters (RHQ) of 22 SAS was a commcen and the Hereford Base Station, known as 'Receivers'. I joined one of the shifts in Receivers. The workload depended on whatever radio sked was due to take place. The out-stations included all the SAS operations and training locations. In 1976, Masirah acted as the relay station for the troops deployed in Oman on Operation Storm. We also acted as the control station for training, including SAS Selection. In addition to weekdays, I also worked every second weekend. Within the year, Op Storm had ended. The British military departed RAF Masirah on 31 March 1977 and the base was taken over by the Sultan of Oman's Air Force. The HF base station at Masirah used by the SAS to communicate to SAS troops fighting rebels in the south of Oman was closed down.

The Sunday morning shift was dreaded by one and all as the weekly SITREP would come in from Op Storm. The SITREP was an encoded signal of typically 600-letter cypher groups. At fifty cypher groups per page, this was a twelve-page signal. The SITREP had to be laboriously taken down letter by letter by the radio telegraphist and then handed to the cypher operator to be decoded. This meant only the cypher operator on the shift on a 'need to know' basis was able to see the plain language version of this classified message addressed 'CO 22 SAS Eyes Only'.

On my first Sunday shift I was instructed to sit alongside the control operator and copy the signal to see how I got on. I passed the test and was soon working live operational links. Nowadays, with 'real-time' online encryption, a good keyboard operator can send a twelve-page message in thirty minutes or less, in other words the message will be transmitted as fast as he can type. This wasn't quite so simple using Morse code. It would often take most of the shift to copy the message down, particularly when the frequencies would fade as the ionosphere would rise and fall. Every time this happened, we would have to change frequency, which required one of us to jump on a bike outside the back door and pedal like mad to the other side of camp with the key to the transmitter hut. Once there, you had to power down the high-tension stages of the transmitter, pull out a drawer and insert a new crystal and then re-tune it while trying not to burn your arm on the red-hot valves inside. Sometimes it would require two or three frequency changes before you could carry on receiving the SITREP. Bradbury Lines was rebuilt in 1981 and to create space the transmitter site was moved to a secure location 15km away.

I enjoyed my time in Receivers and was soon no longer surprised to see the CO coming in to read a signal as it was being decoded, such was the pace of life providing comms support to the SAS. I built up a good reputation for myself while working in Receivers, but it was now time to join D Squadron. I was informed that they would arrive back in Bradbury Lines at a certain time and I should make myself known to Mac, the D Troop (Signals) Staff Sergeant. Mac shook my hand and welcomed me to the troop. He was a big guy, ex 216 (Para) Signal Squadron, and like several other members of the Signal Squadron, had passed SAS Selection. Mac had served in a Sabre squadron for several years before returning to the Signal Squadron. As well as the four sabre troops in D Squadron of Air, Boat, Mobility and Mountain, there was also D Troop. Mac told me that there would be a troop party on the very next evening in a local pub and I was invited. I turned up at the appointed time and when I asked the landlord where the party was, he looked me up and down before nodding to the stairs at one side of the bar. The party was upstairs for a bit of privacy and security even though it was a pub where the SAS drank among friends who watched each other's backs. I was soon introduced to all the characters in the troop before getting stuck in to the free booze. Later Mac took me to one side and informed me that the troop had a week's leave, and then we would start our new job at a nearby training camp. He told me to report for duty at D Squadron lines at the end of the leave period and to wear scruffy jeans, boots, T-shirt, fleece jacket, woollen hat and a warm coat!

The new job was training operatives preparing to deploy to Northern Ireland on undercover work. Most of the instructors were SAS, but there were others involved which needs no further comment. I found myself sticking numbered paper dots inside map books for the first few days. The only heating inside the hut was a single-bar electric fire so I soon discovered why Mac had told me to wear warm clothes! My next task was to assist our radio technicians to install covert radios into civilian cars. The installation included various 'add-ons' for hands-free operation of the radios. Our vehicle mechanics improved the performance capability of the cars and also added various items and disabled others. All these enhancements were vital, whether we were operating in cities or making 'drop-offs' and 'pick-ups' in rural locations. The following week I was shown how to man the control station in the ops room and, speaking a form of abbreviated voice procedure interspersed with codewords and spot codes, I learnt how to control the cars on mobile surveillance operations.

On quiet days they let me have a go at close quarter battle (CQB) shooting. Weapons I fired included the Ingram M-10 sub-machine gun and the Walther PPK automatic handgun. The ranges had wooden obstacles on them to simulate opening a door or climbing through windows. I would regularly drive an unmarked car to carry out comms tests within a fifty-mile radius of Hereford, operating in both rural and urban environments. We kept an official letter signed by the Chief Constable of West Mercia Police in an envelope in the glove compartment. We called this the 'Get out of Jail Card'. The letter requested any police who pulled us over for speeding or any traffic infringement to phone the West Mercia Police Operations Room for advice. If they did phone up, they were merely told to leave us alone and not to arrest us. Although only a scaley (signaller), I was allowed to sit in on 'O' groups (orders prior to a task) and attend 'prayers' (daily updates). The work rate was intense when training was underway and then we would have some time off before starting the whole cycle again. Occasionally I would be used to simulate the role of a terrorist (known as an X-Ray). Whenever this happened, I was able to observe the trainees under test conditions while working mobile and when going 'foxtrot' (on foot). I continued in this role for six months until Mac told me I would be deploying to Belize in Central America the following week and to get a haircut before I went!

D Troop was short of manpower in 1977. The comms detachment going out to Belize had a corporal in charge, although with acting sergeant rank. This was a common practice in Hereford at the time, and luckily for Harry he was, as the signals detachment commander or 'pronto', able to live in the comparative luxury of the Sergeants' Mess. One big plus for Harry was that he lived in a two-man room, compared to our four-man basha. Harry liked a drink and was overjoyed to discover just how cheap the duty-free booze was. There was, however, a downside to Harry's sleeping arrangements when he learnt he was sharing a room with a lay preacher from the Salvation Army. This good-intentioned character would spend hours on his knees every evening praying aloud with his arms held aloft. The teetotaller was not quite the drinking buddy Harry was expecting!

The SAS were in Belize to patrol the jungle border with Guatemala, a country that claimed the whole of Belize as its missing province. It's worth noting that Belize was still a British colony at this time. The international airport had very few flights, but they included the weekly VC-10 flown by RAF Transport Command, bringing in new arrivals for their six-month tour at Airport Camp or one of the smaller bases in the country.

My role was to man the radio nets in the SAS ops room at Airport Camp. The SAS troop and embedded signals detachment were in country for a three-month tour. We used the PRC-320 as the base radio on the forward net while the SAS patrols still used the very reliable and much-loved PRC-316. The patrol signallers would bash out their encrypted messages to us in Morse, only switching to voice if they required a helicopter for a casualty evacuation (CASEVAC). We also manned the rear link communicating directly to Hereford using offline encrypted letter cypher, again using Morse, but with high-powered HF transmitters and receivers. I enjoyed my time in Belize and made use of the squash courts, swimming pool and home-made weights, plus a daily run, to keep very fit.

I was able to deploy to the jungle for a week and the D Squadron guys taught me all the basics for living in it. This was another plus for when I attempted SAS Selection. I was also given the opportunity to test-fire the AR-15 assault rifle on the ranges. Our jungle mission was to build a Helicopter Landing Site (HLS). I learnt how to correctly sharpen and use a machete to hack away at the secondary jungle while assisting 'Hoss' Ligairi, our Fijian SAS sergeant, to tamp the plastic explosive (PE) for the larger tree trunks. When Hoss shouted 'Fire in the hole!' we all knew it was time to take cover as another tree was about to be blown up as we cleared the HLS. We had one casualty during the week when an infantry soldier, who was there clearing the scrub, was injured when he stupidly stood up to take a photo of Hoss blowing a tree when he should have been taking cover. As the tree exploded and flew in all directions, a large tree branch went spinning through the air and broke the soldier's knee cap. It was the first time that I had to send a CASEVAC message and then switch to voice to arrange for an urgent helicopter casualty evacuation. Within two hours the soldier was being winched on board a Scout helicopter (as the HLS was still under construction). We had to inflate and send an air marker balloon up through the jungle canopy as our new HLS was not marked on the pilot's map. The balloon was 'DayGlo' orange and could be seen for miles around.

We eventually came to the penultimate day in the jungle and Hoss was doing the calculations to work out the correct weight of the explosive charge for a massive hardwood tree which he had left for last. I remember him sitting down on a fallen tree trunk and licking his pencil with furrowed brow. After about five minutes he called me over and asked that I check his calculations. I looked at the formula, which was all new to me, and noted that the calculations were in the Imperial System using pounds and ounces which made it all the more difficult. I eventually came up with a figure of four pounds of PE, whereas Hoss had come up with four ounces! We checked it again and this time I also came up with four ounces, but Hoss came up with four pounds! Hoss turned to me and asked me how much PE was left in the box. I checked and told him there were thirty-two sticks making a total of 16lb. Hoss looked at the sky for a few seconds and turned to me and said, 'I remember from my demolition course, I was told if all else fails remember there is one calculation which always gives the correct answer and that is P for Plenty. Tamp all thirty-two sticks into the tree-hollow. I will return in twenty minutes.' Hoss left me to puzzle the wisdom of his decision while I tamped away moulding the PE into shape. When I was finished, Hoss inserted the detonator and laid out the detonation cord before instructing everyone to take cover 100 metres away. Finally he called out 'Fire in the Hole!' before blowing the tree. Immediately the air was sucked out of my lungs and the blast wave blew over our prostrate bodies. I looked up and saw clouds of smoke and dust, and then, incredibly, it started to rain matchsticks! When we approached where the tree had been there was just a huge crater in the ground – which got everyone grumbling as we had to fill it in and only had two small spades. We finished the HLS by last light and the next day it was our turn to fly back to Airport Camp. It was an great experience when a small Scout helicopter, followed by a much larger Puma helicopter, flew in to pick us up at our new HLS. As we took off, we could see the full extent of our efforts, and yet within a few seconds the HLS was lost to the sea of green that is the jungle canopy.

Later, we all had a few beers in the NAAFI. Several of the badged members of D Squadron who were drinking with the D Troop signallers told me what a good job I had done arranging the CASEVAC helicopter. I felt chuffed and knew that I had made the right choice coming to 264 to work with the SAS. Hoss bought everyone a round of beers. Now, if ever there was a gentle giant, but with the killer streak when required, it was Hoss. He was in great form that night because his leave application had been approved. Hoss was going to his home in Fiji for two months. This 'long leave' with a free plane ticket was granted to our Fijians every three years due to the difficulty and expense of flying to Fiji from the UK. The orderly sergeant had great difficulty getting us to vacate the NAAFI that night!

Before leaving Belize, I was also able to visit St George's Caye just offshore from Belize City, where the British Army had an adventure training centre. We spent the weekend kayaking, sailing and fishing.

After my return from Belize, I was granted a week's leave. On return to duty, I was presented with my beige beret by OC 264. I had completed my one year's probation period and could now proudly wear the SAS beret with Royal Signals cap-badge. The presentation was very informal, I just knocked on the OC's door and Paddy invited me to come in and sit in one of the armchairs. Then he came from behind his desk to sit opposite me and we had a quick chat before he handed over the sand-coloured beret and shook my hand.

The next week I reported to the gym for my 'Pre-Para' course. The course was run by the Quarter Master Sergeant Instructor (QMSI) who was responsible for physical fitness training and development. The attached arms included signallers, medics, clerks, storemen, and mechanics. The course was a week of intensive physical fitness assessments, including ten mandatory tests identical to the tests that the Parachute Regiment are subjected to on their infamous 'P Company' pre-parachute training course. Jim, the QMSI, had been the QMSI for the Para depot in Aldershot only the previous year. We were under no illusions that this was to be an easy option, although one saving grace was there was absolutely no bullshit on the course, unlike P Company. The tests included 'milling', which was a form of toe-to-toe boxing with instant dismissal if you stopped boxing, even for a moment. I managed to knock down my opponent, but then ran out of steam and dropped my guard. He saw his chance and knocked me down, although I was back up on a count of three. The QMSI was the referee and he held both our arms in the air at the end of the bout to signify an even contest. We also had a 'stretcher race', 'log race', ten-mile tab, indoor running circuits in the gym, high-level confidence course, assault course, and so on. I passed the course, but quite a few dropped out. This now qualified me to attend a military parachuting course when a vacancy came up.

My next role was to deploy to Northern Ireland with D Squadron. The squadron had three weeks for our work up training, spending a week of this time on a training area where even the attached signallers from D Troop learnt how to cope with action on ambush, first aid, range work and a final exercise where we put everything together. We were issued with Browning automatic pistols at the start of the week together with live ammunition. For the whole week we were expected to carry the weapon fully loaded and cocked with one round in the breech twenty-four hours a day. This included sleeping with the handgun under my pillow. I remember the orderly officer from an infantry regiment coming into the NAAFI to close the bar at chucking out time. I thought to myself the officer would be apoplectic if he discovered we were all carrying loaded weapons!

We eventually flew to Northern Ireland and took over some basic accommodation consisting of portable buildings behind the RUC police station at Portadown. Every building was heavily fortified with sandbags and anti-mortar netting on the roofs. We even had a pipe range to test-fire weapons before deploying on operational patrols. I began shift work in the operations room controlling several VHF nets which in those days were still 'in clear', i.e., our radios lacked online encryption. For communications security, we relied on abbreviated voice procedure, coloured spot codes to disguise locations and brevity codes which gave short term protection over the radio. Working as a soldier in Northern Ireland was very difficult with many restrictions on how we could operate. At least the SAS were able to operate undercover, which gave D Squadron a huge advantage compared to conventional troops.

After a couple of months, I was sent back to England for my military parachute course. The course took place at Number 1 Parachute Training School, RAF Brize Norton. We assembled in front of the training hangar with a huge sign displaying the motto 'Knowledge Dispels Fear' hanging over the massive hangar doors. The jumps began with clean fatigue, then jumping with equipment, before a night jump and then the eighth and final jump which was a 'SIM-32 with equipment'. This final jump was when thirty-two paratroopers jumped simultaneously from each side-door of the C130. In effect, this achieved a 'zipping' of the jumpers from each door into a continuous line of sixty-four paratroopers all in the air at the same time. Disaster almost struck. Our RAF instructors were under supervision themselves and were using our jump to qualify as parachute despatchers. Unfortunately they never gave us the one second separation required between parachutists jumping out of both side-doors. As I saw the green light and jumped from the aircraft via the port side exit, I was immediately struck by the parachutist exiting from the starboard side exit as we collided in the slipstream. With a mighty clatter I was almost knocked senseless, and then I realized he had passed through my rigging lines and snagged. Meanwhile to add to my problems my rigging lines were wrapped around my neck and reserve chute! I somehow managed to extricate myself and could see my canopy was only partially inflated. I was also in severe twists, i.e., my rigging lines were all wrapped round each other instead of flying separately. I shouted out a warning to other parachutists in the air that I was in trouble by calling out the standard warning, 'Steer away, I'm in twists!' That gave us a bit of spare room to manoeuvre, but I was conscious that time was running out as it only takes about thirty-five seconds from jumping out of the plane at 800ft until reaching the ground and a lot less time if the canopy is partially deflated. I also had another very urgent problem in that I had to lower my equipment which was a jerrycan full of sand strapped to my thighs. This 'equipment load' would definitely break my legs if it was still there when I hit the ground. At that moment, I started falling the full length of my rigging lines as the other parachutist below me was 'stealing' the air from my canopy. I thundered past him like a freight train and then suddenly my canopy fully deployed. But this time his parachute started to collapse. Now we had about another ten or fifteen seconds of flying time left to sort this mess out, so I followed the Standard Operating Procedure (SOP) that had been drilled into both of us. I shouted to him to pull hard on his back risers while I did the same. Immediately both canopies separated and opened normally. I just had time to release my equipment to dangle below me on its tethering rope and get my feet and knees together before we both hit the ground a few seconds later, still tangled together. I could scarcely believe neither of us had been injured, although we were both badly winded from the hard landing.

Within the hour we had been transported back to RAF Brize Norton by bus and once there we had a 'wings' presentation ceremony. I was very proud to wear my para wings for the rest of the day and then having a few beers with the other members of the course, mostly from the Parachute Regiment, but also a few Royal Marines. The next morning, I reverted to civilian clothes and drove to Hereford. A few hours later I took a train from Hereford to Liverpool, travelling back to Northern Ireland via the Belfast overnight ferry. I was met by a couple of signallers in an unmarked car and was soon back in Portadown. Once there, I carried on as normal and whenever I had a quiet night shift as the control station radio operator, I studied my 'O' Level German correspondence course.

After my tour of duty in Northern Ireland, I requested an interview with the Education Officer back in Hereford and outlined my desire to pass a few 'O' levels, or GCSEs as they were called a few years later. The Education Officer was very supportive and told me he was a linguist running language courses in several different languages that were of interest to the SAS, ranging from Arabic to Norwegian. He suggested that I use the language lab in the evenings to brush up on my German conversational skills and he would enter me for the next 'O' level exam. The education officer also helped me apply for another correspondence course in 'O' level Maths. After a few weeks, he came to listen to my efforts and informed me I was ready for a day-trip to the Army School of Languages to take the Colloquial German exam. This exam should be retaken every three years to stay in-date. I drove up to Beaconsfield with two other candidates, both from D Squadron, one was the squadron commander and the other was Sergeant Lofty Arthy. Lofty was a member of Mountain Troop and needed the language qualification before deploying to Germany for his Mountain Guide Course with the Bundeswehr (German Federal Army). We all passed the exam and I was pleased that I had spent a few hours chatting to the Squadron OC on the journey back from Beaconsfield, in English of course! The OC had never spoken more than a few words with me before so it was nice to be noticed in a positive way. Sadly, Lofty died in the Falklands War in the SAS Sea King helicopter crash.

I was advised by Geordie, who had taken over from Mac as the D Troop 'pronto', that he had nominated me for the Royal Signals Detachment Commanders Course at 11 Signal Regiment in Catterick Garrison. Gaining a pass on this course was a mandatory requirement in Royal Signals before you were eligible for promotion to full corporal. The course covered foot drill, weapon handling, marksmanship, stores accounting, leadership and infantry minor tactics. 11 Signal Regiment was the Royal Signals military training depot and not a place I enjoyed visiting. There was an unbelievable amount of bullshit on the course and I hated every minute of it. But that didn't prevent me from passing the course as top student.

There were plenty of other things keeping me busy, and on my return to Hereford I was assigned as D Squadron Commander's signaller on the counter-terrorist team. The team was known within the regiment as the Special Projects (SP) Team. We had an intensive work-up period which included training with some new radios. I also had to maintain all the radio pagers and was responsible for charging the batteries on the team's electronic devices, which gave me an opportunity to test out a night-scope for the first time. 'Wow, it's true, you really can see in the dark!' The D Squadron SAS members initially concentrated on Close Quarter Battle (CQB) for the assault group, while the sniper group concentrated on marksmanship. The CQB skills were practised in a building specially adapted for the purpose and known as the 'Killing House'. As the tempo increased, we came together to practise various scenarios. As the squadron commander's signaller, I was expected to follow him into the scene of activity for post-assault procedures. At the end of this phase, the incident would be handed back to the police who would retain primacy both before the SAS assault phase and immediately after. When we were deemed ready to take over the SP team from the outgoing sabre squadron, we had a final exercise of thirty-six hours duration. I managed to participate in some of the training activities while I was on the SP team, including abseiling from a helicopter onto the roof of a building.

Towards the end of my stint on the SP team I was promoted to full corporal. We had a full-blown counter-terrorist exercise every month. On one exercise, I was taken off my normal duties. This one time I played the role of chief terrorist in a fictitious German terrorist gang. The scenario had me and a few other 'terrorists' holding a number of hostages in a medium-sized passenger aircraft. At first I only spoke in German, which gave the police a headache trying to locate a negotiator who could speak the language. It was an incredible experience to be on the receiving end of the assault when it eventually went in. Once the terrorists and hostages were separated, the incident was handed back to the police. At the end of exercise, we departed within minutes. The lucky ones flew back to Hereford in helicopters, the rest of us returned in a fleet of Range Rovers.

On another occasion, the Prince of Wales, HRH Prince Charles, came to visit the regiment and this included a look at the SP team's equipment in our hangar before driving over to the 'Killing House' to observe our shooting skills. Not for the first time, I was chosen to be a live hostage, sitting amongst several full-sized mannequins representing terrorists. Prince Charles and his retinue were escorted into a roped-off area and given a briefing of what lay before them, which was a simulated coffee bar with a cafe-style counter top plus a few tables and chairs. The lights were then turned off as the briefing continued in the dark, before the assault group entered and proceeded to shoot the terrorists using powerful 'Streamlight' flashlights attached to their Heckler & Koch MP5 sub-machine guns to illuminate the targets. It wasn't a pleasant experience to have the light shone directly into my eyes and neither was having over twenty hot empty shell cases drop into my lap. When the shooting was finished, the lights came on and the team lined up to meet HRH. When Prince Charles reached me he shook my hand and turned to the Squadron OC and said next time I should be given a folded blanket to catch the hot empty cases from the 'blank' ammunition falling on my lap. You should have seen Prince Charles's face when he was told that we only used live ammunition in training!

Our six months on the SP team were drawing to a close and we handed over to the next squadron to take on the counter-terrorist role.

My next trip with D Squadron was a six-week jungle training exercise in Brunei. I spent it being mentored to take my turn as the senior signaller on a future deployment. The senior signaller, whether of the whole troop or a smaller, deployed detachment, was always known as the 'pronto'. The use of this word was common across the whole of the British Army, in the same way that other appointment titles are used: 'Sunray' for commander or 'Starlight' for medical support. In addition to the rear link, we also manned a forward link to the jungle base camp and acted as a guard station if any of the SAS patrols couldn't make direct contact with the jungle base. Halfway through the exercise I was given the opportunity to go on a one-week jungle training course, run by 22 SAS Training Wing. This was a great opportunity for the D Troop signallers on the exercise to see the jungle at first hand. During the training we learnt trapping, demolition charges, anti-personnel mines, patrolling and tracking, which added to my knowledge of SAS jungle operations.

On arrival back in the UK we were sent on leave for Christmas, then the New Year started with a three-month deployment to Belize. This was my first deployment as the 'pronto'. I was temporarily promoted to sergeant for the deployment and was accommodated in the Sergeants' Mess. The SAS team comprised a composite SAS troop from D Squadron, six signallers from D Troop, plus the SSM acting as our ops officer and the SQMS who handled our logistics support, which included helicopter resupply to deployed patrols. We also had a couple of Gemini inflatable boats with outboard motors. These were occasionally used to patrol the Sarstoon River which marked the southern border with Guatemala, but more often than not we used them to get out to the small islands known as 'cayes' where we would go most weekends. The cayes were a great place for R&R and we always had a barbecue, went swimming and generally chilled out for the day. We often saw large salt-water alligators in the estuary as we set off from Belize City and also the occasional shark in the shallow water near the cayes.

I was very fit after the first month and growing in confidence now that I was controlling the forward and rear radio comms. One day during our deployment in Belize, I was out running with some of the SAS guys when it suddenly dawned on me that I was ready to attempt SAS Selection. My decision was made easier by the encouragement of one of the SAS sergeants, Sid, who made me truly believe in myself. Sadly Sid was one of those great guys who died in the SAS helicopter crash in the Falklands War.

When I returned to Hereford, I went to see the SSM of 264 (SAS) Signal Squadron to discuss my wishes to attempt SAS Selection at the earliest opportunity. Mick agreed the time was right and I was booked onto the January 1980 course. I was then told to go and have a chat with the Signal Squadron commander. The Squadron OC, Paddy, was a really nice bloke and also SAS-badged. Paddy made me feel a valued member of the Signal Squadron and confided in me that there were plans underway to make the embedded sabre squadron signal troops even larger. In future, all the sabre squadron signals troops were to have a staff sergeant or warrant officer class 2 Yeoman of Signals in command instead of a staff sergeant radio telegraphist as was the case when I arrived in Hereford. Yeoman of Signals (YofS) was the term for the army's comms manager and YofS were widely acclaimed for their technical and operational management skills. Paddy was keen that I pass SAS Selection, enjoy three years in the regiment and then go on a Yeoman of Signals course before returning to command one of the signal troops embedded in an SAS sabre squadron as a staff sergeant Yeoman of Signals. Now to be honest this didn't interest me at the time, but as I was becoming smarter by the day, I kept my thoughts to myself. I was then told to go and have a chat with the WO1 YofS who commanded the Signals Training Troop. Vic, yet another SAS-badged signaller, listened to my plans and then arranged that I would return to 264 and join the Signals Training Troop as an instructor until I went on Selection.

My role in the Signals Training Troop was to train patrol signallers from the SAS and SBS. This was a great opportunity for me to meet SAS troopers from the other three squadrons, i.e. A, B and G Squadrons, and also members of the SBS. Knowing all these guys was very useful in the future, particularly during the Falklands War as I knew some of the G Squadron guys and also a few in the SBS. I spent most of my time instructing Morse code, but also taught other subjects, including voice & telegraph procedures, antenna theory & propagation, signals codes and radio equipment.

I sat the German Language 'O' level exam in May 1979, which I passed with a good grade. I was also informed that I would soon be going to Catterick for six weeks to attend a crypto course and thereby qualify as a cypher operator.

Meanwhile, I went tabbing alone on the Brecon Beacons mountains every weekend. I soon became 'bergen fit' with the stamina and endurance that comes from days spent walking up the hills and running down them. This type of stamina training carrying weight is totally different to that achieved by merely running or walking. Occasionally I would tab with others, and on one occasion I had a day on the hills with a returning SAS trooper who was retaking SAS Selection after being RTU'd (returned to unit) for fighting. Pete was being allowed to return to the regiment subject to passing the first month of SAS Selection culminating in the 'Endurance' march. What struck me about Pete was he had an uncanny eye for the lie of the land and didn't waste a scrap of energy unless he had no other choice. The day out with him taught me not to lose height unless it was absolutely imperative. I discovered that sometimes it made more sense to contour around a feature, which although a longer route, actually saved you time and energy. Another soldier that I trained with on the hills in the autumn of 1979 was Harry. We became good friends and Harry told me a little about his background and previous military experience. Harry was originally from Glasgow, brought up in the school of 'hard knocks'. His escape route proved to be the Parachute Regiment, where he served in 2 Para. After this, Harry told me that he had emigrated to South Africa and served for several years in their Special Forces (SF), where he experienced close quarter combat and was truly battle-hardened. Now back in the UK, Harry was determined to pass SAS Selection no matter how hard the ordeal.

To attend the Royal Signals Crypto Supplement Course, more usually known as the 'crypto course', you first had to hold Developed Vetting and also be a class 1 radio telegraphist or data telegraphist. I drove up to Catterick to attend the course at 8 Signal Regiment. It took place inside a high-security compound, surrounded by razor wire and known as the 'funny farm'. Everyone on the course was searched on arrival and departure every day. All the classified equipment and keying material was kept in security vaults. Even our notes were classified 'Secret' and destroyed at the end of the course. We finished with a comprehensive written examination. I came out as top student and also equalled the all-time best score.

When I returned to Hereford, I carried on working in the Signals Training Troop and it gave me great satisfaction to see the SAS and SBS patrol signallers pass through with excellent results for most of them. Meanwhile, I had managed to save up some money while I was away in Belize so decided now was the time to buy a sports car. The car was a white MGB Roadster with wire spoked wheels and was my pride and joy for the next couple of years. However, it was soon December and the SAS Selection course was scheduled to begin in early January.

Before beginning Selection, some final words of advice were given to me by D Squadron's SSM. Lawrence (WO2 Lawrence Gallagher BEM) sat me down in his office with the door shut and told me that SAS Selection would be the hardest thing I would ever attempt in my life and the only chance of success was to keep going whatever happened. He reminded me that the only way you can fail SAS Selection is if you voluntarily withdraw from the course or if you are hospitalized. In an attempt to inspire me he reminded me of the macabre joke, if you could call it that, which was circulating around the regiment at that time: 'Death is nature's way of telling you that you have failed SAS Selection.' This pep-talk only made me more determined to keep going whatever the odds. I asked Lawrence, if I was successful would it be possible for D Squadron to claim me and could I be posted to Boat Troop? He said he would see what he could do but made no promises. The sergeant major's parting words to me were ominous. He told me that I would be totally ostracized by D Squadron while I was on Selection, and furthermore I was banned from the squadron lines and was to be treated like a pariah so there could be no accusations of favouritism. I felt like a monk about to start a pilgrimage. Although I didn't realize it at the time, I had been working towards SAS Selection from the day I was born. Sadly, Lawrence was to die in the SAS Sea King helicopter crash in the Falklands War.

Chapter 3

SAS Selection

I was nervous when we all gathered in the Blue Room, which was at that time the main room in the largest building in Bradbury Lines. There were over 240 soldiers and 36 officers gathered there for the start of 22 SAS 'Winter Selection' 1980. I arrived without rank on my uniform and wearing a navy-blue beret with Royal Signals cap-badge. I had also removed my parachute wings. This was an attempt to appear as nondescript as possible to give the instructors less ammunition to chastise me. As I looked around at the other candidates, including many from the Parachute Regiment, other infantry regiments, a few Royal Marines and quite a few from the various technical corps, I wondered what special spark had to be inside me to pass SAS Selection? I had prepared as well as possible and now all I could do was give it my all.

The CO of 22 SAS, Lieutenant Colonel Mike Rose, soon took to the stage and his pep talk lasted all of sixty seconds. He stated that nobody fails Selection as everyone who attempts it will gain something from the experience. He then went on to say that many are called but few are chosen to serve in 22 SAS. With that, he wished us good luck, said most of us would not be seeing him again, and departed. We were then introduced to OC Training Wing who soon handed us over to the SSM. John 'Lofty' Wiseman was the sergeant major's name and he lost no time in informing us that all of his staff were to be obeyed instantly and all were to be addressed by the term 'staff' regardless of the instructor's actual rank. However, once you pass Selection it is all first name terms, although the officers are called 'Boss'. Lofty later became famous for writing the *SAS Survival Handbook*, based on his experiences in 22 SAS.

We had each been issued with a mountain of kit the day before and it was soon to be put to use with a vengeance. Within minutes we were organized into squads and handed over to the QMSI at the gym for the Basic Fitness Test. This was a standard army test consisting of a fifteen-minute run over one and a half miles, immediately followed by an individual best effort run on the return route. My finishing position was halfway down the pack. I was playing the 'grey man', that is don't be recognized as a front runner and don't lag behind. After the timed run, we immediately put on our combat jackets and helmets and carried weapons and bergens for a Combat Fitness Test. This was a timed march over eight miles and an army-wide test. I was shocked to see that half a dozen men failed to complete these tests. They were driven to the train station and returned to unit (RTU'd) the same day. We spent the remainder of the first day revising our map-reading knowledge.

A few days later we participated in the dreaded 'Fan Dance'. The name comes from 'Pen-Y-Fan', which is the highest mountain in the Brecon Beacons. It had been snowing all week, so going twice over the summit of Pen-Y-Fan would be even more difficult than usual. We were told to stay together as a squad and keep up with the instructor. The weather conditions were poor, but even so I had the good sense to remove my army pullover from underneath my smock as the fast pace was more than enough to keep me warm. Anyway, there was absolutely no stopping for a rest. Once again, I played the grey man, keeping a few places behind the instructor and never getting up to his shoulder. I noticed one or two very fit guys who were trying to engage the instructor in small talk which I don't think helped their cause at all. The route started at Torpantau Station and the first checkpoint was the summit of Pen-Y-Fan. From there we ran downhill to the Storey Arms before turning around for the return leg. Overall, the route covered 24km and for some of the guys was a brutal introduction to tabbing at speed over mountainous terrain.

On the second week, we ran up a hill about 3km from Bradbury Lines. There was a trig point on top and from there we had a great view of Hereford City, including the cathedral and other key landmarks. The viewpoint looking down on Hereford permitted each of us to calibrate our prismatic compass. To be honest, I hardly ever used mine, preferring to use a Silva compass that I had tied to my chest pocket to avoid the possibility of dropping it. By now we were going up to the Brecon Beacons several times a week and practising our navigation in pairs. We worked every day and most evenings and the workload was unforgiving.

One evening on the mountains I was with my designated partner and running downhill. Suddenly I fell through a snow-bridge and ended up standing in a stream up to my groin in freezing cold water with only my head peeping out over the snow. Try as I might, I simply couldn't get out and I was in danger of being swept under the snow by the fast-flowing current which would likely have proved fatal for me. Fortunately, two other candidates found us there by accident and helped my buddy to pull me out of the stream.

Test Week consisted of a daily tab operating alone. We were told by the Directing Staff (DS) that everyone was assigned different routes so it would be pointless to follow anyone else from checkpoint to checkpoint. The wear and tear on your body rapidly degrades the performance that you are capable of giving. Cut-off times were never given so you just had to give it your best effort. At this time there was an outbreak of food poisoning that spread through us like wildfire. A few guys reported sick with diarrhoea and vomiting and were pulled straight off the course never to be seen again. I dosed myself up with Imodium and just got on with it even though I could have shit through the eye of a needle! I had stomach cramps early on during Test Week and was really ill, but kept my predicament to myself. On one particular tab, I was getting more and more delayed by being forced to squat down and empty my bowels every thirty minutes or so. At the end of the day I was seriously dehydrated, but kept going by drinking plenty of water with electrolyte sachets dissolved in the water and somehow made it to the end of the tab, despite having eleven or twelve shits along the way! I finished in last place that day. The next morning Taff, who was taking over from Lofty as the Training Wing Sergeant Major, called me over and strongly advised me to improve my times or else. Fortunately once we were out on the hills I felt much better, and as a bonus most of the snow had melted. I completed my tab that day halfway down the list of finishers. Hoss Ligairi from D Squadron was by now an instructor with Training Wing and was manning the last checkpoint on top of a mountain. As I staggered into the checkpoint, he looked at me with his deadpan face and steely-eyed stare and then his face burst into a huge grin and he laughed aloud when he saw the state of me. This cheered me up no end and he added a few words of encouragement: 'Go on Tony, it's all downhill to the finish. You can do it!' That was the only time during the whole of Selection when an instructor gave me any encouragement, so it meant a lot to me at the time.

That was also the day we had a no-notice night tab a couple of hours later after finishing the daytime tab. We arrived back at the trucks and were told to break open our emergency ration pack that we always carried and cook ourselves a hot meal. Then we were trucked over to the next valley before being dropped off one at a time just after last-light to start our lonely trek through the mountains. Somewhere along the route my ankle started swelling up and I started to limp. Things were no better on the next day which was the penultimate tab. The march on the final day was known as 'Endurance'. Meanwhile I realized that I had 'tendonitis' and could only limp along slowly while grimacing with pain. Somehow I survived the day, but my time was once again borderline. I felt like throwing my hand in as there was no way I could carry 65lbs on my back, plus belt-kit weighing another 10lbs and a 9lb rifle while trying to walk forty miles over the mountains in winter.

I had a hot shower back at camp, sorted out some dry clothes, took a couple of prescription painkillers, and slit the side of my boot to get it on over my badly swollen ankle. I also taped up my back which had been rubbed raw from carrying the bergen. After a few hours' sleep it was time to parade at the armoury to collect our rifles and climb on the trucks for an 0200 hrs drive out to the Brecon Beacons and the start of 'Endurance'. I thought fuck it, I would rather fail by collapsing on the mountains than jacking it in outside the armoury in front of all the other guys. We set off at one-minute intervals from somewhere near Talybont Reservoir and the route took us directly up a steep climb and then on to high ground. It was about 0330 hrs when it was my turn to start. I took another couple of strong painkillers and tried to hide my limp from the instructors. I basically just went head down and arse up into the wintery snow squalls. My tendon was excruciatingly painful for the first half hour and going uphill didn't help matters. Then slowly but surely the pain started to recede and I began to regain full movement in my ankle. I can only assume that once I had warmed up, the tendon began to move freely. If it is possible to smile while giving it your maximum effort and all the time going straight up a steep climb then I was smiling! After another twenty minutes I made the first ridge and things became a bit easier.

Sixteen hours later I had not only traversed the Brecon Beacons to the west but had turned around and via a different route returned to the east and was finally approaching Talybont Reservoir and the finish. There had only been about ten hours daylight and it was dark again with not even a glimmer of moonlight to guide my path. I followed the edge of a fir tree plantation steeply downhill towards the reservoir. Suddenly I slipped in the mud and plunged downhill sitting on my arse out of control. A sheep fence stopped my descent when a few strands of barbed wire hit me in the face and chest and ripped open my forehead just above my eyebrows. There was no time to stop and appraise the situation as every second counted. I struggled to my feet and carried on. Suddenly the reservoir dam wall sprang into sight as the moon shone through the clouds. I ran the last 400 metres along the top of the dam wall and finished 'Endurance' with my face covered in blood. I was elated to discover that I had finished in third place out of thirty-six finishers! That was all that was left of the original 280 candidates who had started Selection four weeks earlier. I have no idea why my performance improved dramatically on that day? Perhaps the longer distance suited me? Perhaps it was because I was over the diarrhoea? Then again it could have just been luck or divine intervention? The Medical Officer (MO) was on hand to clean up my face and put some 'steri-strips' on the gash to close the wound. To this day I have no idea why I felt so strong after suffering all week from diarrhoea and then tendonitis.

Next up, we spent a couple of weeks practising infantry minor tactics, and I must have carried out over fifty section attacks until I could do them in my sleep. Since finishing test week, I had stopped exercising as much as possible in a bid to get my body fully rested and also get rid of the tendonitis. We did however manage to fit in the SAS swimming test of 1,000m swimming breast-stroke while wearing army trousers, shirt and a web-belt with a full water bottle attached.

We were given a long weekend off before flying out to Belize in Central America for our jungle training, an essential prerequisite to passing SAS Selection. Our first week in Belize saw us board three Puma helicopters for the flight out to a rubber plantation. On arrival we took over some semi-derelict rubber processing sheds for our lectures and sleeping accommodation. On our first afternoon we were each told to cut a log into one-metre lengths with our machetes. This required teamwork to select a tree, chop it down and then cut it into lengths. Naturally everyone tried to grab one of the lighter ones as we knew we would be carrying the logs quite a bit. We then paraded with our logs and the DS swapped the logs about so that those with a thinner, lightweight log were given a thicker, heavier log and vice versa!

Each morning began at first light with callisthenic exercises using our logs and then a 5km run still carrying our logs on our shoulders. We then spent all day, and long into the evenings, developing our patrolling skills and learning what to do in the event of a contact with the enemy. The contact drills were exhausting, especially when sometimes you had to carry a 'casualty' in a fireman's lift and still keep on firing from the hip as you withdrew to a 'rally point'. Contact drills were always carried out using live ammunition so we had to be switched on to avoid an accident. We spent most of one night lying prone in an ambush position, all the time being bitten alive by mosquitoes and ants. I suspected there would be a member of the DS sitting behind us keeping watch so I just suffered in silence until the ambush was initiated a few hours before dawn.

One day we spent several hours learning how to camouflage ourselves to SAS standards. Then as a test we were given an area in which to blend in with our surroundings. An instructor approached the four sticks marking our patrol stand just as one of our number fired his rifle negligently. Unusually, we were only carrying rifles loaded with blank ammunition at this time otherwise the instructor could easily have been shot. Immediately the instructor called out my name and asked if it was me who had fired the negligent discharge. Fortunately for me the culprit stood up and admitted what he had done. I think my name was being bandied about as the other three members of my patrol were all from the infantry and the instructor assumed that as I was the only man from a technical corps it must have been my mistake.

The next day we flew to a location in the virgin jungle and set up camp with the instructors one side of a river and ourselves on the far bank. We were told to set up our patrol locations in a wide crescent. I had already cut down some saplings and made my A-Frame bed, tied a rattan line to my stand-to position and was showing the other patrol members how to do the same when the RSM turned up. I think my efforts were noted, but nothing was said by the RSM. A week or so later, while out on patrol, I spotted a 'fer-de-lance' snake coiled right in front of us, both the lead scout and number two had already passed by and had almost stepped on it. I brought this to the attention of our instructor using sign language. This was evidence that I had been keeping observant. Fer-de-lances are one of the largest and most deadly snakes in Central America. They are a particularly aggressive type of venomous pit-viper and will often strike without warning. During the day fer-de-lance snakes will lie coiled among leaves on the jungle floor, where their long, thick bodies can be difficult to spot. All communication in the jungle was by sign language (although whispering was allowed when absolutely necessary). Talking at a normal volume was strictly not permitted.

An hour or so later the lead scout literally walked off the top of a cliff and the second man tumbled after him. I was third man and just managed to stop myself falling over the cliff edge. As I was carrying the radio, I was able to erect a wire antenna thrown over a couple of nearby trees and establish comms direct with the guard station at Airport Camp. I informed them to stand by for a CASEVAC signal. Meanwhile the instructor climbed down ten metres onto the massive rock slab on which my two colleagues were now sprawled on the river's edge. The instructor climbed back up the cliff face after twenty minutes having given first aid to the two casualties. He told me to establish contact with Airport Camp and warn them to stand by for a CASEVAC signal. He looked impressed when I informed him that I had already done this and the helicopter crew were standing by. I also told him that I had contacted our jungle base camp and the RSM and 'Starlight' (chief medic) were already walking along the river bank to our location and expected to be with us within the next forty-five minutes. The two guys were later CASEVACKED to Airport Camp after our 'Starlight' had examined them. That left just the two of us still standing in our patrol. As I was the patrol second-in-command, I assumed command and was asked by the DS what the revised plan was. I decided we would carry on and after shouldering the extra loads continued with our mission. The mission was to cache a heavy ammunition box in a deep hole that we dug. Then I took bearings and paced out the distance from prominent trees and boulders before entering all this in my notebook. After completing the mission, the two of us compiled the cache report.

The jungle training involved lots of live firing and patrolling, often staying out overnight. The two of us left in our patrol combined with the remnants of another patrol to make a five-man patrol for the remainder of the jungle phase. After every patrol we were required to write up a report that same evening and hand it in after stand-to the next morning. I was soon elected by the other patrol members to write all the reports, one or two of my colleagues not being particularly good at writing with 'joined-up' sentences. We practised our shooting relentlessly and I soon became adept at putting a 'double-tap' into the chest of the target, followed by an aimed shot to the head. After conducting a live firing exercise along a jungle lane, where we would put into effect all our 'contact drills', we would be permitted to check our targets. It was reassuring that all of us had become excellent shots with so much practice and every target was riddled in the head and chest. One highlight of the trip after three weeks was a river crossing with our bergens tied together as a flotation aid and rifles draped over the top of the bergen raft ready for instant use while we swam alongside. When this activity was finished the instructors told us to strip off to 'bollock order', i.e., naked, and have a full body wash in the river. Now this was my first proper wash in over three weeks and I didn't need to be told twice. We must have stunk but had become immune to the pungent smells as we merged into the jungle and became as one with it.

The final exercise of the jungle phase involved a Close Target Recce (CTR) of an enemy camp that the DS had constructed. This required us to get in close to the camp by day without being spotted by the DS and sketch all the key points and defensive positions. We spent several hours redrawing the sketch map, plans and other diagrams to support the report that I had written with contributions from everyone in the patrol. We attacked the camp just before first light on the next day. Later that morning we were flown out of the jungle back to Airport Camp. This concluded the jungle phase and we then had two days R&R at Airport Camp before flying back to the UK via Washington DC.

Our first morning back at Hereford was filled with trepidation. We formed up outside the Training Wing office. Those that had their names called out were told to go to the Blue Room. That left fourteen of us standing there, including one officer. We were told to wait. After about ten minutes, Taff, the sergeant major, came out to speak to us. We were expecting bad news as nobody had paid us much attention, but the news was everything I had been hoping for. 'Well done men. You have successfully passed the jungle phase of Selection and will now move on to the field-firing phase.' I didn't know whether to laugh or cry, such was the emotional roller-coaster that we were travelling on. We deployed to Sennybridge for the field-firing phase of Selection, which included live firing on a variety of infantry support weapons. I fired the

84mm Carl Gustav anti-tank shoulder-launched missile. We also carried out extensive training with the GPMG in the Sustained Fire role. This weapon requires a two-man crew and can lay down fire at 750 rounds per minute at ranges out to 1,800 metres. I was given two 66mm M72 LAW (Light Anti-Armour Weapons) to fire and marvelled at the weapon's simplicity. Additionally, we spent several days 'fighting-in-built-up-areas' in a specially constructed village.

We had a free weekend and then, as always, the tempo increased. We had poor weather, including heavy mist, low cloud base and rain. We were learning about Helicopter Landing Sites (HLS) and lighting patterns for night-time landings. This was more difficult than it might seem as we didn't have any Night Vision Goggles (NVG). We would wait in total darkness until the sound of the helicopter rotors were close to our location. At that time, we would switch on our army flashlights with red filters to light up the HLS in a prearranged pattern. The light cast was very dim, but it was just enough for the pilot from the SF flight to see and gave him an indication of what direction to approach and then land at the HLS.

The next morning, we received a lecture on parachute air resupply and spent the afternoon packing our own resupply pack with a dummy load of a box filled with sand. On top of this 'bundle' the resupply parachute would be attached. The resupply bundles were then driven in a truck to RAF Lyneham for loading onto the aircraft. The following day, we deployed onto a large training area and each four-man patrol sent a coded message in Morse. These were received by the Hereford base and one consolidated signal was sent via teleprinter to RAF Lyneham operations centre. There the signal would be read and the pilot of the C130 briefed on his mission. We then had two or three hours to wait before getting into position with our air marker panels while the rain pissed down on us. The weather was very poor and we had been told the drop would be cancelled if visibility fell below 400m. Gradually the weather improved and I assessed the ground visibility to be close to 400m. It was then that I knew the para-resup was on as I was confident the RAF SF crew would pull out all the stops to deliver our bundles. Suddenly we heard and then saw the C130 flying at a very low altitude. The flying was absolutely breath-taking when you consider there were many ground obstacles such as tall trees and electric pylons to take account of in the poor visual conditions. Four runs were made and each time a parachute would drop and then we could hear, and sometimes see, the aircraft as it performed a sharp turn and lined up for the next patrol's turn. Soon enough, our turn came and our air markers were set out upwind of where we wanted the bundle to land to take account of wind drift. We also had to mark our desired point on the drop zone (DZ) with a large white cross. We were delighted when our bundle landed less than 10 m from the designated cross.

Throughout SAS Selection we were often taken on timed runs and had countless tough physical training sessions in the gym. One day we were taken out along the lanes and over the hills for a seven-mile run. The run was interspersed with sprints up a few hills along our chosen route. We were all tired on our return to camp, but immediately we were hustled into the gym for a game of 'murder ball'. Lofty, the outgoing sergeant major, and Taff, the sergeant major designate, led the two teams. I remember the game started with Lofty holding the heavy medicine ball and saying the object of the game was to get the ball into your opponents' net at the other end of the gym. He went on to say there is only one rule, and with the immortal words 'The rule is there are no rules!' Lofty kicked one of the opponents in the bollocks and went charging down the gym with the rest of us in hot pursuit! Soon it was every man for himself and there were many bloodied noses before the game was concluded. Even Lofty lost a tooth, and one of the Selection candidates suffered a twisted ankle in the ensuing *mêlée*.

Another week, and another subject, as we moved on to close quarter battle (CQB). This was a week of working with handguns, sub-machine guns and assault rifles that we would encounter later on when we deployed on operations in Northern Ireland. We did countless house assaults and room clearance drills, often using 'flash-bang' stun-grenades to initiate the assault. We would strip and assemble the weapons many times while blindfolded and kept a loaded and cocked handgun on our person at all times. Some of the weapons the terrorists were using in Northern Ireland at that time were simply ancient. One memorable weapon that I fired during this training phase was the 'Tommy Gun', or to give it its full title the Thompson sub-machine gun, with its 50-round drum magazine firing .45-inch calibre bullets on fully automatic fire. The Tommy Gun was a museum piece. Invented at the end of the First World War, it became the weapon-of-choice for both criminals and law-enforcement agencies during the American prohibition-era of the 1920s and 1930s.

We then stepped up a gear and used our new-found skills and incorporated them into close protection (CP). This was a week's introduction to the skills that a bodyguard would require for VIP protection. The full CP course was four weeks and would come later if and when you became a fully-fledged member of the regiment, but for now this was just an introduction that everyone received during Selection.

We followed this with a week working with demolition charges, including the physical properties of detonators, det-cord and plastic explosive (PE). Once we had experimented with frame charges and then shaped charges we progressed to home-made explosive and made lots of loud noises out on the training area! This was followed up with a similar week practising first aid, including the treatment of battlefield trauma and learning how to insert an intravenous drip.

The final phase of SAS Selection began on Monday 5 May 1980. The Selection course candidates were joined by over one hundred British and NATO soldiers, marines, and pilots for the NATO Combat Survival Instructors Course. We had guest speakers who were former prisoners of war (PoW) from the Korean and Vietnam wars. I was totally absorbed in the first-hand accounts of their ordeals. They spoke about escape and evasion, how to stay sane, survive interrogation and possibly endure years of incarceration. We also studied nutrition and learnt all about calorific intake and the importance of eating enough food to survive when on the run. It might be stating the obvious, but the best time to escape is immediately after capture. This is to avoid the psychological and physiological deterioration that will rapidly set in if you are being physically abused, denied sleep or have no access to food and water.

There was something else going on while I progressed through SAS Selection continuation training at the end of April 1980, something that would have far-reaching implications for the future of the SAS. On the morning of Wednesday, 30 April, six Iranian gunmen forced their way into the Iranian embassy at Prince's Gate in London's South Kensington. With my trained eye, I watched the SP team deploy in their helicopters and fleet of Range Rovers. I assumed, wrongly, that B Squadron were deploying on a counter-terrorist training exercise, although I was surprised that this was taking place on a Wednesday.

As soon as the SP team arrived on scene an Immediate Action (IA) plan was put in place. The IA plan is only used if the situation quickly deteriorates and hostages are shot. It is much better to study the building blueprints and consider all the amassed intelligence before formulating a series of 'what-if' scenarios resulting in detailed planning options for an assault and hostage rescue. Negotiations continued over the following days and by the sixth day the terrorists were becoming increasingly frustrated by the lack of progress with their demands. At this point, the terrorists decided they were not getting anywhere fast so they shot a hostage and pushed his body out of the front door of the embassy. The Cabinet Office Briefing Room (COBRA), headed by the prime minister, Margaret Thatcher, discussed their response. Early that evening they authorized the use of force to release the hostages. Operational control was handed over to the MOD by the Metropolitan Police. While negotiations continued with the terrorists to keep them occupied, CO 22 SAS implemented Operation Nimrod. Soon afterwards, the SP team abseiled from the embassy roof and forced entry through several windows. The raid lasted about fifteen minutes and the SAS rescued all except one of the hostages and killed five of the six terrorists.

The siege at the Iranian embassy had been on the news all over the weekend. I was to find out that evening exactly what was going on when the TV programme we were watching was interrupted with a live broadcast of the SAS assault on the Iranian embassy. I knew straight away that the regiment would be thrust into the limelight after all this publicity. Anyway, I still had a course to pass if I was to join the regiment as an SAS trooper. Later that evening B Squadron started to return to Hereford by helicopter and the remainder in Range Rovers. I heard later that the CO treated the SP team that same evening to a pint in the Officers' Mess!

The combat survival course continued without further interruption. The course began with a few days of mainly classroom-based lectures. There were also trips out to the countryside to identify wild plants and fungi that were safe to eat. The course continued with lectures on resistance to interrogation and the Geneva Convention concerning PoWs rights in captivity. I also learnt how to draw and use a sketch map and how to navigate using a button compass which could be shoved up your backside to avoid being found during a body search.

The second week was spent building bashas out of what materials we could find in the woods. I crafted a hardwood spoon in my spare time and used it for several years on my desert and jungle trips. We had very little food to eat. All I had was a chicken which I killed by wringing its neck, before smoking the flesh over a slow-burning fire as a means of drying and preserving the meat. The highlight of the week was when we killed a couple of sheep by slitting their throats. Then we skinned the carcasses and cut the meat up into joints. A couple of the regiment's Fijian troopers constructed a *'hangi'* cooking pit. *Hangi* is the Maori word for cooking pit. The first step is to dig a large pit and then light a fire nearby which is then covered by rocks that are heated by the fire. When these stones are sufficiently heated the hot stones are placed in the bottom of the pit and covered with food wrapped in banana leaves. Typical food would be whole chickens and joints of meat plus potatoes and other root vegetables such as yams and sweet potatoes. Unfortunately the Fijians didn't have banana leaves, so they substituted army issue bedsheets which were soaked in water and then cut into pieces to wrap the food. Once the food was in the pit, more of the hot stones were added to the top and the pit was filled in with earth. The food was left to cook for ten hours and then unearthed from the pit. This was when things went badly wrong. The bedsheets had been starched and bleached when they were washed and pressed at the laundry and these chemicals had leached out into all the food. When the pit was opened the most delicious looking cooked food was unwrapped before us. Then we were invited to take our pick and have our fill. I noticed the food smelt strongly of soap powder, bleach and starch. I tried to eat some of the meat, but immediately retched. Was it a set-up? No, I don't think so, but what a waste of a huge amount of food. A few of the course members ate the food despite the vile taste, but they soon vomited it back up! Oh well, I just had to go back to eating a broth of dandelion and nettle leaves with some 'road-kill' rabbit.

The last week of the combat survival course was also the last week of Selection. The previous Friday I was told to report to D Squadron's SSM. Now, I hadn't seen Lawrence since the course started in January so was surprised to be summoned by him. Lawrence informed me that if I passed this final week, I would be posted to Boat Troop in D Squadron and would fly out to Florida with the squadron immediately the course ended. In other words, if all went well, I would be an SAS trooper in a little more than eight days. Lawrence then told me to report to the CO's office. The adjutant was waiting for me in the outer office and told me the CO was expecting me and to go straight in. The CO, Lieutenant Colonel Mike Rose, told me that I only had one week left on the course and at the end of Selection he planned to meet with and personally congratulate the regiment's newest SAS troopers. However, he wouldn't be able to congratulate me as I was to fly out to Florida with D Squadron on a joint training exercise with the SEALs. The CO went on to say he didn't want to jinx me by saying congratulations for the moment and wouldn't be shaking my hand just yet. He told me to remain focused and get through what would undoubtedly be a tough ordeal for me. Just as I was about to leave he said, 'Hey Trooper! Don't you want this?' and he threw my SAS beret with the winged dagger cap-badge across his desk which I caught. I stuffed the beret deep in my pocket and ran all the way back to the Blue Room for the final briefing.

The final exercise started the next morning, a Saturday. I showered and dressed carefully and went to the cookhouse determined to eat a huge breakfast! I literally stuffed myself with as much food as I could cram into my mouth as I wasn't expecting to eat again for a few days. I felt physically sick and was groaning from all the food I ate. After breakfast we reported to the Blue Room for the exercise. The first instruction was to strip down to our underpants. Most of our clothes were bagged and tagged. We were only allowed to keep our underpants, army shirt, boots and socks. Then we shuffled slowly to the front of the queue where we dropped our underpants and touched our toes. This is the bit where the search team performed a body cavity search while wearing rubber gloves. The searcher was a corporal from the Intelligence Corps. He didn't stick his finger very far up my arse which was fortunate as there was a five-pound note rolled up tightly in a thin plastic bag pushed high up inside my rectum! Once we had had our bottoms violated, we were thrown a set of vintage battledress trousers and jackets. I was also handed a greatcoat that had seen better days. Interestingly, there were no buttons on any of the clothing. Luckily, there was a piece of baling twine in one of the pockets which I used to hold up my trousers. We were given a few minutes to get dressed and then herded into trucks waiting outside to be driven to a nearby training area. Eventually, we were all sat down in a cold, unlit hangar and guarded by British Army Ghurkha soldiers dressed in Russian military uniforms. We were sitting about 3m apart with our backs against the hangar wall. I was sitting below a broken window. After a while I noticed broken glass on the ground close to me so discreetly put a large shard in my pocket as a cutting edge. Suddenly a few stun-grenades were thrown into the hangar and we could hear automatic fire. The partisans had come to rescue us! All 100-plus 'runners' were quickly crammed into the backs of two cattle trucks and we sped off with the Ghurkhas firing after the speeding trucks as we made our 'escape'.

Once up in the Black Mountains, just over the Welsh border, the trucks stopped and the partisans dragged us out four at a time. We were given a sketch-map and a button compass and told that the partisans had an agent contact waiting for us on the following night two hours after nightfall. We had a two-hour window to make this RV and if we missed this there was a fall-back 'Dead Letter Box' that we could make for on the following night where we would find written instructions in a 'cache'. We were now in the partisans' escape 'pipeline' and had to place our trust in them. The Ghurkhas were also all over the mountains acting as a live 'enemy' or 'hunter force'. If anybody got caught early on, they would be roughly treated and then subjected to tactical questioning (TQ) before being released back into the exercise. I was teamed up with three mates from the Selection course and we managed to evade capture all week, although it was a close call once or twice.

We had very little to eat, except for a single slice of stale bread that the 'agent' would give us every second night at our next agent RV. By the fourth day we were absolutely ravenous. I had retrieved my fiver when I had a shit a couple of days earlier. After washing the plastic bag, the fiver was fine. Meanwhile my mate Frankie informed us that he hadn't taken a shit since the exercise began and he still had a five-pound note inside him that he swallowed in a condom! With our urging, Frankie went behind a bush to take a shit. Suddenly, Frankie shouted out 'Fucking Hell! The condom has dissolved and the fiver's turned brown!' Sure enough, the acid in his stomach had dissolved the condom just enough to let body fluids inside which had then dyed the five-pound note brown! I told Frankie to wash it in the small stream near our position. Frankie spent several minutes washing the banknote, but the fiver remained brown, i.e., the colour of a ten-pound note.

We had spotted a village store the previous evening and one of us had sneaked into the village at night to check opening times displayed in the shop window. We set up an OP late that afternoon just above the village from where we could see the shop. We waited anxiously, and then as closing time approached Frankie furtively walked up to the village store, looking every inch the tramp in his army greatcoat. The three of us stayed in hiding while Frankie was in the shop. Suddenly, Frankie emerged and ran down the road and across the field to our location. He then shouted, 'Run! It's the fucking Ghurkhas!' in his scouse accent. We ran after Frankie for over a mile, mostly uphill, with Frankie running flat out in his army boots with a carrier bag of shopping in each hand and still wearing his greatcoat. We carried on running until we reached a large wooded area where we took stock of the situation. To this day I have a mental picture of Frankie running along with the carrier bags and the flapping tails of his greatcoat. It still seems just as funny to me now as it did on the day it took place.

As there was no sign of a pursuit, we stopped and asked Frankie what had happened when he went in to the shop. Frankie described the little old lady behind the counter looking at him oddly as he entered the shop. Frankie said she obviously thought that he was a tramp. He quickly grabbed four of everything that we had previously listed and put the items on the shop counter: bread, corned beef, cheese triangles, packets of digestive biscuits and cartons of milk. The old lady packed the food into two carrier bags and told Frankie the cost, which was just under £9. Frankie slammed down the two fivers on the counter, one blue and one brown. It was then the old lady asked Frankie why he had given her a ten-pound and a five-pound note? Quick as a flash, Frankie grabbed the carrier bags and hightailed it out of the shop, shouting over his shoulder, 'It's alright! Keep the change!' As Frankie charged out onto the village high street, he spotted a Land Rover full of Ghurkhas about 50 metres from him facing the other direction. He assumed he had been spotted, but luckily for us he hadn't and our race up the hill had put some distance between us and the hunter force. I have never eaten an entire large loaf of bread and a can of corned beef in one sitting before or since, but it tasted wonderful! We spent a most uncomfortable night in the rain, soaking wet lying on fertiliser sacks in a hedgerow, before waking up at first light and eating our cheese triangles and biscuits. We had a long walk to our next agent RV, and there were Ghurkhas, on foot, in vehicles and above us in helicopters over-flying the area. We managed to avoid all contact with them, although we heard dog patrols with the trackers shouting instructions down in the valley. The dogs were barking loudly as if in hot pursuit, but they must have been on someone else's trail as we neither saw nor heard them again.

That was the last food we had until we walked into the final agent RV. The agent gave us a single slice of bread each and then told us to climb into the back of one of two cattle trucks. We waited there while the truck gradually filled with 'runners' over the course of a couple of hours. Once the trucks were full, I wasn't surprised when we came under 'attack' by the Ghurkhas, and the DS immediately surrendered and were spirited away. That left us all in the hands of the Ghurkha hunter force. Soon after this we were driven in the cattle trucks, escorted by a convoy of Ghurkha soldiers in Land Rovers, to a holding area for tactical questioning (TQ). This was fairly low-key 'Geneva Convention' stuff and we were not really roughed up at this stage, although it was cold and damp and we were not offered anything to eat or drink.

Things took a turn for the worse when we were blindfolded and had our hands tied behind our backs. When it came to my turn, I was led outside and pushed into the back of an army truck. I knew this to be the end of the TQ phase and I expected us to be subjected to a disorientation phase before moving on to the dreaded interrogation phase. We drove around, probably in circles for the next hour, before stopping at what I later found out to be a large hangar on a military training area. My hands were untied and I was pushed into a small brick building which turned out to be an ablution block with a few toilets and told by one of the Ghurkhas guards, 'You have one minute for quick piss!' Now I knew that Ghurkhas are prudes and would not look at someone having a piss. This gave me an opportunity not only for a quick piss but also for a drink of water and to splash cold water on my face. The Ghurkhas were waiting when I emerged and they led me, still blindfolded, into the hangar. The hangar had 'white noise' reverberating around the building. I was made to stand against the wall in a stress position. The occasional cough told me there were others in the room and I coughed once or twice to alert the other 'runners' to my presence.

Although blindfolded, I needed to become aware of my surroundings. First, I listened to the generators producing white noise at close to dangerous decibel levels. I was a bit worried that the exhaust pipes may not be venting outside to avoid carbon monoxide poisoning, but after twenty minutes or so I realized all was well. The next bit of excitement came when a couple of Ghurkha soldiers came up to me and one shouted in my ear, 'Take off clothes now! Very quick!' Feigning stupidity, I used this as an opportunity to whip off my blindfold along with my clothes. It took them several seconds before they realized what I had done before screaming at me to put on the blindfold. Nevertheless, I felt like I had scored a valuable victory in the mind-games that I was playing with my captors. I now knew what my surroundings looked like, including three Coventry Climax gennies mounted on trailers. I also saw about twenty 'runners' spaced around the walls in two different stress positions. The Ghurkha guards then gave me a set of army coveralls to wear. This was obviously my prisoner of war (PoW) uniform. The guards took all my clothes away, including socks and boots which would have been a major blow to any escape plan had this been for real. Next they tried to squeeze my bare feet into army gym shoes several sizes too small. This gave me another opportunity to play mind-games. I scrunched up my foot, curled my toes and obstinately refused to let them put the gym shoe on my foot. They started shouting at me and punched me in the back, but still I grimly fought against putting the shoe on. All the time I was standing on a gravel floor that was freezing cold. I stubbed my toe which started bleeding so they went to speak to an umpire. I couldn't hear what the umpire was saying, but the pair of them were shouting, 'Yes Sir! We do it now Sir!' Ten minutes later, my toe was cleaned and a first-aid dressing put on it before they put my feet in a pair of gym shoes that actually fitted. I was really enjoying the mind-games and thought I was well on top. However, as soon as the umpire disappeared, they changed their tune, saying to me, 'You bad man! You do what we say or there will be big trouble for you!' They forced me into various stress positions and then tried to make me do some press-ups. I realized they were already in trouble with the umpire so I just adopted the press-up position, rested on my hands and knees and refused to do any press-ups. Eventually they gave up and put me on my knees with my arms linked behind my head. This is a very uncomfortable position to hold for twenty minutes. Next, I was spreadeagled against the wall for another twenty minutes, and then the two stress positions were alternated for hours on end. Eventually I heard the sound of crunching gravel as the guards approached me and I was dragged away for my first interrogation.

I was forcibly pushed down into a chair and my blindfold was pulled away. Immediately the bright light in front of me hurt my eyes. It took a good twenty seconds of squinting into the blinding light before I noticed the two guards standing either side of me. Then a voice to my side shouted 'Look to your front!' I could just about discern the shape of a person behind the bright light. He started shouting questions at me without waiting for my response like somebody going crazy, 'What's your name? What's your rank? What's your number? What's your date of birth?' He never stopped, not permitting me to reply. Suddenly he stood up and his chair clattered on its side with a loud crash. He came and stood directly beside me and started to scream in my ear. I could actually feel globules of his spit landing on the side of my face. Eventually he tired himself out and walked out of the interrogation room slamming the door behind him. I was left alone with the guards for several minutes before a different interrogator took his place. 'Sorry about that, but he has had a busy morning. Shall we start again?' The second interrogator was polite, trying a totally different tack to get me to reveal more than the big four of number, rank, name and date of birth. Suddenly he started filling in an International Red Cross Committee postcard with my personal details. These postcards are supposed to be given to PoWs so that they can write to their families to inform them that they have been taken prisoner and are being well treated. He asked me to sign the card and handed me a pencil. Now I had been taught on the course that there is no requirement to sign anything as a PoW and it could well be a trick to film you signing a 'so-called' confession document. I picked the pencil up sideways, i.e., placed along the flat of my hand and when he asked me for a second time to sign, I made a fist and broke the pencil. That got me thrown out of the interrogation! If I remember rightly, I had six interrogations spread over about thirty hours. I never gave away anything at all to the interrogators, despite being very, very tired. I even watched a cup of coffee cooling down in front of one of the interrogators that he hadn't touched. I quickly swiped it and swallowed it in one big gulp before the guards could react. One of the interrogators was an attractive female who ordered me to strip off naked before laughing at my manhood which was understandably not feeling very perky at the time. Another interrogator had a plastic bag, with my confiscated uniform inside, which he proceeded to check for contraband. He was more than a little pissed off when he cut his hand on the piece of glass that I had previously stuffed in a pocket!

I was taken to a different room at the end of this phase and my blindfold was removed. When my eyes adjusted to the light there was an army officer wearing an umpire's armband on his upper sleeve. 'I am an umpire. Do you recognize me as an umpire?' After figuring out that this was not a trick – I remembered we had been briefed that umpires could not be impersonated – I told him that I knew him to be an umpire. 'This ordeal is now finished. The interrogations are over for you and here is some soup and sandwiches. Can I also be the first to congratulate you on passing Selection.' With that he shook my hand which was all a bit bizarre after what I had just been subjected to. I was too tired to say much but managed a rather subdued thank you. Then I got stuck into the soup and sandwiches while they asked for my feedback, all the time taking copious notes.

Three hours later I was back in Bradbury Lines packing my bergen as I was flying out to Florida with D Squadron within hours. The rest of the guys who had just finished 'interrogation' returned to Bradbury Lines soon after. I was able to congratulate them all except two. One had started talking during interrogation so was deemed unsuitable to serve in the regiment and had already departed the day before. The other had failed his Developed Vetting, which all SAS candidates must pass, but the details had only come through a few days earlier. The decision was taken to keep him on the course as he would at least qualify as a NATO Combat Survival Instructor, although that was little solace for the guy. Two of them still needed to pass a military parachuting course before being SAS-badged, but the final numbers remained the same. For the 22 SAS Winter Selection 1980, only one officer and eleven soldiers were accepted into 22 SAS from the original figure of 36 officers and 240 soldier candidates. As for me, I was now an SAS Trooper and a very exciting period of my life was about to begin.

Chapter 4

SAS Trooper

As we took off from RAF Lyneham on my deployment to Florida, I reflected on all that had taken place over the last six months since starting SAS Selection. At times I had been pushed to the limits of physical and mental endurance, and I was now fully aware of my strengths and weaknesses. That knowledge proved to be a great asset as I started my new life as an SAS trooper. The D Squadron main party had flown two days earlier in a VC-10. I was to fly with Mountain Troop on board a C130, together with a large consignment of freight.

After an eight-hour flight we landed at Gander Airport, Newfoundland. The runway was covered in a light coating of snow, but we still had a smooth landing. The weather was well below freezing point and I was wearing lightweight tropical uniform with just a woollen pullover and an SAS smock over the top. The RAF loadmaster informed us that a bus would take us to a downtown hotel for an overnight transit. Once there we were given meal vouchers by the reception desk staff so that we could eat in the restaurant. The RAF loadmaster also gave us a time to be ready for the bus to collect us early the next morning. On arrival at the hotel, I shared a room with Roy, originally from the Seychelles. A few years later, in 1984, Roy would attempt to climb Mount Everest with a British Army expedition. Unfortunately he wasn't given an opportunity to summit the mountain due to prolonged adverse weather conditions. Roy went on to become a warrant officer in the regiment and served with distinction. Later he founded his own security company in 1993 after facilitating the private security element of the presidential candidate Sir James Mancham on his return to the Seychelles.

We quickly ate our food in the otherwise empty hotel restaurant and in the space of twenty minutes we were in the bar, which advertised a 'Happy-Hour' with half-price beer! The cheap beer was on offer because the place was like a ghost town and would remain like that until the start of the salmon fishing season. The tourists wouldn't arrive for another month. We had a great night, sharing the bar with about half a dozen locals who made a collection to buy us a round of beer when they saw our uniforms. I was nursing a hell of a hangover as we took off in the C130 early the next morning. We had one more refuelling stop at Bermuda, where we all 'skinny-dipped' at the side of the runway in the crystal blue ocean. Swimming in the sea was a great way to rid ourselves of some mighty hangovers. After that it was back on board for the final leg of our journey to Florida.

The rest of D Squadron were waiting beside the runway at Hurlburt Field when we landed in Florida. They had four SAS Land Rover 'pinkies' and two USAF trucks. We piled our bergens onto the pinkies and then helped the rest of the squadron personnel manhandle the boxes of freight onto the trucks. Hurlburt Field is a satellite airfield to Eglin Air Force Base.

It wasn't long before we all had lunch in the USAF dining hall where the choice of food included three different flavours of ice-cream. The troop was accommodated in a large tent alongside the remainder of D Squadron at a bivouac area within the airfield perimeter. After lunch I found a spare folding cot and put my bergen and daysack beside it. I already knew everyone in the troop and we had a good chat and a briefing for the next day's training. Dick, the Boat Troop staff sergeant, told me I would be a member of his boat crew in one of our Gemini Rigid Inflatable Boats (RIB). Then after a couple of hours we went off for a four-mile run in the glorious sunshine. Soon it was time to take a shower in the communal shower tent that blasted cold water at you from a series of shower roses connected to a fire hydrant outside.

I had worked with Gemini inflatables in Belize so it didn't take me long to learn how to mix the fuel, start the engine, and basically ride around the bay. Then we began to practise all our standard operating procedures (SOP) over the coming days until I became proficient in small boat work. I learnt to tie everything to the boat so it wouldn't fall overboard. This included our weapons, but they were always within arm's reach and we could grab them at a moment's notice. Each day finished with a truck ride back to Hurlburt Field where we hosed down the boats to wash away the saltwater to protect the rubberised fabric. Most of us would run four or more miles after work in small groups. Then it was time for a shower and go and eat some of the great food in the USAF mess hall. My favourite snack at the time was a bacon, lettuce and tomato 'BLT' sandwich, something I had never eaten before. An interesting contrast between us was that the Americans seemed to have about twenty different ways to describe how they liked their eggs fried. Breakfast was a culinary minefield: the bacon was always crispy and often accompanied by French toast or pancakes with maple syrup. I soon figured out that I liked my cooked-to-order eggs 'over-easy'.

The training continued in the same vein all week until the Friday when we had the weekend free. After a shower and a change into civilian clothes we went straight to the Enlisted Men's Club, which was the USAF equivalent of a NAAFI bar. Surprise surprise there was a 'Happy-Hour' with half-price pitchers of Miller Lite and the highlight was they had a stripper! The pretty girl would dance around and finally take her bikini top off and show off her assets for the last song when we copied the Americans and shouted 'Go girl, go!' The final song was always *Funky Town* by Lipps Inc. and every time I hear the song it takes me straight back to that fond memory. While the show was going on, I was sitting next to one of the troop sergeants, Vince, who told me he would look out for me. Suddenly the show came to an end and everyone rushed out of the club to grab one of the cabs waiting outside to go downtown to Fort Walton Beach. I made to follow, but Vince grabbed my elbow and told me to help him gather in the half-full pitchers that were lying about on the abandoned tables. I thought we were just helping the club staff to tidy up, but Vince had other ideas. 'You don't need to go downtown on your first night off. Stick with me and we'll drink this free beer and I will tell you all you need to know about Boat Troop.' We ended up getting pissed and had a good laugh. Vince told me that to be a success in Boat Troop all I had to do was watch and learn. I thanked Vince for his good advice and promised I would keep quiet and learn my new role. Never again did I stay behind to drink with Vince though, as he could drink anyone under the table and he was way out of my league. Besides, the bright lights of Fort Walton Beach were beckoning!

After my first trip downtown we returned in a cab and drove in past the main gate. It was then that I first saw the huge sign next to the entrance: 'Hurlburt Field welcomes the Special Air Service, heroes of the SAS Iranian embassy siege in London'. When the cab driver saw the sign, and realized we were SAS, he wouldn't take any money off us for the fare. That just about summed up the amazing friendship, generosity and trust between the American military, the local township and ourselves. You have to remember at the time that there were US citizens being held hostage in Tehran after the Iranian 'students' overran the American embassy. Also, some of the helicopter crews that took part in the rescue attempt were from Hurlburt Field, so people in our immediate vicinity were suffering. There was another sign beside the first that stated how many days had passed since the US hostages were taken. The rescue attempt was known as Operation Eagle Claw. It was a USAF operation on 24 April 1980 to rescue more than fifty embassy staff held captive at the US embassy. The operation resulted in failure after encountering many difficulties, including sand being sucked into helicopter engines causing catastrophic failure. Due to the many problems, the operation was aborted, but then disaster struck as one of the helicopters crashed into a C130 containing military personnel and additional on-board tanks full of aviation fuel. A fire resulted that destroyed both aircraft. Eight service personnel died and many others were badly burnt.

The following weekend saw the arrival of a platoon of Navy SEALS who were to work alongside us for a month of joint training. They slept in the tent next to Boat Troop and we cross-trained with our respective RIBs. Then we moved on to more advanced training, taking advantage of the huge fleet of helicopters available at Hurlburt Field. We trained in many amphibious techniques including helicopter 'cast and recovery' where you jump out of a helicopter wearing a wet suit. We first jumped at ten knots from 10ft and progressed to thirty knots from 30ft which meant you hit the water with a mighty slap if you didn't enter the water cleanly. Then we lined up in the water ready to climb a rope ladder back into the helicopter. This is much more difficult than it sounds! We also drove the Gemini boats straight up the ramp of a Sikorsky HH-3E helicopter, nicknamed the 'Jolly Green Giant', that was hovering on the surface of the sea. With a watertight hull, the HH-3E could land on water and it had a large rear door and ramp. It was an awesome experience to see the water gushing out of the helicopter's decking as we took off.

We also had available a USAF missile recovery launch which would normally put to sea to recover spent fuel tanks from missiles which had been fired to high altitudes over the sea from the nearby test-firing ranges. What struck me about the SEALS was their equipment was second to none. One glaring example of the contrast in kit was when the crew of the USAF launch asked the SEALS and ourselves to fit radar reflectors to our RIBs so that they could spot us on their radar at night. Immediately the SEAL RIBs were able to erect aluminium poles with compact radar reflectors. One of our troop sergeants, Colin, said we would have some fitted for the next day. That evening Colin cut some branches off the pine trees near our tent and manufactured 6ft poles. Then he used catering-size baked bean cans which he scrounged from the mess hall and hammered these onto plywood boards which he then nailed to the poles. The next day the USAF launch crew and the SEALS roared with laughter when they saw Colin's DIY radar reflectors, but we had the last laugh as they worked perfectly. We continued our training with water jumps from C130 and Caribou aircraft before parachuting out of Huey helicopters for a night jump.

We had some great nights out downtown with the SEALs and built up a long-lasting rapport and mutual respect for each other. Many of the bars in Fort Walton Beach were owned by the same guy. His name was Mr Cash, and every one of his drinking establishments had a plaque over the door with an inscription which stated, 'Open every day of the year unless Cash dies'.

We usually spent Friday and Saturday nights downtown drinking, but Sundays was our rest day. After a lie-in I would go for a run before lunch. Afterwards most of Boat Troop would go to the large outdoor swimming pool on the airbase. I always swam lengths for forty minutes.

Our month's training with the SEALS was soon over and they departed. We still had three weeks to continue training by ourselves. I was proficient enough by now to act as coxswain and would take my turn steering the boat at its maximum speed of twenty-five knots. I spent the next weekend diver training before it was time to train on the Klepper folding kayak. Now I had kayaked in several different types of single and double fibreglass kayaks, but never a Klepper. The design is based on a wooden folding frame with aluminium fasteners, with solid bow and stern pieces, and a series of ribs and stringers, over which is stretched a pliable, rubberised, canvas skin. It is a two man carry, i.e., one man carries the skin and the other a bag with all the 'bits' inside. It is very heavy, particularly if you have tied it on top of your bergen already full of your kit including patrol radio, ammo, water and rations.

I was a member of a four-man patrol and took the front seat in one of the Kleppers. The patrol commander, Chippy, was in the rear seat to steer the boat using pedals at his feet attached to the rudder via steering lines. The patrol insertion was exciting stuff, being towed several miles behind a couple of Geminis before releasing the towing lines and skimming off into the darkness. That was the easy part, before a tough five-hour paddle across the bay and up a wide, deep river against the current, before arriving near our selected target. Chippy was quite tall and thin with a mass of blond hair. He didn't look particularly tough, but that was a disguise and he made the five-hour paddle seem easy. Another training mission was to paddle up a creek into a swamp. Once the Klepper insertion was complete, we completed a close target recce (CTR) before staying overnight on a small island. The island was covered in mangrove and was the home of several alligators. Fortunately, I slept in a hammock and tied it high off the ground that night!

Before leaving Florida, we were told that our next task back in the UK was to attend individual training courses. The regiment had three individual patrol skills: signaller, medic and demolitionist. I was already a patrol signaller, but needed a second skill so requested to go on a patrol medic course. I was very pleased when my request was approved.

The patrol medic course lasted twelve weeks, including a four-week attachment to a large NHS hospital. I learnt many things, including anatomy & physiology, battlefield trauma, emergency dentistry, emergency childbirth, vaccinations, administering analgesia and fluids, basic psychiatry, and suturing. We also studied haematology – the diagnosis and treatment of blood-related diseases. While studying haematology I researched my blood group. I knew my blood group was rare, but what I read astonished me. I discovered that, in the UK, only one person in sixty-seven has B negative blood. Furthermore, it is mainly found in Romany gypsies. Now this 'eureka' moment took me straight back to a distant memory. I recalled that my grandfather, Thomas, married Mary an Irish Romany gypsy, who had both sadly died before I was born. Grandfather Thomas was sent to Dublin in 1914 to buy cavalry horses for the British Army at the onset of the First World War. I am sure his wife Mary would have been able to provide him with a few contacts from among her family still living in Ireland. So, now I realized that my granny had left me the most precious of gifts: her blood to live on in another generation.

That explained to me why I had the 'wanderlust' and was indeed a pilgrim, always wanting to travel somewhere new, 'beyond that last blue mountain barred with snow, across that angry or that glimmering sea.' The instructor on the course pointed out that our knowledge of anatomy & physiology was very comprehensive and should make passing GCSE Human Biology a mere formality. I passed the GCSE exam with a good grade a few months later.

There was a running boom in the 1980s and marathon fever was gripping the UK. I decided to run a marathon myself at the earliest opportunity. I started to progressively increase the length of my longest training run each week. I was soon running fifteen miles on this single run each week. Many of us would stick to running for much of our fitness training. Looking back with the benefit of hindsight I think this approach was wrong and I used to weight-train at least twice each week. I also rode a bike and paddled my kayak on the River Wye.

Immediately after the patrol medic course, D Squadron started training to take over the SP team for a six-month tour of duty. The first week we were issued a special fire-retardant black suit with integral hood, respirator, Browning 'Hi-Power' 9mm pistol and an MP5 sub-machine gun. All my equipment, including personal weapons, was kept in two canvas holdalls. The hangar was built to armoury standards so there was no need to lock my weapons inside a gun locker. I was allocated to the Blue Team, the other team being the Red Team. Each team had an 'assault group' and a 'sniper group', plus a small command group including signallers. For the first couple of weeks, we trained together. Most of the guys had been on the SP team before and I knew the set-up from my days as a support signaller. Now I just had to refine my CQB skills for the assault role and get used to abseiling and 'fast-roping' from a helicopter while wearing a respirator and throwing stun-grenades as we made an explosive entry into a building. We all had an assessment on the ranges as an introduction to sniper rifles and I scored quite highly. That evening I was assigned to the Blue Team sniper group. I was issued my two sniper rifles, one with a day-scope and one with a night-scope, and both manufactured by Parker-Hale, probably among the very best rifles available on the market at that time. After zeroing the rifles, I transported them in customized weapon cases in the back of our Range Rover. I was also issued with a 'ghillie suit', a type of camouflage clothing used by snipers to blend into their surroundings in a rural situation. The suit is covered in strips of hessian cloth to which is added natural vegetation to improve your personal camouflage. During our three-week sniper course, we refined our shooting skills, using aids such as wind tables and laser rangefinders. Phil (Staff Sergeant P.P. Currass QGM) was our instructor and led the sniper team. Phil sadly died in the SAS helicopter crash during the Falklands War.

I was also sent on a police advanced driving course for a week during the work-up training for the SP team. Anyone can drive a car faster than 160kph down the motorway, but try driving at 100kph along winding country lanes when a tractor may be just around the next bend and the road is only single-track! To make it even more difficult, the driver had to keep up a running commentary of what was taking place in front, behind and at both sides of the vehicle all the time you were in the driving seat. One day we had a tyre blow-out at more than 160kph; luckily we had 'run-flat' tyres or the vehicle could have overturned. We completed the week's training by spending a day on skid-pans practising high speed hand-brake turns and other advanced driving techniques.

While we were busy on the SP team, Bradbury Lines was being completely rebuilt with a unique design for our highly specialized skills. The camp was renamed Stirling Lines to commemorate David Stirling, the founder of the SAS. We had a new gymnasium, including a mock-up of the inside of a C130 transport plane for parachute training. When you jumped out of the C130 side-door, you had a controlled descent in a harness while hanging from a wire. We also had an aquatic centre for diving, swimming and small boat work. There was a high diving board which we all had to jump off in full assault kit, and many other innovative features. The new-build also provided a modern RHQ building, commcen, 'Receivers' base station, squadron offices, briefing rooms, an indoor theatre, garages, boat workshops, improved facilities for the SP team, a parachute centre, dining hall, officers' mess, WOs' & sergeants' mess, soldiers' accommodation, and NAAFI Club. We also had a new rugby pitch and running track.

Every month the SP team would have a major exercise with police involvement. One month all the hostages were American and we were joined by the US counter-terrorist team for joint training. The SP team deployed first while the American team were mobilised and flew to the nearest RAF airfield direct from their base at Fort Bragg before finally arriving at the exercise location. I met up with my American counterpart and together we 'relieved in-situ' an SAS sniper at the rear of a large building with more than thirty rooms. The terrorists were holed up with their hostages somewhere inside the building. The American sniper was a big man, about 6ft 4in and probably weighed 300lbs. When I asked him how he had grown so large he replied in monosyllables, 'M and V'. When I asked him what that meant he elaborated slightly, telling me M and V stood for 'meat and vegetables'. When the exercise finished, I had an opportunity to look at the American team's comms set-up. They were talking in voice transmissions direct to Fort Bragg over a manpack-sized radio. I was amazed when it was explained to me that they were using tactical satellite in the UHF band with real-time encryption. This was absolutely cutting-edge comms equipment in those days. Little did I know it at the time, but the SAS would borrow a couple of these URC101 tacsats the following year to communicate back to the UK during the Falklands War. We finished on the SP team in January 1981 and then it was straight on to another tour in Northern Ireland.

We deployed to a new base in Northern Ireland and I spent a lot of time in South Armagh working undercover. It was a difficult area to operate in and I was pleased to see the back of the place. I had a more enjoyable time working in Fermanagh before spending short periods in Belfast and Derry for specific short-term operations. When I arrived in Belfast, I was taken on a familiarisation drive into the nationalist areas of the city, including Falls Road. There were plenty of murals depicting the PIRA 'freedom fighters' painted onto the gable walls of terraced houses. Before every operation we sat down and had a 'Chinese Parliament'. This is where every trooper is allowed to give an opinion on the planning and execution of what is about to go down. I was surprised the first time this happened when my suggestion to use a different approach route to a target was discussed, accepted and included in the revised plan.

We had an impressive assortment of personal weapons in our NI armoury. If we were masquerading as infantry soldiers, we would carry the 7.62mm Self Loading Rifle (SLR), the standard British Army rifle at that time. We also had a choice of the Armalite M16 and its various derivatives, including the Colt Commando which was more suited for CQB. Additionally, we had the Heckler & Koch HK53 assault rifle and the larger 7.62mm calibre HK G3 which had greater stopping power. We tended to carry the G3 rifle on rural patrols, where we might need to take part in a firefight at a distance exceeding 200m which was about the maximum effective killing range of 5.56mm assault rifles.

A major problem that we had to contend with at the time was the placing of illegal vehicle checkpoints (VCP), manned by several armed members of the IRA. Occasionally we would be out alone in an unmarked car and inadvertently drive into one of these well-placed checkpoints. The wisest course then was to bluff your way through, while all the time being prepared to shoot your way out of trouble using only a Browning Hi-Power 9mm calibre handgun, or perhaps an MP5K sub-machine gun could be grabbed from the car bag at the feet of the front passenger. More than one member of D Squadron had pushed a pound note into the collecting tin that was raising funds for the families of the 'Hunger Strikers' at an illegal VCP in a rural situation rather than blow their cover. The 1981 hunger strike was the second hunger strike by Irish republican prisoners in NI, and was aimed at breaking the resolve of the British prime minister Margaret Thatcher. One of the hunger strikers, Bobby Sands, was elected as a Member of Parliament during this time. The hunger strike was called off after Sands and nine others starved themselves to death.

D Squadron went to Greece in the summer of 1981 for two months. I was one of twelve squadron members allocated a place on a four-week Greek language course. The course had twelve weeks content yet we only had four weeks to complete the syllabus, not the first time the SAS had demanded maximum effort from me! The plan was to learn the vocabulary, and master how to write in the Greek version of Cyrillic script. The language officer was a fairly new member of Training Wing's education department and he gave us a pep talk informing us that Greek is much harder to learn than most other European languages. He went on to tell us that he held a classical languages degree in Greek and Latin.

I probably spent sixteen hours a day learning the language before we flew to Athens. On arrival we met our counterparts from the marine commando element of the Greek Raider Forces. These raider forces, known as 'Dynameis Katadromon' (ΔΥΝΑΜΕΙΣ ΚΑΤΑΔΡΟΜΩΝ) in Greek, have evolved from the Sacred Squadron, a Greek SF unit who were closely linked to both the British SAS and SBS from Second World

War days. Their motto is *'O Tolmon Nika'* (Ο ΤΟΛΜΩΝ ΝΙΚΑ), which translates as 'Who Dares Wins', so we felt an immediate affinity with them. They had an amphibious role and Boat Troop trained side by side with them. All of the junior ranks were conscripts, but instead of the normal twelve months they had volunteered to serve eighteen months as their initial training was longer than in conventional units. Nowadays the unit is part of the 1st Raider/Paratrooper Brigade and consists of a Special Forces unit with both army and marine elements. All Raiders wear a green beret with the Greek national flag on the left arm.

One of the marines in the Raider Forces had a British mother from Newcastle. His name was Georgios and he was allocated as our language tutor. We would take a Greek language class every evening after our normal training ended. Within minutes of starting our first class together he started laughing aloud and announced to us all, 'Hey guys, I don't know who has been teaching you Greek, but he must be about 2,000 years old!' What Georgios meant was our language officer had been teaching us classical Greek and not modern Greek! This meant much of our previous month's language learning had been a complete waste of time as my head was full of phrases that went something like, 'Hail, O Nikos, how art thou on this day of splendour?' Being a fast learner, it didn't take me long to learn the modern language.

We worked closely with our Greek counterparts and, as they were conscripts with only a small personal allowance for toiletries each month, we were pleased to buy their beer and socialised with them at every opportunity. We had several memorable nights out with them. I was given the task of teaching them how to assemble a Klepper folding kayak. This would normally have been easy enough, but I had to do it in Greek! They were superb swimmers and I soon discovered being able to swim one mile simply wasn't up to their standards. We were each given a swim buddy to improve our swimming technique and Dimitris was allocated to me. Dimitris had a wonderful swimming style which consisted of swimming on your side wearing swim-fins and a mask. He took two large double strokes underwater then bobbed his head out of the water and sucked in a huge breath before going back underwater and repeating the sequence again and again. I copied the technique with some difficulty and was then able to swim about two miles across the bay in one go at quite a fast pace. After a two-minute rest, we swam straight back! I suffered the next day. I was so stiff that I couldn't get off my camp bed! I stuck at it though and swam two or three miles each day.

We spent several days learning how to conduct a beach recce, where we used plumb lines to record the depth of water. The next part of the process was to dive to the seabed to assess whether there were any underwater obstacles to hinder an amphibious landing force. All this information was recorded on waterproof boards with wax pencils. This was followed a few days later by an introduction to underwater demolitions.

The Raider Forces and Boat Troop spent a couple of weeks living on the beach side by side in two large tents. The beach was fairly isolated and the area behind the beach was covered in low-lying scrub. One day after training had ended, one of the Raiders asked me if I had ever eaten snake. When I confessed that I hadn't, a couple of them went into the scrub to hunt for snakes. After about ten minutes they came out with a small snake that they promptly roasted on the fire we had going on the beach. There was just enough meat for a couple of mouthfuls each. Then it was time to walk the two miles into town for a few beers.

The following week we went parachuting and fitted in eight jumps and qualified as Greek military parachutists. Seven of the jumps were from a C130, but one water descent with equipment was from an antique Nord-Atlas aircraft which shook from every rivet. I was so glad to jump out of it before the engines failed! We had a presentation that Friday afternoon and I was presented my Greek parachute wings and a certificate written in Greek awarded to me from the *'Dynameis Katadromon'* (Raiding Forces). I also attended a one-week diving course. Our final exercise saw us conduct a night water jump and then be given a ride in a boat to the shore north of Thessaloniki, before walking many kilometres to the top of Mount Olympus, at a height of 2,918m. We then carried out night patrols for the whole week. Once we returned to barracks, we had a huge party on our last night. In typical Greek style, all the plates were smashed at the end of the meal. The next morning, we ate fried eggs off squares of newspaper for breakfast as not a single plate had survived the party!

I made strenuous efforts throughout the exercise to speak Greek. A few days after our return to Hereford I passed the language exam and scored high enough to achieve first place.

Within two weeks we deployed to Belize again. This was early August 1981. We had a couple of weeks patrolling in the jungle where we quickly refreshed our skills. I really enjoyed my time in the jungle, particularly when we set up makeshift firing ranges. One weapon I enjoyed firing was the M79 stand-alone grenade launcher firing 40mm single shot grenades. The same grenades are also used in the more modern M203 grenade launcher usually underslung on the M16 assault rifle.

On return to Airport Camp, we went on a week's diving course at St George's Caye. This is where the British Army Adventure Training Centre was based. I was very pleased as we were on an advanced course and by the end of the week I managed to dive to 43m (140ft) in the Blue Hole, 70km from Belize City. This is a world-class destination for scuba divers attracted by the opportunity to dive in crystal-clear waters. As we didn't have any tasking, we spent an additional week at St George's Caye on their basic kayaking course. I was pleased to finally master an eskimo roll.

The next day we returned to the mainland, but still there was no tasking for us when we arrived at the SAS ops room in Airport Camp. Later that day, an immediate signal arrived informing us that we were to undergo CP training. We were then to provide close protection for some Very, Very Important Persons (VVIP) who would be arriving to represent the UK when Belize would achieve independence on 21 September 1981. I then underwent four weeks of intensive training to learn all the CP skills required of a bodyguard. I was assigned as the driver of the rear blocking vehicle. My main role was to deny any vehicle space to overtake the convoy with orders to ram them off the road if necessary. I had an old, but powerful Cadillac, the VVIPs had smart limousines.

On completion of our training, we waited at the airport for the VVIPs' aircraft to land. Down the steps came HRH Prince and Princess Michael of Kent accompanied by Lord Carrington, the Secretary of State for Foreign and Commonwealth Affairs. We had a few hectic days looking after our VVIPs before the Independence celebrations. One highlight was on a trip from the harbour back to Government House we passed a small fire station with a vintage fire engine parked in front of it. Suddenly Prince Michael spotted the vehicle and allegedly exclaimed, 'Good God! It's a Dennis open-top. Probably manufactured in about 1936. Stop the car!' The next minute our well laid-out plans to protect the VVIPs went awry when Lord Carrington continued with the front blocking car and his own vehicle. Meanwhile our two cars were caught in a huge crowd of well-wishers surrounding Prince Michael who by now had climbed behind the steering wheel of the vintage fire engine demanding that someone take a photo of him. The luxury limousine became hemmed in by crowds and the only car available was my own. A decision was taken to drive him to safety in case there was a rogue element among the hordes. The next minute Prince Michael and his personal aide climbed into my car and I was instructed over the radio to try to catch up with the other vehicles a mile or so ahead of me on the busy highway. I drove as fast as I dared and caught up with them within ten minutes and the glitch was soon forgotten.

Independence Day was a long day that culminated in the flag lowering and raising ceremony at sundown. I felt a little sad at seeing the Union Flag go down on a British outpost but also happy that the people of Belize would achieve their independence. There was a formal dinner for the VVIPs and other invited dignitaries at Government House and we remained on duty. I stood discreetly in a corner watching proceedings and ready to take on any threat that manifested itself using my handgun as a last resort. I was absolutely dying for an alcoholic drink which of course wasn't permitted. At 9 pm I was detailed to stand guard outside Princess Michael's bedroom, Prince Michael having the adjoining bedroom with an internal connecting door. There was live music going on downstairs and I could look over the mezzanine balustrade and down onto the scene below. Princess Michael came upstairs thirty minutes later, accompanied by a female flunkey. The princess enquired what was I doing there and I informed her that my job was to provide personal security for her from outside her bedroom door. She looked me up and down and thanked me for protecting her. Then she surprised me by asking if I would like an alcoholic drink. I explained to the princess that this was not permitted, but thanked her anyway for the kindness shown. She had a final question for me which was what would I like to drink if this was permitted? I answered rum and coke and she said goodnight to me with a little smile on her face. Ten minutes later, the flunkey returned with a tray upon which was a bottle of coke, a glass and a small bowl of ice cubes. Great! I thought this coke is just what I need to quench my thirst. Surprise, surprise, some of the coke had been poured away and there was a generous measure of rum in the bottle along with the remaining coke. Cheers Ma'am!

The next morning before we drove them to the airport, and out of sight of the TV news crews, HRH Prince Michael accompanied by Lord Carrington came to thank us for our efforts over the previous days. Prince Michael said we had done a great job and presented the Troop with a signed photograph of himself and Princess Michael in all their finery. Then it was Lord Carrington's turn. He surprised us by asking how much a beer was in the NAAFI? Quick as a flash one of us shouted out two Belizean dollars. Lord Carrington opened his wallet with a flourish and said 'Here's a fifty dollar note. That should be more than enough to buy you all a beer with my grateful thanks.' A few minutes later we loaded the limousines up with our VVIPs and sped off to the airport. Mr George Price, the first prime minister of the newly independent Belize, was there to wish them farewell. We had finished our mission and flew home ourselves the very next day. As I sat in our own VC-10 for the flight home, I cast my mind back to my first trip in the jungle as a 'scaley'. That was when Hoss Ligairi, among others, had shown me the ropes. Now I had heard only that day that Hoss had retired from the regiment a few weeks before. By the time I returned from Belize, Hoss had already departed for Fiji. Apparently he planned to join the Fijian army and I thought that would be the last I would ever hear about him. I was wrong. Hoss, or to give him his full title, Colonel Ilisoni Ligairi, retired from the Fijian army in 1999 and a year later was a member of an armed gang that stormed the Parliament Building in Suva. The gang kidnapped the prime minister, Mahendra Chaudhry, and other members of the government. Ligairi was a key member of the gang and was reported to be a close friend and advisor to the coup leader, George Speight.

Soon after arriving back in Hereford, I discovered that I had successfully passed GCSE Maths, which was a huge relief. The next couple of weeks saw D Squadron participating in a large-scale exercise in the north of Scotland. This required us to be isolated in a Forward Mounting Base in Herefordshire for the first week of the exercise carrying out helicopter assaults against a few isolated buildings to simulate a control tower and a crew room similar to our target airfield in Scotland. When the order to deploy was given we flew in two CH47 Chinook helicopters by night at little over wave height up the North Sea and landed about 2km from the base. We advanced cautiously and established a forming up point (FUP) 200m from the perimeter fence. From there Mobility Troop carried out the assault on motorbikes, while the remainder of D Squadron set up a fire support base of mortars and GPMG. We were back in the helicopters within thirty minutes of the assault going in. Then it was time for more training and I spent several days studying sea charts and learning about coastal navigation. We had some leave over Christmas, although it was my turn for guard duty on Christmas Day. Soon it was January 1982 and we flew to Kenya for troop training.

We flew to Kenya with only one refuelling stop at RAF Akrotiri in Cyprus. After an overnight stop in Kahawa, we travelled to Impala Farm, 20km north of Nanyuki. This was a five-hour trip by army truck. The farmhouse was derelict except for a few rooms that still stood at one end of the original building. When we arrived a row of 160-pounder tents had already been pitched, five men to each tent. One of the remaining rooms at the farm had a couple of fridges and shelving to provide us with a shop where we could buy toothpaste, soap and even a cold beer. The fridges in the 'shop' were powered by generators as was a single light bulb for each tent. We were at an altitude of about 1,400m, so although it was very hot by day it was cool in the evenings. There was a large rock outcrop 250m distant so Mountain Troop went rock-climbing. Mobility Troop were driving their pinkies, while Air Troop were parachuting from two British Army Scout helicopters on detachment from 656 AAC Squadron. That left Boat Troop on dry land without any navigable water in sight so we went patrolling.

The ablutions and latrines were primitive. We had a wheeled water bowser for washing with taps along the rear of the trailer. You simply half-filled a washing bowl and placed it on a folding table to wash and shave. The toilets consisted of several open-fronted plywood cubicles. There was a long wooden bench above a connecting trench with spaces to sit at. The open fronts of these 'thunder-boxes' meant we had a fantastic view of Mount Kenya in the distance. One morning the sergeant major, Lawrence, went for a crap. He took the end cubicle and once he got nicely settled someone set off a green smoke grenade which wafted under his cubicle. It took Lawrence about three seconds to realize what was going on and another three days to scrub the greasy green smoke particles off his private parts!

It was only a few years since all rear link comms to Hereford were transmitted via offline encrypted Morse code. Then more recently we had switched to online encryption using teleprinters over HF radio-teletype circuits. This exercise brought about another technical advance as we deployed a TSC-502 satellite comms terminal for the first time with D Squadron. The TSC-502s had been used for a couple of years with the SP team, but this was the first time they had been used for a 'green army' task rather than 'black ops' tasking for the SP team. This enhancement meant the squadron commander could have daily conversations with the CO and ops officer via a secure voice channel. Simultaneously, we had a radio-teletype channel for signal messages. We also had a daily news bulletin printed out from a long roll of teleprinter paper which included sports news. Every Saturday there would be a crowd of us trying to see the results for our own teams. It would be several minutes before I could get close enough to read the Tranmere Rovers score!

Every day we tabbed around the area getting acclimatized. While out patrolling we saw many wild animals. The giraffes would let you get within 50m before ambling off, eventually breaking into an awkward run. Whenever we were out and about, if we looked to the south we could see the immense bulk of Mount Kenya with its snow-capped peak about 60km from our location. I had started learning Swahili from a phrase book the week before deploying to Kenya. My few phrases came in useful whenever we came into contact with the local people.

Meanwhile, Air Troop continued with their free-fall parachuting. One day they were jumping in our vicinity while we were passengers in Mobility Troop's Land Rover pinkies. With nothing better to do we drove towards the DZ with the intention of making a brew and having a chat. Suddenly we noticed three SUVs with black and white 'zebra stripes' painted on to each vehicle. They obviously had the same idea and were also driving towards the DZ. When we arrived at the DZ I was amazed to see several beautiful young ladies dressed in tiny shorts and flimsy vests emerge from the almost new SUVs. It transpired that the young ladies were all French, mainly models, and were staying at the estate of a French billionaire who was currently managing his business portfolio back in France. The man in charge of the group sought out the squadron commander and invited him for a drink that evening. The ladies would join them and he requested that the OC bring the officers with him *pour une petite soirée entre amis*. He also said that twenty of *'les soldats'* could arrive later for a few beers. Each troop were allocated four places, but unfortunately I wasn't one of the lucky ones. One of my mates, Topsy, returned later that night and said the house was simply amazing. There was also a private airstrip with a large hangar where the owner kept two of his planes, and there was a rhino sanctuary! Topsy went on to say that he was introduced to several of the girls, one of them a famous French movie star and the remainder models or budding film actresses. There were many photos of famous guests who had stayed at the lodge. The house was called Ol Jogi Ranch and was full of art and fine furniture. The owner at the time was the French billionaire and fine art dealer Daniel Wildenstein who died in 2001.

Topsy went on to say that as Boat Troop were due to travel to the coast, north of Mombasa, the following week for a diving course, we were all invited to stay the night camping next to the owner's beach house which was on our route. The journey by truck to Mombasa took about fourteen hours and was very tiring. We called in at the port refinery to pick up four full petrol drums for our outboard motors. A couple of hours later we pulled up at this huge house on a private beach south of Malindi. The house manager was British and showed us where we could set up camp about 100m from the main house. He offered to get the cook to prepare a meal for all eighteen of us, including our REME fitter and a diving instructor from the Royal Engineers. Our troop boss, Ted, declined but agreed we would accept a huge bowl of boiled rice to supplement our army rations. Ted then returned from the house and informed us that we had all been invited up to the house for a beer at 7 pm. In the meantime we could go for a swim in the sea and there were some basic showers there. I had a quick swim and a shower and then the house manager strolled up. I asked him how far the private beach extended and he said, 'Three miles in that direction and four miles in the other direction.' I was well impressed!

We had a couple of beers that evening in a huge, airy lounge in the main house when suddenly the group of girls arrived that we had seen the previous week. There was a shortage of chairs so one of the girls sat on the arm of my comfortable chair and tried to talk to me. Unfortunately her English was non-existent and my French wasn't much better. In an effort to communicate with her I remarked that she looked like the famous and very beautiful American actress Farrah Fawcett. This remark broke the ice and she blushed while her friends rushed off to get the latest copy of a French magazine. The very same girl who was on the arm of my chair was on the magazine cover with a headline in French that described her as 'The French Farrah Fawcett'!

The next morning, we continued our journey to the north of Malindi, finally arriving at our destination at Ngomeni. We set up camp on the beach and unrolled razor wire to create a makeshift enclosure, inside of which were about six tents, four Gemini RIBs, outboard motors, a diving compressor, a couple of trucks and a Land Rover. The next day was spent getting all the boats inflated and the outboard motors tested. I helped Topsy get the compressor going and we filled the diving tanks. On the following day our instructor said we would carry out the standard Royal Engineer diving course but would work extra hours and both weekends to compress the course into eighteen days. There followed a very comprehensive course and I discovered that a lot of the coursework was designed to see if you could cope with diving in difficult conditions. To ascertain if you suffered from claustrophobia, we often dived with blacked-out masks to simulate nil visibility. We also sat on the seabed wearing weighted diving belts in fairly shallow water with a plastic bucket on our heads and breathing the small amount of air inside. Whenever the air ran short, we would place a hand on top of the bucket to indicate we required a puff of air from the instructor's demand valve. This little game lasted an hour. The instructor had several spare compressed air tanks on the seabed to ensure he would have enough air for all of us. It may have seemed a bit silly at the time, but it certainly instilled confidence in us. We made several night dives, roped up to a dive partner. We also practised underwater navigation with a compass board. One day while we were on the diving course, Daniel Wildenstein's yacht dropped anchor opposite our tented camp. I managed to spot a few bikini-clad beauties frolicking on board, but they only stayed an hour or so and didn't come ashore. After the diving course was finished, we had a few days travelling north along the coastline in our Gemini RIBs to recce the area and saw the occasional Arab dhow. We were close to the border with Somalia and this area became notorious in the ensuing decades due to the kidnapping of tourists for ransom. Three weeks or so after arriving at Ngomeni we drove back to Kahawa to offload the heavy equipment for its imminent shipment back to the UK.

Soon afterwards, after an overnight stop at our squadron base near Nanyuki, we drove up to Archer's Post for the field-firing phase. Day after day we practised with our support weapons, including the GPMG and the 66mm LAW. We also had an 81mm mortar on call for indirect fire support. On our last evening we set up an ambush position a short distance from a prominent rock feature which had been fitted with 'Figure 11' targets which could be pulled upright using pulleys and rope. One man was detailed to lay in dead ground to pull the targets up at a predetermined time which was unknown to us. I was given the honour of initiating the ambush as soon as the targets came up and I fired off a 66mm LAW followed by five full magazines from my AR-15 assault rifle. We had been given orders to fire off all our ammunition and the one-way firefight continued for about fifteen minutes. The tracer ammunition showed how accurate our shooting was.

After a night at Impala Farm we redeployed to Mount Kenya, where we worked with Mountain Troop. I got to know their troop commander, John Hamilton, and thought he was very charismatic. Sadly, John (Captain G.J. Hamilton MC) was to die in a firefight in the Falklands War.

The mountain had different types of vegetation according to the altitude. We patrolled up to 2,250m in virgin rainforest. John advised us that there were wild elephants everywhere and these could be highly dangerous, especially if you got between a mother and her calf. Because of this we slung our hammocks on trees overhanging cliffs at night (roping ourselves in) to avoid being inadvertently trampled in our sleep. We saw several elephants as we patrolled, and their dung-balls were everywhere to indicate that there were more in the vicinity. Soon it was time to return to Kahawa and our final exercise.

We had an 'O' Group at Kahawa the next evening. Our orders were to move to Eastleigh Airbase, near Nairobi, and from there carry out a squadron-sized insertion onto a high plateau east of Nanyuki. The plan called for a parachute insertion and then carry out a CTR on a rebel base before mounting a squadron strength assault to rescue the hostages. When we kitted up with our parachutes at Eastleigh, we were informed that the reserve chutes were a new model. I didn't give much thought to this as I could see the rip-cord handle to pull in an emergency and as far as I was concerned that was all I needed to know. What I had failed to appreciate was there could be an issue because the reserve pack straps were longer than normal, making the reserve chute very loose when strapped to my main harness. The height of our planned DZ, and the high temperatures, meant that we would descend faster than usual, meaning our landings were going to be hard. When you couple these two factors together it was perhaps unsurprising that quite a few of us were hit in the face by the reserve parachute pack which swung up on landing. I was particularly unlucky as the reserve pack broke my nose and cut my upper lip quite deeply. I was also concussed and blacked out for a few seconds. The DZ had many undulations and rocks which was probably what caused Vince from Boat Troop to break his leg with multiple fractures when he landed. Paddy from Mobility Troop suffered the misfortune of having a long thorn from a blackthorn bush enter his eyeball and snap off. Cedric the Squadron OC badly bruised his heels and was unable to walk. A Scout helicopter was waiting at Nanyuki and was soon on the way. One of our patrol medics, Topsy, sutured my lip in the twenty minutes or so that we had to wait for the helicopter to arrive. Vince was put on a stretcher and Paddy and I joined him inside the aircraft to be CASEVACKED to Nanyuki Cottage Hospital. Cedric decided to remain on the DZ and eventually took a Land Rover ride back to Impala Farm where he recovered over the next few days.

Meanwhile Paddy and I carried Vince inside the hospital on the stretcher. The Kenyan nurse on duty was a big lady and said the doctor was on the way and we could leave Vince with her. She took some convincing that Paddy and I were also casualties! The doctor soon arrived, and after a cursory glance at Paddy and me, we were asked to wait while he dealt with Vince. With nothing else to do we were invited to take a bath and I had my first hot bath for six weeks! When the doctor was finished with Vince, he removed the blackthorn from Paddy's eye and fitted him with an eye-patch. Eventually it was my turn for treatment. The doctor, who was Scottish and quite young, said the sutures in my lip were fine, but my nose was definitely broken. He informed me that I was to be sent to a Nairobi hospital for my fractured nose to be set under general anaesthetic. I asked him what was the procedure and he said they would basically get hold of my nose and pull it straight. I asked him to do it there and then, but he said it would be too painful without anaesthetic. Being a cocky young trooper, I told the doctor I couldn't spare the time to go to Nairobi for several days and he should just pull my nose straight there and then.

Finally, the doctor agreed to tweak my nose, but told me it was going to hurt. He then yanked my nose this way and that for what seemed like several excruciating minutes before pronouncing the job done. He told me to look in the mirror, which is when I realized my nose was about the size of an orange. Luckily it settled down over the next week, although I was prescribed antibiotics and had to bathe my nose and lip in antiseptic solution every six hours. Instead of re-joining the exercise, it was decided I was to be used as a truck driver to deliver nightly water resupplies to the patrols. A few days later we returned to Kahawa and soon afterwards flew back to the UK.

The following weekend I ran in the Wolverhampton Marathon. This was the first of eight marathons that I ran over the next five years. I also joined Hereford Athletics Club and the following year was presented with my county colours for running in the 5,000 metres at a track and field event at Haverfordwest. I also represented Herefordshire in the Wales and West Midlands cross-country leagues. My fastest time for the marathon was 3:05 (Hereford Marathon 1984). I joined Wye Valley Runners in 1984, a new running club based in Hereford, and made many friends in the years that I remained with the club.

We had a week's leave at the end of March 1982, before training for Northern Ireland. Those who had already attended NI training with the regiment were given various advanced courses to attend during the first week of the training. For my part, I attended a one-week photography course. We were taught photography for surveillance purposes prior to our pending deployment. We set up 'hides' taking many photos of cars and their occupants as they entered and left Stirling Lines. We then spent hours in the dark room learning how to develop monochrome film. We used monochrome as the photos could be developed much more easily and quicker than colour film. During the photography course I heard news of a rumoured invasion threat of the Falkland Islands by Argentina.

Chapter 5

South Atlantic Bound

Diary Entry Thursday 1 April 1982
Falklands War Diary – dedicated to those who never came home.

This is my war diary covering the invasion of the Falklands which started during a photography course I was attending on Thursday 1 April 1982. During the day I heard news of a rumoured invasion threat of the Falkland Islands by Argentina. Hourly, the news of an imminent invasion of the Falklands became stronger. On Friday morning various news reports stated the Argentinians had landed while official British government reports denied this. At 0800 hrs the BBC news stated 'invasion of Falklands imminent'. Actually, the invasion had begun before first light that morning and the 'Argie' flag was flying over Government House by this time.

Looking back at my diary entry after all these years there are some vivid memories that jump out over the intervening timespan. The photography course was in preparation to deploy to Northern Ireland, where my duties, among other things, would include covert surveillance where good quality photos of likely suspects would be essential. I started the diary on the day we departed, writing in a spare notebook that I took with me. On return from the Falklands War, I had a couple of weeks leave and used one week to copy my diary into a scrapbook which allowed me to match up various photos and printed memorabilia with the diary entries.

Diary Entry Friday 2 April 1982
My photography course finished at lunchtime on the Friday and I went home to prepare for the Hereford Marathon on the Sunday by doing a final run before resting on the Saturday.

The Hereford Marathon on Sunday, 4 April 1982, was to be my second marathon and I was hoping for a 'personal best' time. The NI work-up training was to continue after the weekend.

Diary Entry Saturday 3 April 1982
I woke up with a sore throat and the beginning of a cold which was a bit worrying as the marathon was only twenty-four hours away. I went to a point-to-point race across the border into Wales and gambled away a few pounds on the horses. I knew a few people at the point-to-point and I was asked if I expected to deploy to the Falklands. I said no, which is what I believed at the time as nobody had said anything to me the day before when I was still in Stirling Lines. Just before midnight I went to bed after laying out my running kit for an early start the next morning. There was a phone call almost as soon as I put my head on the pillow. 'Come into work tomorrow,' said the voice on the other end of the phone without any trace of excitement or emotion. I could guess what this was all about. The next day was a frenzy of preparation and of course the Hereford Marathon ran without me.

On Sunday morning, the Brigadier, CO and 'Head Shed' briefed us all on the situation, which didn't tell us that much. We spent all that day in Stirling Lines sorting out equipment to be packed. We were informed that we could have the evening off and the next morning before reporting back for duty after lunch on Monday. We were instructed to wear uniform and advised to pack plenty of warm items. I also stocked up on toiletries, reading material, a few bars of chocolate and chewing gum. At the time I thought we would probably be back in Hereford within weeks once diplomacy had been given time to resolve the issue.

Diary Entry Monday 5 April 1982
I was given the Monday morning off work to sort out essential 'personal admin' such as say farewell to family and friends and call in to the bank for a spare cheque book. We boarded a couple of nondescript civilian coaches and drove to RAF Brize Norton taking off for Ascension Island later that evening.

Before leaving home, I read in my Atlas that Argentina had a population of 25,384,000 people with Buenos Aires as its capital. The Falkland Islands were not mentioned and were tiny specks on the map. We travelled by bus in uniform, carrying weapons to RAF Brize Norton where we caught our VC-10 aircraft to Ascension Island. Arrived at Ascension very early in the morning and had a meal in the American military mess-hall. Ascension is a volcanic island in the Atlantic, south of the equator. We spent several days on Ascension and used the time test firing our weapons, kayaking, boat training etc. On the beach one day we witnessed hundreds of turtles hatching out. We even helped some of them to the sea.

I also learnt that the Falkland Islands were over 6,800km from the UK and about 500km off the coast of Argentina. On boarding the VC-10, in uniform and carrying our personal weapons which was highly unusual, we taxied to the take-off position at the end of the runway. For security reasons the pilot had been handed the flight manifest showing that he was transporting members of the Royal Wessex Rangers to Ascension Island. The Royal Wessex Rangers were a fictional British Army infantry regiment featuring in the 'Spearhead' television drama series. He obviously knew who we really were and warmly welcomed us on board. The pilot promised to get us to Ascension in as short a time as was possible and he and all his crew wished us good luck in whatever mission and hazards we would face.

I bought a couple of newspapers in Hereford before departure. I read the headline stories of the Argentinian invasion of the Falkland Islands. I discovered that the enemy forces comprised a mix of Argentinian marines, infantry conscripts and SF. I also learnt a little of the geography and conditions that I could expect to find if we ever reached the Falklands. To be honest, I had never heard of the Falkland Islands and assumed it to be a group of islands somewhere off the coast of Scotland, simply because the name sounded vaguely Scottish. When we arrived at Ascension Island, I discovered that the airfield was named 'Wideawake Airfield' and there were many Americans on the island. While waiting for a couple of buses to take us to the American military mess-hall, I watched RAF personnel unloading Wessex helicopters and a large amount of airfreight from an enormous Belfast cargo plane. The Belfast was formerly an RAF aircraft but had been sold off due to defence cuts a few years previously. We were eventually found accommodation in a single-storey schoolhouse at Two Boats Village. We slept on the floor in our sleeping bags and were happy as long as we were fed and watered. There followed a few hectic days of fitness and weapon training. We also practised launching our boats from a nearby beach for troop level activities.

It was amazing to see the RAF engineers fit the rotors onto the Wessex helicopters and then taking them on a test flight within hours of arriving on Ascension Island. The use of this airfield was absolutely critical to the success of the retaking of the Falkland Islands, by now given the name Operation Corporate. Although a British dependency, the 10,000ft runway was built and maintained by the Americans to support their space programme. Just three aircraft movements a week was the normal air activity at the airfield before the Falklands War. By mid-April 1982, aircraft activity peaked at 400 aircraft movements per day, including helicopter flights to the task force ships anchored offshore.

Diary Entry Thursday 8 April 1982
Embarked on RFA *Fort Austin* by Lynx helicopter, sailing at dawn on Friday. It took a while getting used to being on board a ship, but the RFAs are comfortable, certainly more comfortable than the fighting ships of the Royal Navy. The *Fort Austin* had a comparatively large bar with beer at thirty pence a pint. Hot cross buns on Good Friday. We also practised boat stations and emergency stations. Weapon training for the next few days.

The civilian-manned Royal Fleet Auxiliary ships provide logistical and operational support for the Royal Navy warships worldwide. I soon discovered what a great bunch of characters the crew were, although quite a few were 'batting for the other side'. The RFA crew became our fans and they liked to sit on the stores' pallets shouting encouragement, and the occasional sexual innuendo, as we kept fit below decks by running along the 'Burma Road'. This was the nickname for the main starboard and port passageways, wide enough for two fork-lift trucks to pass each other, that we used as a circular route to run laps protected from the weather. In this way we would run for forty minutes or so after the day's training.

I had bought a copy of the Ascension Island's weekly newsletter. I now had an opportunity to read the newsletter and it cautioned all on Ascension 'to be discreet in their overseas correspondence and telephone calls. It would be tragic if an unguarded remark put someone's life in danger.'

While on *Fort Austin* we took the opportunity to assemble our Gemini RIBs and using a winch put them over the side and took them for a spin around the ship. The SBS also put one of their Geminis in the water. We noticed their outboard engine was in better condition than our own which had seen better days. We saw a killer whale that actually swam under our boat, but as it was only 5m long and well behaved we didn't feel threatened by its presence.

Diary Entry Saturday 13 April 1982
RV with HMS *Antrim*, HMS *Plymouth* and RFA *Tidespring* (tanker). I watched resupply at sea (RAS) of fuel by line and vertical replenishment (VERTREP) by helicopter of food and ammunition. We cross-decked by Wessex helicopter; Boat Troop to *Antrim* and the remainder of D Squadron to HMS *Plymouth*, RFA *Tidespring* and HMS *Endurance* which joined us later. I was now on-board HMS *Antrim*, a fast destroyer...

It was a shock to the system to be on board HMS *Antrim*. Launched in 1967, she was a fairly old ship but at least she was quite large and boasted a flight deck with her own helicopter. Luckily for me, I had been on board a Royal Navy warship for a week in 1973 so at least I knew 'Navy Speak' for things like galley (dining hall/kitchen), mess (place where the crew sleep and socialise according to their rank or rating), heads (toilets and washrooms), 'scran' (food), 'a wet' (a hot brew of tea or coffee), ship (never call a warship a boat!), 'pusser' (refers to official Royal Navy/Royal Marine issue equipment), 'nutty' (chocolate bars), 'the jack' (a special tap which dispenses boiling water), the bow (the front of the ship), aft (the rear section of the ship), the stern (the blunt end of the ship), 'pongos' (army soldiers) and 'Royals' (Royal Marines).

Diary Entry 14 April 1982

Getting used to being on a destroyer. No space anywhere, I sleep on the deck in a junior ratings mess in my sleeping bag. Most of the junior ratings were 'hot-bedding', meaning the triple bunk-beds had a different person sleeping in each bunk every four hours around the clock according to their 'watch system'. For our benefit, the remainder of the junior ratings soon started hot-bedding. This meant it freed up several bunks for us to sleep in. The bunk made for a more comfortable sleep but they were narrow and I banged my head every time I woke up for the first few mornings until I got used to there being another bunk above me. The beer is rationed to two small cans daily per person. There are no salad vegetables and potatoes are strictly rationed. The crew are ordered up on deck in the afternoon and we follow them. We steam past HMS *Endurance* as she sails in the opposite direction and on command our crew give them a rousing three cheers for their sterling work in South Georgia. *Endurance* is quite a small ship, painted red for her role as an Antarctic survey vessel and nicknamed 'The Red Plum' due to her colour. It is hard to believe they have given the 'Argies' a run for their money. I remained on deck and an hour later an RAF Nimrod maritime surveillance plane flew over and dropped operational orders in a sealed canister for the captain's eyes only. We speculate that we may be going to South Georgia first as we are fourteen days ahead of the main task force.

Many of the junior ratings were only 18 or 19 years old and they treated us with a great deal of respect. On that first evening they were rushing around cleaning the junior ratings mess and were adamant that we had to pack away our kit and smarten ourselves up for 'Captain's Rounds'. This was the captain's routine evening inspection as he made his rounds of the ship. Eventually we heard whistles and feet slamming together as each Mess in turn stood to attention and 'piped' the captain's arrival. There was no way Boat Troop were going to look smart whatever we did, but we played the game and rolled up our sleeping bags and stood to attention when Captain Brian Young, Royal Navy, came down the ladder to our Mess. Fortunately for us, Captain Young saw the need to relax the normal rules of being 'shipshape and Bristol fashion'. That evening the captain's daily briefing was televised on the ship's CCTV to give us all an update. He started by welcoming the new arrivals and informed us that we were sailing with HMS *Endurance* as a new addition to our task force which now comprised five ships. The junior ratings cheered when Captain Young announced there would be no more 'Captain's Rounds' for the duration of hostilities. Then he gave us the news we had been waiting for. We were going to liberate South Georgia!

Diary Entry 16 April 1982
We have spent the last week practising our Troop skills, in my case boat skills. After a week of checking and assembling our Gemini boats and confirming all our drills on board HMS *Antrim*, we finally had a chance to put it into practice. The ship slowed to a few knots to maintain headway and then we lowered five Gemini RIBs over the side. Our little inflatables seem very small alongside the destroyer. The weather was still fairly warm, but we expect it to get much colder soon as we sail further south.

The Geminis were attached by their four corners to webbing straps. I was the junior crew member of callsign 17 Alpha and therefore the first to stand on a Gemini and be lowered by a mechanical hoist into the sea on the starboard side. The other two men, i.e., the troop captain and coxswain, scrambled down rope netting to get into the boat alongside me and then the outboard motor was lowered down to us. Once the outboard motor was attached to the gunwale, we started it up and made a couple of circuits of the ship. This was quite a complicated procedure and it took several attempts for the five RIBs to get into the water and cruise around in formation. We tried it again after a mug of tea. We were a bit quicker on this second attempt, although our Johnson 40 outboard motors were temperamental. Knowing a bit about two-stroke engines, I was concerned that our problems would be worse when we arrived off South Georgia due to the extreme cold when trying to start the engines in Antarctic waters.

The weather did indeed worsen over the next few days as we crossed from the South Atlantic into the Antarctic Ocean (also known as the Southern Ocean). We had a force twelve hurricane a few nights later as we passed through the 'Roaring Forties'. It is common to experience strong westerly winds in the southern hemisphere between the latitudes of 40 and 50 degrees. These can reach hurricane force and are caused by air being displaced from the Equator towards the South Pole, the scarcity of landmasses to temper the wind and the Earth's rotation.

The captain came up on the public address system to announce to all of us that this was the worst weather he had sailed in throughout his long career in the Royal Navy. Captain Young also said that if anyone wished to see the weather for themselves, they were welcome to come and take a look from the lower bridge. I was one of those who took him up on this opportunity. Spindrift reduced visibility as I tried to peer out into the darkness. Soon my eyes became accustomed to the gloom. I was enthralled by the power of nature unleashing its forces to cause the waves to crash over the bows while the ship shuddered as it struggled to make headway through the mountainous seas. There were ominous creaks and groans coming from the very bowels of the ship. It didn't feel possible that we could survive the night as we crashed our way through the hurricane on our way to South Georgia.

Even elite Special Forces have to muck in and help out on fatigue duties on board a warship. I was nominated with my troopmate 'Topsy' to report to the galley to help with the clean-up caused by the continuing storm conditions. There were quite a few 'matelots' (sailors) on the same fatigue duties, so we worked together. Everything had to be tidied up in the galley, and after sweeping up some broken crockery we were detailed to tie down the Formica-topped tables and stacking chairs which were sliding from side to side as the ship crashed through the storm. The weather got the better of us though and it was impossible to stack the chairs without them being knocked down as the ship lurched through the treacherous seas. The galley floor was soon covered in margarine, sugar and ketchup, which made it very slippery. In the end we gave up and sat on the upturned tables and enjoyed 'dodgem car rides', laughing our heads off as we slid up and down astride the tables skidding across the galley floor.

No matter what the weather, we were making steady progress towards South Georgia and as the storm receded the ships in our task force, now officially designated Task Group 317.9, were able to stick to the agreed sailing formation while the plans for the liberation of the islands were put together. We had arrived off the coast of South Georgia by the morning of 21 April 1982. Operation Paraquet was the operational name for the retaking of South Georgia. The crew soon changed the name to 'paraquat', a strong weed killer, and this alternate spelling was often used as we arrived close to South Georgia to weed out the Argies!

Chapter 6

South Georgia

It was known that the Argentinian forces were based at Grytviken and Leith. These were two former whaling bases and Grytviken was also the base of the British Antarctic Survey (BAS). The Argentinian marines flew their national flag at these former whaling bases in an attempt to add legitimacy to the scrap-metal merchants who had already begun to salvage the scrap metal. The Royal Marines left on the island to provide some level of defence had defiantly taken on the superior forces of the Argentinians before being taken prisoner. The Royal Marines were led by Lieutenant Keith Mills who commanded a detachment of twenty-two marines. Lieutenant Mills was advised by signal from the UK to defend South Georgia in such a way as to ensure that the Argentinians were seen to be the aggressors when they captured the main base at Grytviken and the smaller outpost at Leith. Lieutenant Mills was also cautioned not to incur any loss of life during any confrontation. The confrontation occurred soon enough.

On the morning of 3 April 1982, the Royal Marines fired a burst of machine-gun fire at an Argentine Puma helicopter. Other marines reported seeing the tracer hit the helicopter before it turned away belching smoke and crashed on the other side of the harbour. There followed an intense firefight between the British and Argentinian marines. An Argentine naval vessel, the ARA *Guerrico*, a modern frigate carrying Exocet missiles, entered the narrow opening from Cumberland East Bay leading into King Edward Cove where there was a jetty to tie up alongside the BAS buildings. The frigate immediately came under fire from the Royal Marines who fired their 84mm Carl Gustav and 66mm LAW shoulder launched weapons. The Royal Marines scored several hits including one that hit just underneath the Exocet launcher on board the *Guerrico*. The ship did an abrupt about turn and steamed back out into Cumberland East Bay from where it put down inaccurate fire with its 100mm gun onto the Royal Marines' defensive positions. Deciding they had put up a good enough fight to prove the Argentinians had acted aggressively, the Royal Marines surrendered. Subsequently the twenty-two Royal Marines and the BAS scientists were put on board the Argentine naval vessel ARA *Bahia Paraiso* and taken to Rio Grande. From there they were airlifted to Montevideo and reached England on 20 April. This still left some BAS scientists at outlying field sites who remained undetected.

There had been regular planning conferences on board HMS *Antrim* as Task Group 317.9 approached South Georgia. The Royal Navy, Royal Marines, SAS and SBS officers discussed what the best course of action would be, especially in consideration of the unpredictable weather conditions. Eventually, after much debate, it was decided that the SAS would go in first to set up an OP overlooking Leith, and the SBS would go in soon afterwards to set up their own OP near to Grytviken. It was agreed that Mountain Troop would fly from HMS *Antrim* to land by helicopter on Fortuna Glacier. From there they planned to walk to their selected OP near to Leith. The SBS section would leave soon after from HMS *Endurance*, with HMS *Plymouth* in close support, flying in two Wasp helicopters. Unfortunately 2 Section SBS were prevented from landing that night due to a fierce blizzard that blew up out of nowhere. The SBS were able to get ashore at Hound Bay the following day and succeeded in crossing Sörling Valley, but still some distance from Grytviken. The SBS section were recovered by helicopter on 24 April, having been unable to get their Geminis across Cumberland Bay which was strewn with small pieces of floating ice known as 'brash'.

Diary Entry Wednesday 21 April 1982
Mountain Troop move onto Fortuna Glacier by helicopter. The Troop soon discovered that movement was extremely slow and difficult due to the terrible weather conditions and the many wide crevasses that they encountered. They had no choice but to halt and bivouac for the night. One tent blew away and further movement the next morning proved impossible. Late on the morning of 22 April, Captain John Hamilton, the Troop Commander, was forced to radio for immediate rescue. A blizzard had been blowing all night and most of the next day until just before the rescue when conditions improved slightly. The rescue attempt used three helicopters. Two Wessex 5 'troop-carrier' helicopters stayed well back from the Wessex 3 as the

pilot tried to find a gap in the cloud cover to locate Mountain Troop. To aid him in this he had an anti-submarine warfare radar which gave the crew some capability in collision avoidance, a facility the Wessex 5 helicopters did not possess. Eventually they were running low on fuel and had to return to HMS *Antrim* before a second attempt. This second attempt succeeded in locating Mountain Troop and they were quickly put on board the two Wessex 5 aircraft. Again the weather worsened and the first of the Wessex 5 helicopters crashed very soon after take-off. Lieutenant Commander Stanley RN, flying the Wessex 3, picked up the downed aircrew and SAS troopers and started to fly back to *Antrim* when the second Wessex 5 crashed with the remaining ten SAS on board. After establishing that they had all survived the crash, Ian Stanley flew back to *Antrim* to refuel and then returned to the crash location, but this time with the SAS Squadron Commander and two patrol medics on board. I was sent on this flight as a patrol medic and remember climbing on board the Wessex 3 with another medic and the Squadron Commander. We carried our patrol medic packs and several sleeping bags to try to help them on the ground. I caught a glimpse of several wide crevasses with deep blue glacial ice plunging into the depths of the Earth. Then suddenly we were over one of the crashed helicopters and I caught sight of some of the troopers waving up at us. When we located them, contact was made using a small radio known as a tactical beacon equipment (TACBE). By this means, the pilot of the Wessex 3 ascertained that everyone was alive and not too seriously injured. Ian Stanley was informed that several required first aid and they were all suffering varying degrees of hypothermia. They were instructed to wait while the helicopter returned to *Antrim* to drop off the SAS Squadron Commander and the two patrol medics, myself included. Then the pilot bravely took the decision to return with his aircrew, i.e., co-pilot, observer and aircrewman, in an otherwise empty helicopter and with a lightened fuel load. Against all the odds, the single helicopter picked up the ten SAS troopers and two downed aircrew in one lift. Mountain Troop were forced to abandon all their equipment except for personal weapons. It was a miracle when Lieutenant-Commander Stanley finally landed them all safely on the deck of *Antrim*.

To compensate for the loss of the two Wessex 5 helicopters, HMS *Brilliant* was diverted from the main task force with her two Lynx Mk 8 helicopters to support an eventual assault on South Georgia. Some months later, the Wessex 3 pilot, Lieutenant Commander Ian Stanley RN, was awarded the Distinguished Service Order and his crew were Mentioned in Dispatches. The Wessex 3, nicknamed 'Humphrey', would eventually be displayed at the Fleet Air Arm Museum at Yeovilton in Somerset where she remains to this day.

Diary Entry Thursday 22 April 1982
Mountain Troop were now safely back on-board ship, although quite a few of them had cuts and bruises from their two helicopter crashes. Now it was the turn of my Troop.

I had a chat with a few of my mates from Mountain Troop soon after they arrived. They were all a bit shook up and relieved to be back on board a ship. Phil (Staff Sergeant P.P. Currass QGM) had a large wound dressing on his forehead above one eye, but the others were remarkably unscathed. I also shared the banter with Paddy (Corporal R.E. Armstrong) and Paul (Corporal P.A. Bunker). By a cruel twist of fate all three were destined to die in the SAS Sea King helicopter crash.

Diary Entry Friday 23 April 1982
In the early hours of the morning on 23 April, Boat Troop set off from HMS *Antrim* in five Geminis. The objective was to reach Grass Island in Stromness Bay to set up an LUP overlooking Leith and Stromness Harbours. At first everything went well. The sea was remarkably calm as we were lowered over the starboard side of *Antrim*. The destroyer screened us from the wind as we grouped together on the starboard quarter. *Antrim* then sailed off into the night and almost immediately a squall was upon us and the wind dramatically increased in force. The wind pushed the boats apart from each other, waves started crashing over our heads and the outboard motors started failing one by one…

One of the outboard motors failed immediately after *Antrim* sailed and left us to our own devices. Then callsign 17 Alpha, the boat that I was in, had its engine cut out abruptly a minute or two later. One of the RIBs, 17 Echo, turned back and took two boats in tow, but then its engine failed too leaving 17 Alpha, 17 Bravo and 17 Echo in severe difficulties. Meanwhile 17 Delta took 17 Charlie in tow and succeeded in dropping the crew of three with their boat at Grass Island. 17 Delta then returned to look for the other three boats, but saw nothing in the darkness. Eventually Delta's engine also failed, and with a supreme effort the crew managed to paddle ashore on a headland several miles distant from Grass Island where they remained until rescued after the enemy surrender. The three Geminis without functioning engines were initially tied together but this threatened to overturn the boats and we were forced to cast off from each other. This soon left us all over Stromness Bay and being forced out to the open sea in atrocious weather conditions. The three of us on 17 Alpha had little choice but to take turns paddling with the two small paddles while the third crew member tried to start the outboard motor using a starter rope as there was no electronic ignition on our ageing engine. We were completely shattered by now, although the paddling kept us warm, too warm in fact as we were wearing waterproof immersion suits over our uniforms. When my turn came to have a go at getting the engine to start, I went through the motions like the others had already, but to no avail. In desperation I sprayed gasoline directly into the carburettor and over the top of the engine. Finally the engine sparked and there was a brief flash of flame as the gasoline caught alight, and then the engine cut out. I thought this 'flame-out' may have helped to clear out the carb and also warm up the engine. I tried this highly dangerous procedure a second time with nothing to lose. This time the engine back-fired a few times and started to run, albeit none too sweetly. Wasting no time, we sped directly to Grass Island. The outboard motor cut out a couple of times on the way, but we managed to restart it by pulling the starter cord immediately before the engine had a chance to get cold. We didn't see the other two missing boats on the way to Grass Island. Only three Geminis had made it to Grass Island, meaning Boat Troop were now reduced to just nine men. Two boats, 17 Bravo and 17 Delta with a total of six crew members, were missing.

Once ashore my priority as troop signaller was to encode the message that the troop commander, Ted, had just written. All messages were encoded using one-time pad (OTP). The use of OTP encoding was a slow and laborious method, but at least it guaranteed operational security. I wasn't due to make radio contact until after first light, but I broke radio silence and advised D Squadron SHQ on board HMS *Antrim* that two Geminis were missing and their crews were in great danger due to the very poor sea conditions caused by the storm. Lieutenant Commander Ian Stanley took off in his Wessex 3 at first light to try to find the boats and conducted a grid search outside Stromness Bay. The conditions were still stormy with gale-force winds. The helicopter came to within four miles or so of our position at the start of the search and for a few seconds I actually saw the Wessex flying at about 300 feet just below the cloud base searching for the two Geminis. The Wessex then vectored onto a likely search grid which took them over sixty miles from shore. The helicopter was running short of fuel and was at the outer edge of the search area when, suddenly, 17 Bravo turned on their TACBE and this helped guide the helicopter to their position. The boat crew had waited until they had visual sighting of the Wessex to ensure it wasn't an enemy helicopter. Chippy and his crew were then rescued using the aircraft's winch. One of the Gemini's crew, Brummie, used a knife to slash all the air compartments and the boat was abandoned in a sinking condition. Meanwhile, the final Gemini, callsign 17 Delta, had been pushed close to a rocky promontory that jutted out into Stromness Bay, and with the greatest of difficulty the crew were able to paddle ashore. The crew of 17 Delta stayed under a rocky overhang and maintained radio silence until after hostilities ended. It was only then that they finally made radio contact and requested recovery. Until that time everyone had expected the worst possible news about their chances of survival.

I could send Morse as fast as anyone else in D Squadron. Some people struggled to master Morse, but I just had a natural aptitude for tapping out the code. This meant I was usually designated as the patrol signaller, or when the four patrols in the troop operated together I was nominated as the troop signaller. When we were on Grass Island, I would break radio silence twice a day. During these radio skeds, I would keep the task force informed of developments. All messages were encoded using OTP. Ted, the troop boss, would write the SITREP and then I would encode it. Half a page of writing would typically mean a thirty-group message. This would take me about two minutes to transmit. With the additional transmissions of establishing comms and then acknowledging the message, plus an additional wait while it was decoded and a final acknowledgement given, a typical sked would take fifteen minutes. Whenever I was transmitting Ted had the unenviable task of turning the hand generator to give a booster charge to the radio battery. While Ted didn't enjoy this enforced exercise, it at least kept him warm and also was a good incentive to keep messages short! The PRC 320 radio that I was carrying was heavy, but we were only walking short distances as we moved around so it wasn't too much of an encumbrance. While in our LUP on Grass Island, we saw a Boeing 707 aircraft flying on a course that took it along the coast of South Georgia. We reported this and I later discovered that it was an Argentine Air Force aircraft fitted with an electronic warfare suite making a reconnaissance flight to try and locate the British warships. We continued to observe and monitor the movements of the Argentinian marines at Leith all that day and into the next.

We only had a single, serviceable outboard motor when we left Grass Island on the second night. We had tried the night before, but couldn't manage to get even this one outboard motor working. We had more success on the second night when it stuttered into life. We then used this Gemini to tow the other two boats slowly until 100m from shore. We cast off and paddled silently the short distance until we made landfall. This was on the Stromness side of the ridge between the two whaling stations out of sight of Leith Harbour. We hauled the boats out of the water and hid them in the rocks above the high water mark. We then sent a patrol to check out Stromness whaling station. They cleared the buildings quickly, which mostly consisted of large sheds and warehouses. There were also some amenity buildings and offices, typically only one or two rooms in size. We soon confirmed that Stromness was uninhabited, which we already suspected from our observations from Grass Island. Stromness sat at the head of the bay surrounded by precipitous high ground, and behind that the mountains closed in. It was eerily quiet, more like a movie set than a real-life place which had once been a hive of activity. We left five men at Stromness commanded by Colin. Ted decided to leave the PRC 320 with them and I carried a lighter VHF radio forward to the OP. The plan was that I would transmit messages to Colin's VHF radio and he was to relay these via Morse back to HMS *Antrim*. Our four-man patrol ascended the ridge behind Harbour Point and set up an OP on high ground less than 400m from the whaling station at Leith.

We had seen a few lights burning at Leith as we were setting up our OP, and at first light on Saturday 24 April we heard a siren before we saw the Argentinian marines come running out for their morning 'stand-to'. This gave us the perfect opportunity in our OP to count the marines and identify their weapons and also where they had set up their defensive positions. I sat with Ted while he wrote out a signal to send to *Antrim*. The message was fairly lengthy as it detailed the Argentinian dispositions at Leith. The message was duly passed to our patrol at Stromness over the VHF link and then onward to *Antrim* via Morse using the HF radio.

On the morning of Sunday 25 April, I sent another long message via Stromness. This time we confirmed that we were ready to attack and we requested naval gunfire support be stood by for when the attack went in, with our recommendation that H-Hour be an hour before first light the next day, i.e., Monday 26 April. The message was acknowledged fairly quickly, but Colin advised me that permission to close down was denied and we were told to wait. The waiting continued for about two hours. Suddenly, the control station on *Antrim* asked Colin to stand by for a message, and when Topsy, acting as signaller, decoded this a few minutes later it gave us the startling news that we should do nothing as a surrender was being negotiated. We only had this small piece of information, and we spent hours speculating what could have happened to cause this sudden turn of events?

> ### Diary Entry Sunday 25 April 1982
> When we received the message over the radio 'Do nothing, surrender being negotiated,' little did I realize at the time that the Argentinian submarine *Santa Fe* had just been attacked by Royal Navy helicopters. A quick attack on the Argentinian garrison at Grytviken by Royal Marines and Special Forces ensued. At that moment the Grytviken garrison, together with the crew of the submarine, were in the process of surrendering, although Leith was still holding out…

The attack on ARA *Santa Fe* began on 25 April with the Wessex 3 from HMS *Antrim* dropping two depth charges onto the submarine when she was spotted on the surface sixteen miles south of Cumberland Bay. These depth charges straddled the submarine and caused internal damage to ballast tank and trim controls. This initial attack was followed up by a further attack by a Lynx helicopter from HMS *Brilliant* before they were joined by Wasp helicopters from HMS *Endurance* and HMS *Plymouth*. The submarine was faced with little choice in its crippled state but to return to Grytviken.

We didn't know at the time, but a decision was made to land whatever force could be mustered out of the few Royal Marines available, together with SF from the SBS and SAS. This was because M Company, 42 Commando, was still 200 miles out to sea on board RFA *Tidespring*, our replenishment oiler/tanker. The ad hoc force landed by helicopter on the far side of Brown Mountain to screen them from Grytviken. This was after a naval gunfire support bombardment which deliberately avoided firing directly at the Argentinian marines in the BAS buildings, but was rather a show of force. The first wave of British attackers advanced through the Grytviken whaling station and across an unmarked minefield towards the BAS buildings. At this point white flags were seen to be flying from the buildings. The Argentinians at Grytviken, under the command of Captain Luis Lagos, surrendered without a shot being fired. Meanwhile D Squadron's sergeant major, Lawrence Gallagher, proudly hoisted the Union Flag on a nearby flagpole.

While all this was going on, the small detachment of Argentinian marines at Leith repeatedly refused to surrender when contacted by radio from HMS *Endurance*. They did, however, permit the scrap-metal merchants, more than forty of them, to walk towards our new position next to our boats on the Stromness side of Harbour Point and allow us to process them prior to repatriation. We had by now been joined by most of D Squadron, who had been dropped off in small numbers by helicopter and later the remainder by boat from HMS *Plymouth*. When they joined us we were informed that one of their number, Benny from Mobility Troop, was a Spanish speaker. Suddenly the scrap-metal workers started approaching our position where we were waiting in the rocks above the shoreline. They were singing as they walked along, presumably to let us know they were coming so that we didn't shoot them. Benny was instructed by the Boat Troop OC to issue instructions in Spanish to the scrap-metal men. They were to be told to stop, put their hands in the air and then approach in one long line to be searched for weapons and contraband. I watched Benny's face go into contortions while he struggled to digest all this information. Finally he blurted out, *'Buenos Dias!'* and that was all he was able to say in Spanish! We all burst into laughter and even the scrap-metal men joined in. Even I knew *Buenos Dias* meant Good Day, and as it was actually night-time he had used the wrong words. With those two words Benny confirmed to us all that if you don't practise a language, you lose it. He suffered the piss being taken out of him for weeks. We searched the scrap-metal men and confiscated the bottles of whisky and rum that they had stolen from the BAS store. We did however allow them to keep the bottles of Argentine wine that most of them had jutting out of the pockets of their winter coats. As a footnote to Benny's performance as a Spanish speaker: despite his poor performance as a linguist, he was still a superb soldier and would go on to become RSM of 22 SAS.

The next morning, on Monday 26 April, the three Boat Troop patrols returned to the high ground to monitor the situation. Meanwhile, HMS *Plymouth* and HMS *Endurance* sailed close to Leith and persuaded the Argentinian force there to surrender or be on the receiving end of a naval barrage. The leader at Leith, Lieutenant Commander Astiz, finally signed the second set of surrender documents in the wardroom on board HMS *Plymouth*, following on from the first surrender at Grytviken. Lieutenant Commander Astiz was a former intelligence officer and had been heavily involved in running a secret detention and torture centre for political prisoners. Reportedly up to 5,000 political prisoners were interrogated, tortured and murdered there, earning Astiz the nickname *El Angel Rubio de la Muerte* (the Blonde Angel of Death). While the surrender was taking place, Boat Troop were already flying back to HMS *Antrim*. This included the crew of 17 Delta who had remained under their rocky overhang until finally rescued by HMS *Plymouth* after hostilities ended.

Diary Entry Monday 26 April 1982
Boat Troop were finally back on board HMS *Antrim*. We had been lifted off South Georgia by one of HMS *Brilliant*'s Lynx helicopters. After the short flight we were given a hot brew and a debrief, including the exploits of other Squadron members at Grytviken. I managed to obtain a copy of the surrender document signed by Captain I.M. Lagos at Grytviken. He was the Commander

of the Argentinian Forces in occupation of the islands of South Georgia. I didn't however manage to acquire a copy of the Leith surrender document, which was signed by the infamous Lieutenant Commander Astiz.

It was on 26 April that I heard the story of the first-day covers. A member of Mountain Troop, Des, was a keen philatelist and when told to search the post office at Grytviken he lost no time in finding and setting the date stamp for the day of liberation, i.e., 25 April 1982. Des then proceeded to stamp twenty each of two different first-day covers that he found. He then destroyed the remainder. I still have two in my possession. Some were lost in the Sea King helicopter crash on 19 May 1982, when several members of Mountain Troop perished.

We were informed that all SAS and SBS in the South Georgia Task Group were to be cross-decked to HMS *Brilliant*, a modern type 22 frigate, for onward passage to join the main Falkland Islands task force. Before leaving HMS *Antrim*, I was handed a copy of the 'Scum', the *Antrim*'s unofficial newsletter. It contained a cartoon of an SAS trooper, it was actually Brummie from Boat Troop, being served breakfast in his bunk by a jolly jack tar as a thank you for our exploits on South Georgia. That evening we were taken across to *Brilliant* by her Lynx helicopters. It was now full steam ahead to the Falklands!

Chapter 7

Falkland Islands before D-Day

Diary Entry Tuesday 27 April 1982
The next day I woke up on board HMS *Brilliant*. I had developed 'frost nip' in my fingers and toes on South Georgia. Now that I was back on board a ship the higher ambient temperatures made it worse. As always, I kept my medical problems to myself. We had a celebration drink with the bottles of spirits that were confiscated from the Argie scrap-metal men. We then spent a further two days steaming towards HMS *Hermes*, Britain's oldest aircraft carrier and the flagship of Rear Admiral John 'Sandy' Woodward.

The voyage passed quickly and gave us an opportunity to debate whether this was going to turn into a full-blown war or not. At the time, diplomatic negotiations were progressing and we knew that the liberation of South Georgia had given the British an ace card in their dealings with the Argentinians via the 'shuttlecock' diplomacy of United States Secretary of State Alexander Haig.

Diary Entry Friday 30 April 1982
When we arrived on board HMS *Brilliant*. We were informed that our Task Group 317.9 would meet up with the main naval task force, headed up by HMS *Hermes*. We were also advised that a second task force, the amphibious task force, had sailed from the UK and was also headed for the Falkland Islands.

We soon met up with the main naval task force and cross-decked to HMS *Hermes*. This was a huge ship compared to the frigates and destroyers that I had been on board so far. *Hermes* was a conventional aircraft carrier and had on board Sea Harriers, Sea King helicopters and embarked RAF Harrier GR.3 to augment the air capability. Cross-decking all of D Squadron's bulk stores and combat supplies, including ammunition, rations, comms equipment, boats, mountain and arctic equipment, was back-breaking work. It took many hours each time we performed this activity. I was pleased to find out that I now had my own bunk bed and Boat Troop our own mess, shared with Mountain Troop.

Diary Entry Saturday 1 May 1982
We met up with a few of our mates from G Squadron, 22 SAS, on board HMS *Hermes*, and also some of our embedded signallers from D and G Troops, 264 (SAS) Signal Squadron. Within hours G Squadron were to be put ashore on recce tasks. We helped the patrols from G Squadron load up on to the Sea King helicopters on *Hermes* flight deck as they were all carrying very heavy loads, including up to one month's supply of arctic rations for each trooper. Then with a final wave, they took off to the Falkland Islands for their recce tasks. Another item of key interest at this time was that a lone RAF Vulcan bomber dropped twenty-one 1,000lb bombs onto Stanley Airport. This was immediately followed by a total of nine Sea Harriers, from *Hermes* and our other aircraft carrier HMS *Invincible*, attacking the same target. Also two Harriers simultaneously mounted a raid on Goose Green airstrip.

The attack on Stanley Airport included naval gunfire support from HMS *Alacrity, Glamorgan* and *Arrow*. In all, damage was caused to the runway, control tower, other buildings and fuel supplies. My best friend in Boat Troop was called Topsy, the only former RN sailor among his SAS brothers-in-arms. Topsy was a useful mate to have on board ship as his 'navy speak' was second to none. We went with Brummie, another Boat Troop mate, to observe the Sea Harriers land and then followed them down to the flight hangar. We watched in awe as the aircraft technicians checked over the aircraft. One of the Sea Harriers had a large hole blown in its tail fin as a result of enemy action. When Topsy asked how the repair would be made, the response was, 'Oh, we will probably pop-rivet a bit of tin can over it.' I still don't know if he was joking!

G Squadron's SITREPs were coming in to *Hermes* twice a day from the various patrols scattered across the Falkland Islands. There were also a few SBS patrols adding to this intelligence picture. Due to the 'need to know' basis, I knew very little of what they were doing and what they continued to do until after D-Day. I did, however, manage to have a look at a panoramic 'photo-montage' aerial reconnaissance photo of Stanley Airport after the first Vulcan bomber raid. The craters showed quite clearly in the black and white photo taken at an altitude of several thousand feet to show the whole runway. The Sea Harriers were also used to maintain a combat air patrol (CAP) above the fleet to engage any enemy aircraft sent in our direction. Later in the war the Sea Harriers would concentrate on the CAP role while the RAF G3 Harriers would take on the fighter ground attack close support role.

Diary Entry Sunday 2 May 1982
Things were coming to a head. ARA *Belgrano*, an Argentinian heavy cruiser, was sunk with heavy loss of life on 2 May by HMS *Conqueror*, a nuclear-powered submarine. Meanwhile, G Squadron were now on dry land. The fight to regain the Falkland Islands was finally underway.

The *Belgrano* had been caught inside the UK-imposed Total Exclusion Zone of 200 miles around the Falkland Islands. While I was sad at the loss of life, I was pleased that this removed a major threat to our task force. It was also a fact that the Argentine fleet remained in port for the remainder of the war.

Pride of place in my home is a print depicting Sergeant Gordon Mather who was a member of G Squadron. Gordon was awarded the Military Medal for his role in observing and reporting on Argentine enemy positions. The original painting by Peter Archer is currently displayed at Headquarters Mess, Royal Signals. Gordon, like me, was originally from Royal Signals. The print shows Gordon observing a number of enemy helicopters, including two CH47 Chinooks, from his position on Mount Kent. I saw one of these same Argentine Air Force Chinooks four weeks later. It was eventually destroyed by a lone Harrier aircraft in almost the same position adjacent to Mount Kent.

Diary Entry Monday 3 May 1982
Things continue to be very busy now that we are on HMS *Hermes*. We carry out training on subjects such as naval gunfire support and aircraft recognition. We also spend a lot of our time weapon

training. Today I practised on an M203 under-barrel grenade launcher fitted to an M16 assault rifle. The M203 uses the same grenades as the older stand-alone M79 grenade launcher which I was already very familiar with.

Our instructor for aircraft recognition was Flight Lieutenant Garth Hawkins, RAF, who was attached to D Squadron for the duration of hostilities. Garth was accompanied by Corporal 'Mac' McCormack from 244 Signal Squadron (Air Support). Together they made up our newly created Forward Air Control team known as 603 Tactical Air Control Party. Sadly they both died in the SAS Sea King helicopter crash.

All of our squadron briefings and training sessions were held in a large area where passageways crossed. This was known as a 'flat' and we claimed '2 Sierra Flat' as D Squadron's 'classroom'. We soon learned to ignore sailors walking through our 'classroom' as we carried out weapon training and other activities.

D Squadron still hadn't received any mail, although the ship's company already had their first sacks of mail. At least this meant that we were given a few newspapers and magazines which were a valuable source of information about the Falkland Islands. I managed to obtain a copy of the *Hermes Herald*, the unofficial newsletter of HMS *Hermes*. A copy, dated 3 May 1982, showed a cartoon of the *Santa Fe* incident. The cartoon had a caption which made me smile: 'El Capitano speaking! Anyone who can imitate the mating call of a sperm whale is to do so over the loudspeakers now!' We were not the only embarked troops on board *Hermes*. As well as the SAS and SBS there were quite a few Royal Marines on board the carrier.

Diary Entry Tuesday 4 May 1982
Many air raids launched against us, but Harriers from the combat air patrol turned most of them away. That is except for a couple of Super Étendard aircraft flying at low level over the sea which managed to slip through our radar defences and hit HMS *Sheffield*, a type 42 destroyer, with two Exocet missiles. Survivors brought on board *Hermes*, including one who died on the flight deck. Burial at sea. We were also informed over the public address system that a Harrier has been shot down over Goose Green. A bad day for us.

We still haven't received any mail, although the newspapers we received yesterday have helped to relieve any boredom, not that we have much spare time.

HMS *Sheffield* was one of three ships forming a forward anti-aircraft picket to the west of the main task force. One of the Exocet missiles hit HMS *Sheffield* amidships tearing a hole in her hull and starting several uncontrollable fires. Twenty people died and twenty-six were injured. It was the first Royal Navy warship to have been lost in combat since the Second World War. The fires burned for two days. Six days after the missile hit *Sheffield* she sank while being towed.

I also learnt a couple of months later that Vulcan bomber raids by the RAF, codenamed Operation Black Buck, dropping bombs on Stanley Airport and its associated defences, continued for seven missions. Five of these missions were performed, although two were cancelled, one due to weather conditions and the other because of a fault in the Victor tanker fleet that supported the Vulcan bombers. Apparently the enemy after every Vulcan bombing raid made 'craters' out of rings of sand on the runway so that our air reconnaissance photos would show more damage than was true. If this was what really happened, it certainly fooled us at the time.

Diary Entry Wednesday 5 May 1982
Towards the end of the first week in May 1982, mail started to arrive for D Squadron in dribs and drabs. The letters were all dated from early April and they included a couple for me. I also managed to grab a copy of *Navy News* which contained many stories about what was happening in the 'Falklands Crisis'. This was just about the last time that I heard this choice of words before it became the Falklands War. This was inevitable really as the military actions on both sides had escalated rapidly in the last week or so.

It was on or about this date when we all began to realize that we were going to fight in a real war within the next couple of weeks.

Diary Entry Thursday 6 May 1982
Two Harriers lost at sea.

Two Sea Harriers of No. 801 Naval Air Squadron (NAS), HMS *Invincible*, were lost in bad weather, south-east of the Falkland Islands on 6 May 1982. Lieutenant Curtiss and Lieutenant Commander Eyton-Jones RN were lost, presumably after colliding. RIP those brave souls.

Diary Entry Friday 7 May 1982
My birthday! A quiet day. We hear confirmation that our larger amphibious task force has sailed from Ascension with Royal Marines, Paras, Ghurkhas, Welsh and Scots Guards, Royal Artillery etc. We plan our various options now that G Squadron are sending target information back to the ships in our naval task force. I suspect the SBS may also be sending detailed beach recce information for possible landing sites.

We received news that the Amphibious Task Force had sailed from the UK from about 9 April onwards. They had called in briefly at Ascension Island on the way to transfer stores between ships and for even more personnel to be squeezed aboard. I found it incredible when I first heard the names of the Ships Taken Up from Trade (STUFT). They included the cruise liners *Canberra* and *Queen Elizabeth 2*, often called the *QE2*, and the car ferries *Norland* and *Elk*. Later we heard that the schools cruise liner *Uganda* had been requisitioned to be used as a hospital ship. There were many more ships requisitioned from STUFT that were subsequently to be added to the growing list. I managed to acquire a bottle of vodka for my birthday and I shared it with my mates mixed with a packet of lemonade powder diluted with water. My 28th birthday was certainly like no other birthday that I have celebrated before or since!

Diary Entry Saturday 8 May 1982
In the hours before we departed from the UK many of us took the opportunity to complete our last will and testament on a standard Ministry of Defence (MOD) issue form. We were also offered the chance to increase our life insurance at our own cost. I was one of many in D Squadron who took up this offer. Now that things were getting serious, we were issued special identity (ID) cards on 8 May in case we were taken prisoner. In typical British penny-pinching fashion, it was a thin piece of card costing perhaps a penny or two on

which we had to fill in our own details. The piece of card was then slipped inside a flimsy plastic cover. Our normal plastic laminated MOD 90 identity cards were then withdrawn from us and held centrally. This new ID card, together with my dog tags (ID discs), were all I had to prove my identity should I be captured.

The new ID card was known as an F/Ident/189 and stated the following: 'If you are captured you are required, under the provisions of Article 17 of the Prisoner of War Convention, 1949, to give your captors the information set out below so that your capture may be reported to your next-of-kin. When you are interrogated, but not before, tear off the duplicate portion and give it to the interrogator. GIVE NO OTHER INFORMATION...'

Although the intelligence being received from the G Squadron patrols is 'need to know' we had at least been told that they were doing good work ashore. We are itching to get ashore ourselves. We do our best to keep fit and every day I go to the stern of the ship to run up and down. The little covered deck directly above the propellers is where the sacks of potatoes are stored. It is only exposed to the elements on the side facing aft. Most days the flight deck is out of bounds so there is simply nowhere else to exercise. As you can imagine the thousands of crew members and embarked troops are getting through quite a few spuds. Last week the available space to run up and down was about 11m, but now it is up to about 20m as the potatoes are being consumed quickly, despite being rationed. You cannot imagine how much self-discipline you require to run back and forth, with about four other diehards all determined to run for an hour no matter what the difficulties are in achieving this in such a confined space. There is also a space given over to weight-lifting below decks, but there are too many people trying to train and insufficient equipment so I have stuck to my daily run.

Diary Entry Sunday 9 May 1982
Several mail sacks arrived on board *Hermes* today. No mail for me but I managed to get hold of a couple of well-read newspapers and kept the pages relating to the Falklands in a folder that I stored in my holdall.

It was interesting that most of my colleagues would merely scan a newspaper or magazine and make loud exclamations such as 'Would you look at that!', especially when the photo was of a sexy girl. I, however, was an avid reader who literally devoured the print page by page until there was nothing else to read. I still have a few pages carefully torn out of the *Navy News* from April 1982, including a photo entitled 'Bustling scene of Sea Harriers and aircraft controllers on the Hermes flight deck'. There was also a story which began, 'As *Navy News* was going to press, news of the recapture of South Georgia was announced by Defence Secretary Mr. John Nott.'

> *Diary Entry Monday 10 May 1982*
> **Two Harriers strafed an Argie 'spy trawler'. A Sea King helicopter landed on board the trawler and took the crew prisoner, together with their military signalling codes as proof of their activities. The Royal Navy attempted to repair the trawler but it later sank. Argies now have nearly all their ships back in their home ports not wishing to risk them against us. The Argies are still managing to resupply the Falklands though by utilising an air bridge of transport aircraft.**

When I wrote my war diary, I was constrained by the 'need-to-know' basis. This meant that I never mentioned what the other SAS squadrons were doing even though I often knew via official channels or I overhead something. I regularly heard snippets of information about what the SBS were up to also, but again I kept this to myself and never mentioned it in my war diary. The diary note above mentions a boarding party and the Royal Navy attempting to repair the trawler. What it doesn't mention is that I knew it was an SBS boarding party and they were the ones who attempted to plug the leaks on board. I knew several of the SBS guys very well and one of them told me the full details of this little operation. As well as being an instructor who had taught some of the SBS guys on their patrol signallers' course in Hereford, there had been a couple of them on my patrol medic course. I had also trained with them in the maritime counter-terrorism role. The SBS were in control of maritime counter-terrorism, but had the support of the SAS, particularly the boat troops, for terrorism incidents involving 'ships alongside', i.e., in harbour.

G Squadron, 22 SAS, had by now about ten patrols ashore plus a few SBS patrols, all engaged in close observation of enemy positions. The patrols came up on their radio skeds each day and tried to limit their time on the Morse key to no more than a few minutes at a time. The short transmission times were to counter the Argentinian electronic warfare effort. We didn't know, for example, if the Argies were capable of direction-finding in the HF band by means of a base-line. This would require a number of base stations some distance away from the HF transmitter to take a bearing on the signal. Where these bearings intersect each other is the location of the enemy transmitter. The level of sophistication of the direction-finding equipment will dictate how long it takes to plot the lines of intersection.

Meanwhile, a plan was evolving for a recce team from Boat Troop to mount a CTR of the airstrip on Pebble Island, off the north coast of West Falkland. The Boat Troop recce team, consisting of eight men and their four folding Klepper kayaks, moved by helicopter to the mainland opposite Pebble Island. Once there they would assemble the Kleppers and observe the crossing point. There was a rip tide at this point so it was essential to wait for slack water at low tide. I was more than a bit disappointed that I hadn't been chosen to go on the CTR, and busied myself getting my kit ready for when D Squadron mounted the assault on the airfield.

Diary Entry Tuesday 11 May 1982
Once ashore the weather deteriorated, and with rough sea conditions it took two attempts for the Boat Troop recce team to find a suitable launching place to paddle across to Pebble Island. The second location chosen required them to pack up the Kleppers with one man carrying the 'skin' or rubberised fabric and the other carrying the wooden frame plus paddles, not forgetting they also had to carry their personal kit, weapons and radio. This took all night as they couldn't carry everything in one lift. It was only on the second night that they arrived on Pebble Island and were able to establish their covert OP. Two men stayed with the Klepper kayaks and established radio skeds to D Squadron SHQ on board HMS *Hermes*. The Kleppers were camouflaged in the rocks behind a small beach on Pebble Island. The remainder of the recce team went forward to mount surveillance on the airstrip. The assault plan called for the remainder of D Squadron to be airlifted by Sea King helicopters from the flight-deck on *Hermes* direct to Pebble Island to RV with the recce team.

At last the weather improved and the recce team were able to paddle across to Phillips Cove. On arrival at Phillips Cove they left two men there with the canoes. Six men moved off, eventually leaving another two at a Drop Off Point (DOP). Finally, four men moved forward to set up an OP close to the airstrip. Soon it was first light and the men saw eleven enemy aircraft, including six Pucara light attack aircraft, stretched out before them.

Meanwhile, hostilities continued on all fronts. We were required to go about our duties on board HMS *Hermes* carrying 'anti-flash' gear, comprising white-coloured, heat and flash-resistant balaclava and long gloves as our personal protective equipment. These items were worn during air raid warnings and offered protection to your skin from the initial fireball caused by the impact of a missile or bomb exploding below decks.

We heard on 11 May that HMS *Alacrity*, a type 21 frigate, had surprised and attacked an Argentine supply vessel trying to run the blockade around the Falkland Islands. The encounter took place in Falkland Sound, the passage between West and East Falkland. It was a cloudy night and initial contact was made by radar. Eventually *Alacrity* assessed that the target was trying to escape and engaged it with her 4.5-inch gun. The Argentine ship was finally halted by these high explosive shells and a large explosion could be seen from *Alacrity*. The ship was later identified as the *Isla de los Estados*, a naval transport carrying military vehicles, ammunition and several hundred thousand litres of aviation fuel.

Diary Entry Thursday 13 May 1982

We were now in the final planning stages for the Pebble Island raid. We considered what weaponry to take. More than fifty per cent of D Squadron personnel had the AR-15 assault rifle, similar to the M16, as their personal weapon. The remainder carried the M203 with its 40mm underslung grenade launcher. We also had one GPMG belt-fed machine gun for every eight men and about five 66mm LAW rocket launchers. We made up a number of explosive charges, but these were in short supply.

We knew the aircraft at Pebble Island comprised a number of Pucara light attack aircraft plus some other types. These enemy aircraft were well within range of the chosen landing site at San Carlos and could easily have compromised the amphibious task group on its way in. The airfield could have launched air attacks on the British ships and the troops at their most vulnerable point as they approached the beaches. There was also the possibility that a radar installation was situated there. If that was the case it was a top priority to destroy it as the radar could well be capable of monitoring ships entering Falkland Sound.

Diary Entry Friday 14 May 1982
D Squadron were finally given approval to proceed with the attack on Pebble Island. The plan called for HMS *Hermes*, HMS *Broadsword* and HMS *Glamorgan* to steam closer to landfall, but still well to the north of Pebble Island. *Hermes* would stand off at about forty miles with *Broadsword* providing air defence, meanwhile *Glamorgan* was to come in much closer to provide naval gunfire support.

We were briefed on board *Hermes* about the plan for the Pebble Island raid. It was all systems go as we struggled to work out a loading plan to get everyone on board the available helicopters with all the correct weapons and ammunition loaded on to the Sea Kings. The weather was a major problem once again and it forced *Hermes* to steam ever closer to West Falkland to shorten the distance that the Sea Kings would be forced to fly in the ever-increasing wind speed.

After a lengthy delay, D Squadron mounted up by troops into four Sea King helicopters and took off in extremely windy weather to RV with the Boat Troop recce party. Another piece of SAS history was in the making. Not since the Second World War had folding canoes been used to carry out close target reconnaissance (CTR), and now the SAS were mounting a raid on an airstrip. HMS *Hermes* was forced to steam closer to Pebble Island than originally planned due to the heavy winds which reduced the helicopters' range. This meant the arrival would be very late with correspondingly less time on the ground. Finally, D Squadron arrived at the HLS in gale-force winds to join the Boat Troop recce team. Within seconds the Sea Kings took off leaving only the sound of the wind. The troops formed up and the OC, Cedric, gave his final orders to the assembled troop commanders. Then it was time to deploy forward. The time available to launch the attack and then make the helicopter exfiltration RV was very short. Without further delay the troops moved forward to their designated positions, but not without some confusion and last-minute changes to the overall plan. An area had been selected as the squadron RV near Big Pond and it was here that the mortar position was also established. Lawrence, our sergeant major, would also stay here to man the squadron RV and count the men back in after the airstrip raid. The plan called for Air Troop to watch the settlement in case any of the Argie troops decided to take us on. There wasn't time to mount an attack on the pilots and Argie troops in the settlement and instead we concentrated on the airstrip. Mobility Troop were to mount the attack on the aircraft with Boat Troop waiting further back to act as guides and close support if required. This left Mountain Troop in reserve. As so often happens in war, the plan had to be changed before we had even started. Mobility Troop had gone missing during the advance to target and therefore Mountain Troop became the main players on the airstrip with Mobility Troop to be held in reserve when they eventually arrived. Finally everyone was in position and ready for action. The attack got underway with a mortar illumination round to provide light and act as a signal to initiate the assault. Soon *Glamorgan* joined in with naval gunfire support, including star shells for illumination which were supplemented by our own hand-held Schermuley flares. In all, six Pucara light attack aircraft, four T34 Mentor reconnaissance planes and a Skyvan light transport aircraft were destroyed on the grass airstrip that night. They had been destroyed by a combination of demolition charges and small arms fire. After everyone regrouped at the designated squadron RV, it was time to move off to the pick-up HLS. It had been a complete success. D Squadron suffered only two lightly wounded casualties, one had shrapnel in his leg and the other had concussion from when the Argentinians detonated a demolition charge by command-wire out on the airstrip.

Diary Entry Saturday 15 May 1982
The raid on Pebble Island has been a complete success with eleven Argie aircraft destroyed. The tempo of war continued to increase and the Harriers were bombarding the airfield at Stanley most nights while the RAF Vulcan bombing raids continued. An hour or two before last light on 15 May provided yet another surprise. Nine SAS men parachuted into the sea alongside the task force after a long flight from Ascension Island. Eight of the men were from B Squadron, plus one other for separate tasking.

I 'forgot' to destroy my signals codes after the Pebble Island raid and decided to keep them as a souvenir. I still have them now.

The SAS parachutist assigned for separate tasking was Paddy O'Connor, a staff sergeant from G Squadron. Several bundles and other containers were parachuted along with the SAS parachutists. One of the containers contained a small number of Stinger ground-to-air missiles. Paddy had been sent to Fort Bragg to learn how to fire the missiles and had now arrived with them to train D Squadron in their use. The Stingers had been acquired by clandestine means from US Special Forces, but whether this was officially US government sanctioned I have no idea. The missiles were 5ft long and, including the shoulder-launcher assembly, weighed more than 34lbs. They used infra-red heat-seeking technology with an HE explosive warhead. Paddy gave each troop in turn a short introductory lesson to the Stinger. When it was my turn, I remember listening to the noise before it reached a certain high-pitched tone indicating that the missile was locked on to the target. We were scheduled to receive a second lesson from Paddy, but that never materialized due to his untimely death in the SAS Sea King helicopter crash. Soon after, it was decided that Air Troop would operate our limited supply of Stingers.

I met some of my mates from B Squadron when they were brought on board *Hermes*, including 'Donny' who had been one of my instructors on Selection. Within twenty-four hours the B Squadron team had taken off in a Sea King on Operation Plum Duff. The mission was shrouded in secrecy, but it turned out to be a planned recce of an Argentine airbase on the South American mainland. The webbing seats and other items had been stripped from the airframe in an effort to reduce weight and thereby increase the potential range of the aircraft. The destroyed Sea King was discovered a day or two later, 400 miles away near Punta Arenas in Chile not far from the Argentine border. Due to the aborted recce, any likely action by B Squadron, 22 SAS, on the mainland was cancelled. Known as Operation Mikado, this was an SAS plan to use B Squadron to attack the Super Étendard fighters on the ground at their base near Rio Grande, Tierra del Fuego.

The ongoing recces by G Squadron, 22 SAS, and the SBS ashore on the Falkland Islands were now nearing completion. The chosen landing beaches at San Carlos had been designated and it only remained for some diversionary landings to take place before the main beach landings could take place on D-Day.

My knowledge of 'navy speak' was improving all the time so I was able to comprehend that we had a new crisis on board *Hermes* due to a dire shortage of 'nutty' (chocolate bars) in the NAAFI, despite having been rationed for weeks. The NAAFI canteen was manned by members of the Naval Canteen Services who wear naval uniform but remain ordinary civilians in peacetime. One such canteen manager subsequently changed his status from civilian to enlisted petty officer on 15 May when active service was declared. The man, Petty Officer John Leake, on board HMS *Ardent*, was awarded the Distinguished Service Medal for his courage while manning a machine gun during the Falklands War. John had previous experience as a GPMG machine gunner in the army so this enabled him to carry out his duties efficiently.

The shortage of 'nutty bars' was seen as a bigger problem by many of the young sailors than the air raid warnings we were regularly subjected to. As an aside to this story, we in Boat Troop discovered some of our arctic ration packs, issued to us before deploying ashore, had been prised open on the underside. They had then been carefully replaced on the stacked pile so that they looked undamaged. Our ration packs had been stored along a bulkhead in the large space below decks where a film projector was set up most evenings to show movies to the junior ratings. This gave the young 'matelots' the perfect opportunity to remove the 'nutty bars' from the ration packs while the lights were out. It looked at first glance as if the packing tape had dried out as it was still adhered to one flap on the bottom of the cardboard box. However, once ashore Boat Troop quickly found out that all the chocolate bars had been removed from almost every ration pack. It was a big blow to our morale when we discovered this. How we cursed those young ratings!

Diary Entry Sunday 16 May 1982

We listened to the evening 'all hands briefing' over the public address system on *Hermes*. The first news was that two Harriers had attacked a couple of Argie supply ships in Falkland Sound earlier that day. One ship was bombed and sunk in Falkland Sound. Meanwhile the other, *Bahia Buen Suceso*, was tied up at the jetty at Fox Bay and came under cannon fire before casting loose. The ship finally drifted to shore and beached nearby. Another interesting piece of news was that two Super *Étendards* also came in close to Stanley and attempted an Exocet attack on a British ship, but failed to find a target and returned to their base on the Argentine mainland.

D Squadron were informed that we would soon cross-deck from HMS *Hermes* to HMS *Intrepid*, an amphibious assault ship known as a landing platform dock. This transfer was to enable us to be on board a ship that was actually going to be part of the San Carlos landings, as *Hermes*, one of only two aircraft carriers in the task force, could not be risked coming close to shore. We were not, however, to be part of the beach landing at San Carlos. Instead we were to make a diversionary raid in the Goose Green area on the day before D-Day (D-1). We were not told any more at this stage, but thus began two days of packing all our kit onto pallets and into nets ready for cross-decking by Sea King helicopters.

I was given the task of locating all the squadron radio batteries and moving them to an area just under the flight deck where they were to be palletised for the move. I met up with Wally, the D Squadron storeman, who was a corporal attached to the SAS, to ask for his help in locating the items. Wally knew exactly where they were located. We descended about seven decks before we reached *Hermes*'s ammunition magazines and hazardous materials store. The last three decks were negotiated via vertical steel ladders welded to the ship's bulkheads. Minutes after we arrived in the HAZMAT store, we heard a tinny voice over the public address system announce that the ship was now under 'Air Raid Warning Red' status, anti-flash personal protection was to be worn and all watertight hatches were to be closed. With a mighty clang, someone shut the hatch above us and seconds later all the lights went out! Neither of us had a flashlight, which was a big mistake, and to say it was a claustrophobic experience was an understatement. Wally was more than a bit worried as we sat there in total darkness and I had to reassure him that the air raid warning was likely to be a false alarm, even though I wasn't so sure myself. Eventually it was all over and we were able to climb out of our metal coffin. Sadly, Wally died a few days later in the helicopter crash. RIP Wally, you were one of the good guys.

Diary Entry Monday 17 May 1982

Enemy air activity continues, but fortunately for us the CAP turns back most of this probing. We go to 'air raid warning red' status every few hours during daylight hours. This can be a bit stressful as we don't know if an enemy aircraft will try to launch an Exocet missile at us from some distance away. We are also informed on the captain's evening address to the crew and embarked troops that many ships from the amphibious group have joined us. We don't yet know the date, but we do know that we will all land on the islands within days. Our Troop boss, Ted, gets the Troop together for evening 'prayers' when we have our own update briefing and he confirms to us that we will cross-deck to HMS *Intrepid* tomorrow.

I spent an hour with the D Troop signallers on their mess deck and enjoyed the lively banter. They asked me when I expected to go ashore and I told them, truthfully, that there were no details, but it would be soon. As far as I could ascertain, all the G Squadron and SBS recce patrols had by this time been recovered to *Hermes*. I have a lot of respect for what they had all endured, having spent weeks on end living within sight of the enemy, without being able to move in daylight and at times in the most atrocious weather conditions. While waiting to cross-deck to HMS *Intrepid* I learnt that *Intrepid* and her sister ship HMS *Fearless* were Landing Platform Docks (LPD), each equipped with a large flight deck and floating dock. The two ships were able to flood their sterns to enable amphibious landing craft to float in and out. This arrangement was ideal for rapid loading and unloading of troops and stores.

Diary Entry Wednesday 19 May 1982
What a terrible day. A Sea King helicopter has crashed killing many men from D and G Squadrons. The helicopter was involved in cross-decking from HMS *Hermes* to HMS *Intrepid* and had been busy the whole day moving stores and finally personnel from the two squadrons. It was while preparing to land on *Intrepid* that the Sea King crashed into the sea with disastrous consequences. I went on the penultimate lift in the same helicopter. The ships were less than one mile apart. On landing, I joined a small group of soldiers from 3 PARA waiting in line at the galley where I managed to grab a mug of soup as I was chilled to the bone. Suddenly, the ship's public-address system made a broadcast 'Helicopter ditched! Away crash boats! Medical teams standby!' I made my way to the flight deck to see if I could help in any way and was just in time to see Dave H being stretchered away to the sick bay with hypothermia after only a few minutes in the water. I then went with my medical pack to the casualty clearing station which was being set up in the galley. I was one of six SAS medics waiting there, but there were no

casualties for us. We found out later eight casualties were taken to HMS *Brilliant*. There were twenty-two dead, including one Royal Marine crewman. Only two bodies were recovered.

I remember making my way to the galley carrying a medical pack to help establish a casualty clearing station. I was expecting lots of casualties within minutes, but nobody came. We just stood there in shocked silence. A very sad business. It was not until the next morning that I read the definitive list of those who had died in the helicopter crash. They were all good guys and whether from D Squadron, G Squadron or from 264 (SAS) Signal Squadron and other attached arms, they did not deserve to die in such a pointless manner. Years later I was asked to write about one of the signallers, Corporal Stephen Sykes. Here is an extract of what I wrote:

Steve passed the SAS Signals Probation course in 1978 after serving in 604 Signal Troop which is where I first met him. He was a qualified military parachutist and had also recently qualified as a Class 1 radio telegraphist. While with 264 (SAS) Signal Squadron, Steve saw operational service in Northern Ireland attached to G Squadron, 22 SAS.

My last memory of Steve was about an hour before his death. We were sheltering from the weather just off the flight deck on Hermes. I was sharing the banter with Steve, Mick and Paul, all signallers attached to G Squadron. We had been hauling Gemini RIBs, outboard motors, comms equipment, combat supplies, rations and ammunition from below decks and putting it all into nets for cross-decking by underslung load for more than eight hours and were absolutely shattered. While chatting with the lads, Lawrence, the D Squadron Sergeant Major, came looking for me and told me to get hold of Ted, the Boat Troop Commander, and to get all of my Troop on the next helicopter lift. This I did and a few minutes later Steve gave us all a beaming smile and a cheery wave as Boat Troop took off. That was the last I saw of Lawrence, Steve, Mick and Paul. They all died. I am proud to have known Steve and have him as a friend. Steve's last resting place is the South Atlantic Ocean, but his name is recorded in the SAS Regimental Plot at St Martin's Church in Hereford. RIP

Yes, it was certainly poignant writing about a mate after all those years. I had known Steve for seven years, which was a huge chunk of his total life-span of only twenty-five years. He was certainly way too young to die. RIP Steve, Lawrence, Sid, Phil, Lofty, Paul B, Paddy A, Wally, Willie H, Mick McH, Rab, Paul L and all the others who died that day. Most of the dead were my friends. I will never forget.

Diary Entry Friday 21 May 1982

Yesterday, we mounted diversionary attacks to the immediate north of Darwin and Goose Green. Early on Thursday 20 May we had a pep talk from Cedric, the Squadron Commander. He told us that due to the loss of our men there would have to be a redistribution of manpower. Benny was to take over as Troop Staff Sergeant of Mountain Troop and we would deploy in squadron strength for the diversionary attacks we were to mount that night. Each troop would be assigned a target. SHQ would set up the Squadron RV on the western side of Mount Usborne. I was expecting to be issued an M203, but this was changed at the last minute and I took my personal weapon which was an AR-15. We were supposed to be wearing light order: webbing, ammo pouches and daysack, but I was carrying the radio so I decided to carry everything in my bergen which was initially quite heavy due to carrying extra belt ammunition for the GPMG and a couple of 60mm mortar bombs. We left by Sea King helicopter one hour before last light.

We were dropped some way from our target, 'Burntside House', and cautiously tabbed into position. We then had to wait as the other troops got into position for a simultaneous attack. The other troop targets included 'Camilla Creek House' and other isolated houses in the general area north of Goose Green/Darwin. It was finally 0145 hours on 21 May, the agreed time to initiate the attack. Our intelligence reports indicated that there was an Argie platoon in the house, perhaps thirty men, but we didn't know if any Falkland Island civilians were also in the house. Because of this uncertainty and because this was only a diversion, we were told not to fire directly into the house but rather stomp the area with mortars and rake the area immediately around the house with small arms fire. We fired off quite a lot of ammunition and intended to shoot anyone who came out of the house in uniform carrying a weapon. Nobody came out so after ten minutes or so we broke off the attack and disappeared to the north. We had heard simultaneous gunfire at the other four targets so everything seemed to be well coordinated.

Our next objective was to RV with the remainder of the Squadron at Mount Usborne to the north. As we walked, the air raid siren at Goose Green continued for about thirty minutes so we obviously woke someone up. I later heard that SIGINT intercepts had monitored the Argies reporting that they had come under attack by a battalion-sized unit (about 500 men) but had repulsed the attack! We met up with the other troops at the Squadron RV without any problems, although there was a lot of waiting about in very cold and miserable conditions. From the Squadron RV we continued on our epic tab to San Carlos Water, negotiating several stone runs on the way.

The day of the diversionary attacks was a hectic one. When you consider that this was the day after we had lost many of our comrades in the helicopter crash, it was a tall order asking us to go to war in the same type of helicopters. We flew in the dark skimming the waves with the pilots wearing NVG for the very first time on operations. I had never seen NVGs on a pilot before and it was nerve-racking to be in almost complete darkness with just the occasional white crest of a wave showing as I looked out of the Perspex window near me. Some of the guys had started to call the Sea King the 'jinx machine', which I agreed with at the time, although history has proved it to be a very reliable airframe.

We put down a hail of bullets all around Burntside House, including tracer rounds which puts the fear of God into anyone on the receiving end. There were no enemy sighted at our target so the diversionary attack was easy enough. What wasn't easy was the tab to San Carlos Bay. We tabbed for the remainder of the night, across many 'stone runs' and continued walking all morning and into the afternoon. The stone runs were a very difficult obstacle to negotiate, particularly at night when you consider if a stone moved or if you slipped you would likely twist an ankle or worse.

Kiwi, from Air Troop, shot down a Pucara aircraft with a shoulder-launched Stinger missile. The pilot bailed out and we watched him land safely in the valley below us while the aircraft crashed a fair distance

Birkenhead 1957: Third birthday. No toys, just a kitten. (*Author's photograph*)

Cyprus 1972, Salamis amphitheatre. Posing after a few drinks, aged 17. Taken while serving with 644 Signal Troop (UNFICYP). (*Author's photograph*)

Germany 1974 – Rhine Army Parachute Centre. Taken after my first 'ten second delay' free fall jump. (*Author's photograph*)

Belize – helicopter landing site construction – SAS style. (*Carl*)

Belize – Hoss Ligairi sorting out supper. (*Carl*)

Belize – Scout helicopter landing at jungle HLS. (*Carl*)

Birkenhead – Mark Palios as a Tranmere Rovers player. (*Tranmere Rovers FC*)

Florida 1980 – Boat Troop hauling Gemini RIB. (*Author's photograph*)

USAF
MR-65-2110

Florida – Boat Troop loading Gemini. (*P.J. O'Connor*)

Florida – author operating
PRC 316 SAS patrol radio.
(*Author's photograph*)

Florida – Topsy diving with Boat Troop. (*Author's photograph*)

Florida – Boat Troop patrolling in Kleppers. (*Author's photograph*)

Kenya 1982 – Mobility Troop taking a break from troop training. (*P.J. O'Connor*)

South Atlantic 1982 – Boat Troop lowering Gemini into the sea from RFA Fort Austin. (*N.A.*)

South Atlantic – putting Geminis over the side from RFA Fort Austin. (*N.A.*)

South Atlantic – SAS signallers setting up Tacsat on RFA Fort Austin. (*N.A.*)

South Georgia – setting up on Grass Island with snowy mountains behind Stromness whaling station. (*Topsy Turner*)

South Georgia – packing up the LUP. (*Topsy Turner*)

South Georgia – moving by Gemini RIB to Harbour Point in Stromness Bay. (*Topsy Turner*)

South Georgia – Mountain Troop before assault on Grytviken. (*P.J. O'Connor*)

South Georgia – SAS troops boarding two Lynx Helicopters before assault on Grytviken. (*P.J. O'Connor*)

South Georgia – SAS troops emplaning on Wessex Mk III (Humphrey) with HMS *Plymouth* and HMS *Brilliant* in line astern. (*P.J. O'Connor*)

South Georgia – Wasp helicopter landing on HMS *Antrim* on CASEVAC mission post-assault on Grytviken. (*P.J. O'Connor*)

South Georgia – SAS Troops above Grytviken whaling station at ENDEX. (*Carl*)

South Georgia – Grytviken whaling station post-conflict. (*N.W.*)

Falkland Islands – Air Troop with Stinger missile Mount Kent area. (*Carl*)

South Atlantic – Geordie D Squadron pronto on *Hermes* with Harriers and Sea Kings in background. Note GPMG in anti-aircraft role. (*N.A.*)

Above: South Atlantic
– D Troop (Signals) on
HMS *Hermes* with Harrier
backdrop. (*Geordie*)

Left: Falkland Islands –
Bluff Cove Peak on Stag –
GPMG and captured FN
rifle. (*Topsy Turner*)

Falkland Islands –
Bluff Cove Peak is
prominent feature
on right. (*N.W.*)

Falkland Islands – Boat Troop relaxing on Bluff Cove Peak after relief in place by Kilo Company 42 Cdo RM. (*Topsy Turner*)

South Atlantic – RFA *Sir Lancelot* approaching Falkland Islands with the Amphibious Task Group on 20 May 1982. (*Eddie Bairstow*)

Falkland Islands – rigid raiders alongside landing craft with HMS *Fearless* in San Carlos Water. (*Eddie Bairstow*)

Falkland Islands – D Squadron 22 SAS embarking on RFA *Sir Lancelot* in San Carlos Water. (*Carl*)

Falkland Islands – 45 Commando (Royal Marines) advancing on Mount Kent. (*Eddie Bairstow*)

Falkland Islands – 45 Commando (Royal Marines) patrol base near Mount Kent. (*Eddie Bairstow*)

Falkland Islands – Argie Chinook helicopter wreckage Mount Kent Area. (*N.W.*)

Falkland Islands – page from magazine recovered from enemy position. (*Author's photograph*)

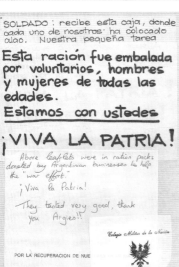

Falkland Islands – leaflet found in Argie ration pack and headed notepaper. (*Author's photograph*)

Falkland Islands –
Pucara at Stanley
airport. (*Carl*)

Falkland Islands – 17 June 1982 – line of prisoners in Stanley with Globe Hotel in background. (*Eddie Bairstow*)

Falkland Islands – 17
June 1982 – surrendered
weapons outside
Falkland Islands
company in Stanley.
(*Eddie Bairstow*)

Falkland Islands – the grave in Port Howard cemetery of Captain Gavin 'John' Hamilton who was awarded the Military Cross posthumously for leading some of the most successful SAS operations carried out during the Falklands War, finally being killed after giving covering fire to a colleague before attempting to fight his way out of a forward observation post when heavily outnumbered. (*N.W.*)

Falkland Islands – graves of 1Lt Ruben Eduardo Marquez RIP and 1Sgt Oscar Humberto Blas RIP, Argentine military cemetery near Darwin – members of 602 Commando Company. Both received *La Medalla al Valore en Combate* posthumously, Argentina's second highest honour. (*Steve Dent*)

Falkland Islands – D Squadron official photograph on board RFA *Sir Lancelot* on cessation of hostilities – Cedric (D Squadron commander) sitting at the front on white line. (*Geordie*)

Italy 1984 – Geordie RIP handover trip to HQ AFSOUTH in Italy before author took over command of D Troop (Signals). (*Author's photograph*)

Hereford – 22 SAS regimental plot at St Martin's Church. (*Author's photograph*)

London – Tranmere Rovers v Boreham Wood play-off final. James Norwood celebrates scoring the winning goal at Wembley 2018. (*Richard Ault*)

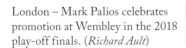

London – Mark Palios celebrates promotion at Wembley in the 2018 play-off finals. (*Richard Ault*)

away. I recall there was some discussion whether we should send two volunteers to tab down to the valley floor and take the pilot prisoner, but the idea was quickly abandoned. In any case it would have been foolhardy to have two of our guys wandering about with a prisoner after last light trying to negotiate a safe passage through 2 PARA's lines. D Squadron were supplied with the Stinger missiles from the USA, but they were in short supply. The missile fired by Kiwi on 21 May was the first Stinger missile ever used in a combat situation and the first to bring down an aircraft. Another Pucara flew close to us, but after seeing his wingman shot down he decided to fly off towards San Carlos Water. We fired two missiles at the plane, but these failed to acquire the target and crashed into the ground in front of the firer, almost wiping out Mobility Troop. We also fired small arms at the aircraft, but this too failed to down the second Pucara.

I would say that the tab was just as hard as the 'Endurance March' that I undertook on SAS Selection two years earlier. We wore white headbands as a recognition signal to 2 PARA as we passed through their lines. 2 PARA were still digging in on Sussex Mountains on the southern side of San Carlos Water. One of the paratroopers asked me if I had been shot as my headband was made out of a crêpe bandage! We finally approached San Carlos Water and I saw numerous enemy aircraft in 'Bomb Alley'. The British amphibious landing had already taken place and there were many Royal Navy warships in San Carlos Water.

We were just in time to see four A-4 Skyhawks bomb HMS *Ardent* and she was hit twice. There was a fireball over *Ardent*'s flight-deck and she later sank. Soon after, I witnessed three hostile aircraft shot down. What I didn't know at the time was *Ardent* had already suffered bomb damage from enemy aircraft earlier in the day further to the south in Falkland Sound. We found out later that several ships had been hit by bombs that had failed to explode. The reason was that to avoid the intense barrage of anti-aircraft fire, Argentinian pilots released their bomb ordnance from very low altitudes. This meant their bomb fuses did not have sufficient time to arm before impact.

At this time there were friendly forces helicopters flying about in our vicinity. Boat Troop took the initiative and started waving at the helicopters using air-marshalling arm signals. We were more than a little surprised when our efforts paid off. A couple of empty Wasp helicopters landed beside us. We told the pilots where we wanted to go and we took off in the direction of HMS *Intrepid*. I was hanging half in and half out of the aircraft and was caught up in the exhilaration of seeing the fleet set out before us. Within ten minutes we landed on the deck of the ship that we had pointed out. We went below to find our kit that we had left behind with the intention of getting into some dry clothes. Imagine our surprise when we discovered that we had landed on HMS *Fearless*, the sister ship of HMS *Intrepid* which was many miles away at that time. We were soaking wet, but fortunately for us the Royal Navy had a solution to our problem. They issued us all with 'Survivor Kits', which consisted of a set of navy-blue trousers, a heavy-duty jersey, navy-issue blue shirt, a pair of warm socks, a towel and gym shoes. This made Boat Troop look like a gang of ruffians. We then handed our uniforms in to the Chinese laundryman on board. After a lot of screaming by him, because we didn't have any laundry numbers, the laundryman was eventually coerced to wash and dry our kit. While our kit was being laundered, we ate some 'scoff' and debated what to do next. The laundryman's antics kept us amused for days, and whenever we saw each other we would shout in a terrible Chinese accent, 'What your fucking number?' It took another eighteen hours until we were back on-board HMS *Intrepid*.

While we were operating in the Darwin/Goose Green area, the SBS were busy just north of San Carlos at Fanning Head. It was here that twenty-five men from 3 Section, SBS, attacked a force of sixty Argentinian troops. The presence of these enemy forces on headland that overlooked San Carlos Bay threatened the whole landing. The SBS landed by helicopter and then attacked the Argies using small arms and GPMG machine guns. They were supported by naval gunfire from HMS *Antrim* that was controlled by a naval gunfire observation officer the SBS had with them. The SBS also had a Spanish speaker who gave the Argies an opportunity to surrender, but this was refused. The Argies fled, leaving behind eleven dead and six who were taken prisoner.

Chapter 8

Falkland Islands from D-Day Onwards

Diary Entry Saturday 22 May 1982
D-Day has been and gone. The SBS killed eleven enemy yesterday at Fanning Head and took six prisoners. The Paras and Marines are digging in on the ridges and hills surrounding San Carlos Water. One of my mates in the SBS told me that he witnessed the Argies shoot down two British Gazelle helicopters. Apparently, the Argies shot at least one survivor swimming in the sea after the first helicopter crash-landed, but the SBS were too far away to help. The Argie prisoners said they hadn't eaten for four days and after a hot meal on board a ship they were surprised how well the British treated them. HMS *Antrim* and HMS *Argonaut* both have unexploded bombs on board and the bomb disposal teams are busy. Today has been one long air raid on our ships. Lying on a bunk on board HMS *Intrepid* I heard bombs exploding nearby and ricochets from spent cannon fire and empty cases landing on the deck above my head. To keep us out of harm's way we were ordered to remain below deck which was hard to stomach. The sight of all our ships in San Carlos Bay, from the Royal Navy warships, RFA landing ship logistics, a Townsend Thoresen car ferry, a Geest banana boat (*Geestport*), SS *Canberra* etc. You name it, it was there! The 'whole shebang' was a sight that I will never forget.

Most of the requisitioned STUFT ships had temporary helicopter pads fitted to their aft decks and two or more Oerlikon 20mm cannons or Bofors 40mm guns in the anti-aircraft role. Meanwhile, Boat Troop felt helpless being unable to help and we were itching to get back on dry land.

During the SBS firefight with the Argie troops, two British helicopters passed overhead and were fired on by the Argies using machine guns. The first helicopter, a Sea King, escaped unscathed, but the pilot of the second helicopter, a Gazelle, was fatally wounded, but he still managed to crash-land the aircraft into the sea. The pilot, Sergeant Andy Evans, and the other crewman were thrown out of the aircraft. Argie troops fired at them for about fifteen minutes as they struggled in the water. When the firing finally ceased, the other crewman, Sergeant Ed Candlish, managed to drag Evans to the shore, where he died. A few minutes later, the Argie troops shot down a second Gazelle, killing Lieutenant Ken France and Lance Corporal Pat Giffin.

Diary Entry Monday 24 May 1982
CO 22 SAS has arranged that D Squadron have the use of several helicopters so that we can leapfrog forty miles into enemy territory. This will hopefully give the Marines an opportunity to advance forward into the vacuum that we create once we have eyes on the ground. HMS *Antelope* sunk.

While our planning to get up on Mount Kent was progressing, the power brokers back at joint headquarters (JHQ) at Northwood in the UK were in deep discussion with the planning staff on board HMS *Hermes*. Their consensus was the enemy threat at Goose Green needed to be dealt with and 2 PARA were given the mission. As this was going on, Boat Troop carried out a map study of the Mount Kent area with the remainder of D Squadron. We didn't know it yet, but on landing in the Mount Kent area we would be allocated Bluff Cove Peak as our troop's objective.

Diary Entry Tuesday 25 May 1982
We have received several Royal Marines and Paras on board HMS *Intrepid* as casualties. Today the task force shot down nine Argie planes. The Royal Navy 'clearance divers' have been busy checking the hulls of various ships anchored in San Carlos Water close to land as a deterrent to the Argies trying to attach limpet mines to them. Personally, I think this is extremely unlikely to happen. HMS *Coventry* was bombed by A-4 Skyhawks and quickly sank. *Atlantic Conveyor*, carrying vital supplies, including many helicopters, was hit by two Exocet missiles. A raging fire caused catastrophic damage to the ship and she finally sank while under tow on 28 May.

It was extremely frustrating being stuck on board HMS *Intrepid*, but things were moving at last. We spent the day conducting a map study of the Mount Kent area and worked on our outline plans, the basics of which were to infiltrate several high points and thereby provide mutual support, all-round defence, defence in depth etc – these are some of the principles of defence that all soldiers learn. G Squadron had already deployed a recce patrol on Mount Kent in early May and reported that it should be possible to get an SAS squadron up there. We sent a recce party by helicopter to Mount Kent. The remainder of the squadron were to deploy there a couple of days later, but this was delayed due to the sinking of HMS *Coventry* meaning all available helicopters were diverted for search and rescue missions. The weather was also rapidly deteriorating in the Mount Kent area causing a further delay.

HMS *Coventry*, a Type 42 destroyer, was sunk by four A-4 Skyhawks on 25 May. She was stationed along with HMS *Broadsword* providing anti-aircraft defensive cover for ships and ground troops in San Carlos Water when she was hit by two 1,000lb bombs. *Coventry* capsized within twenty minutes with the loss of nineteen men.

I met the former captain of HMS *Coventry*, David Hart Dyke, in 1998 when he was the Clerk and Chief Executive of the Worshipful Company of Skinners, a livery company of the City of London. I found him to be a charming and unassuming man who spoke with quiet dignity of the loss of his ship and members of his crew.

Diary Entry Wednesday 26 May 1982

A raging fire caused catastrophic damage to *Atlantic Conveyor* yesterday. *Atlantic Conveyor* was a Ship Taken Up from Trade (STUFT) and was requisitioned by the Ministry of Defence (MOD) at the start of the Falklands War. D Squadron was due to fly up to Mount Kent on the night 26/27 May. We took off in three Sea King helicopters, but were immediately caught up in a bombing run by enemy A-4 Skyhawks. While waiting on the ground at Ajax Bay with rotors turning, several bombs were dropped less than 200m from us. The target appeared to be the nearby ammunition dump next to the British field hospital. At least one bomb went through the roof of the hospital, but luckily failed to explode. The hospital had been established in a disused meat processing factory and the bomb was caught by the tail fin dangling over the heads of the medical staff. Talk about divine providence! We finally took off but in the poor weather conditions were put on the ground in the wrong place. We then spent a couple of hours working out where we were. The helicopters returned and as it was so late we were forced to return to San Carlos Water. It wasn't until the next night that we finally got up to Mount Kent.

The Sea Kings would hug the ground when flying. Whenever Argie aircraft were reported anywhere near us the helicopters would land in dead ground with rotors turning. The ammunition dump and field hospital formed part of the logistical build-up to create a Force Maintenance Area. I later discovered that the *Atlantic Conveyor* carried a cargo that included six Wessex helicopters, eight Sea Harriers, and six RAF GR.3 Harriers. The Harriers were all flown off *Atlantic Conveyor* before she was hit and sunk. A Westland Lynx helicopter was destroyed in the fire as well as three CH47 Chinook helicopters. There were originally five Chinook helicopters; one was left on Ascension Island and one was already in the air when the two Exocet missiles struck. It was the loss of these ten helicopters that meant British troops had to march across the Falklands to capture Stanley. The Royal Marines called it 'yomping' and the Parachute Regiment 'tabbing'. This last term had also been adopted by the SAS. Twelve men died on the *Atlantic Conveyor*, including the ship's commander, Captain Ian North, who was posthumously awarded the Distinguished Service Cross. This was the first British merchant vessel lost at sea to enemy fire since the Second World War.

Diary Entry Thursday 27 May 1982
Finally, two troops of D Squadron got up onto Mount Kent, arriving in the early hours of 28 May. The other two troops joined us a few hours later. I was pleased the weather was still very poor as that meant we got in without the enemy seeing us. However, the helicopters hovered for a long time trying to find a flat piece of land to put us down safely so the Argies must have heard us. Once the helicopters departed, we got our bearings and spent the remainder of the night getting into position.

We flew to Mount Kent on 27 May, stopping briefly to refuel near the Ajax Bay Field Hospital ('The Red and Green Life Machine') which had been set up by British Forces the week before. The hospital was commanded by Surgeon-Commander Rick Jolly, who was awarded the OBE after the war. He also received the *Orden de Mayo* from the Argentine government for his efforts in treating many wounded enemy soldiers and pilots. The award refers to the May Revolution that led to the birth of the nation and is one of the highest decorations awarded by Argentina.

I was happy when the mighty clatter of the helicopters faded away and we could sort out our night vision. Boat Troop only had one pair of NVG, but even that was an improvement over the situation in South Georgia where we had none. We did however get our hands on a few more pairs of NVG after some firefights with Argie SF. We spent all night getting into position on separate high points for each troop, including a separate point on a ridgeline for our 81mm three-man mortar crew. Boat Troop were allocated Bluff Cove Peak and in turn the position was subdivided into interlocking arcs of fire with a four-man patrol taking each sector. I was with Ted, the troop boss, together with John and Simon, both corporals, as callsign 17 Alpha. Our patrol took one of the Boat Troop arcs of fire. Another high point was occupied by Air Troop looking towards Stanley. That left SHQ, Mobility and Mountain Troop to our east along a ridgeline.

Diary Entry Friday 28 May 1982

We now have the entire Squadron on separate high points in mutual support. We know there are enemy positions to the west, about 2,000m away, and very heavy enemy concentrations to our east, 5,000m distant. An hour before last light eleven enemy helicopters, mainly UH-1 'Hueys', a CH47 Chinook and a Puma, flew between our locations, possibly taking reinforcements to Goose Green. Extremely poor weather with high winds, sleet and snow. We knew more or less exactly where the enemy forces were, as our advance party, who arrived on Mount Kent during the night of 24/25 May, had brought a thermal imager with them. This required a separate gas bottle full of coolant and was extremely cumbersome to carry. Boat Troop sent a clearance patrol out as far as Estancia House, but returned within a few hours. Later that same night, two enemy patrols, each about eight strong, were dropped by two helicopters close to Air Troop's location. Air Troop quickly set up an ambush and a ferocious firefight erupted which lasted for twenty minutes. One of the SAS troopers, Dan, was shot in the upper thigh and first aid was given. Boat Troop were too far away to ascertain who was friend and who was foe so we withheld our fire.

The aerial photos of the Mount Kent area showed lots of stone runs which we were getting quite familiar with. Regarding the terrain, someone said at the time, 'The Falklands are just like the Yorkshire Dales, but with stone runs and more snow.' We soon sorted ourselves out and, as befitting the junior patrol member of callsign 17 Alpha, I was on first stag. Eleven enemy helicopters flew by just before last light. After it quietened down, everyone settled down for night routine, i.e., no cooking or lights, with just the four men on stag about 50m apart in our sangar positions.

It would have taken perhaps twenty minutes to set up the radio and antenna and encode a message calling for a Harrier to come and shoot up the enemy helicopters. They only hung about for a few minutes so there was no point in sending the message. Air Troop also requested permission using a short-range VHF hand-held radio on the squadron net to fire one of their remaining Stinger missiles at the helicopters. This request was denied by SHQ to prevent revealing our presence on Mount Kent. We did however report that they had been there on our next radio sked, but the helicopters never returned while we were in the Mount Kent area.

Soon afterwards, I heard the sound of a helicopter at last light, and saw what appeared to be a Puma in the fading light, but I couldn't be certain. The helicopter turned on a landing light which made me think it must be enemy as our pilots used NVG. I alerted the remainder of my patrol, but when they joined me at the OP, the helicopter had already taken off again after only a few seconds on the ground. We later discovered that there was actually a second helicopter that was out of our view and together they had dropped off two Argie SF patrols from the 3rd Assault Section of 602 Commando Company. It was confirmed over the squadron radio net that the enemy patrols were moving in the general direction of Air Troop who quickly set up an ambush to welcome them. The ambush was sprung in total darkness. It was all but impossible to wait for all the enemy to enter the killing zone before springing the ambush so it was inevitable that some enemy SF were able to escape the way they had come. One of the SAS troopers, Dan, was shot in the thigh. Air Troop also took a second casualty, Connor, but he was not too badly wounded compared to Dan. The enemy patrols suffered several casualties from this action, but managed to get away in the darkness. The next morning much of their equipment was found abandoned near to Air Troop's position.

We got into a routine quite quickly up on Bluff Cove Peak. I was sent with Brummie to fill a jerrycan from a stream on the second night as we were running short of drinking water. My basha was basically a couple of flat stones about 2m long and touching each other to provide overhead shelter. The stone slabs provided me with plenty of cover and some protection from the wind. There was just enough space for me to crawl under the stone slabs with my sleeping bag wrapped in a waterproof groundsheet. There was no Gore-Tex bivvy bag for me although I had finally been issued with a civilian olive-green Gore-Tex jacket a few days earlier. The quilted jacket had been procured from Cotswold Camping by the regiment along with their entire stock of Gore-Tex items. We were very pleased when we received these items.

Diary Entry Saturday 29 May 1982
Most of the Falkland Islanders were being kept virtual prisoners out on the 'Camp', the name the islanders call everywhere outside Stanley. Some of our Troop members went forward when we patrolled to Estancia House and spoke with several people at the house. One of the men was from the Pettersson family. I met up with some other members of the Pettersson family later when we finally reached Stanley.

I was at an SAS reunion in 2004 and Dan was there. We got talking over a pint or two. When I queried Dan about his war wound, he very kindly dropped his trousers to show me the scars!

Diary Entry Sunday 30 May 1982
Two stragglers from last night's enemy patrol came close to our position at first light. They were possibly seeking shelter among the rocks. Their lead scout came into the position via a blind spot in our arcs of fire which was unavoidable due to the topography of Bluff Cove Peak. While this was happening, the other enemy

soldier waited among the rocks nearby. Don had little time to react and quickly fired a short burst at the Argie and shouted out 'Stand-to!' to alert us to the threat. Don had hit the soldier in the throat who ended up falling among some large rocks nearby. Next, the enemy soldier threw a grenade at Don as Don shouted 'Grenade!' to warn the rest of us. Luckily for Don, he had built a low sangar out of rocks around his sleeping position and the grenade exploded the other side of the rocks a few feet from his head and body. Don received two pieces of shrapnel in the middle of his back and another piece to his side, but he could have come off much worse. Don wasn't finished though as he stood up and fired off two more short bursts of fire into the enemy soldier, while calling out 'Stand-to!' several more times. Meanwhile, I managed to get within 10m of the enemy soldier who was still lying between the rocks. Nobody was sure if he was alive and therefore still presented a threat to us? While I was trying to get into a position to shoot him, he was shot by Ginge, one of my troop mates, who came to Don's assistance from his position to the rear of Don's sangar. Now Ginge didn't do things by half and he fired several short bursts from his GPMG machine gun at less than 10m range. That finished the poor soul. Don shouted from patrol to patrol to check everyone was OK as we regrouped and took stock of the situation. Brummie proceeded to render first aid to Don and a CASEVAC was requested over the Squadron radio net. It was then that we heard from Mountain Troop over the radio that there was another enemy soldier crouching behind rocks about 50m from our location and below us. One of the Troop corporals, Simon, carried out a clearance patrol with two others and shot the Argie officer dead. Simon told me afterwards that he had no choice but to shoot when the enemy officer pointed his weapon at him and fired, managing to get off just one shot before being killed. This second dead man was a First Lieutenant. I searched the body of the first dead Argie. He was a First Sergeant carrying an FN rifle with a folding stock, 9mm Browning handgun and a bayonet for his FN. We quickly confirmed by their uniform and ID documentation that they were professional, SF soldiers.

We later confirmed that the SF forces soldiers were from 2nd Assault Section of 602 Commando Company, and the dead Argentinian soldiers were First Lieutenant Ruben Eduardo Marquez and First Sergeant Oscar Humberto Blas. They were not stragglers from 3rd Assault Section who had stumbled on Air Troop's position, but a separate twelve-man fighting patrol contrary to what I had written in my diary entry. Two of us were told to bury First Sergeant Blas and another two troop members had the task of burying First Lieutenant Marquez. Topsy and I searched Blas and bagged any items of interest, including a notebook, a family photo, rosary beads and one of his ID discs, leaving the other disc on the body. I recall the chain holding the ID discs had broken when a bullet pierced the chain, so we put the remaining ID disc in his pocket. One of my mates wiped blood off a bar of chocolate he found in a pocket of the dead man and scoffed the lot. The bagged items were handed over to Ted, our troop commander. We kept the FN rifle to add to our firepower. The ground consisted of an inch or so of peat directly on top of solid rock with some grass and ferns sprouting here and there. There was no way we could have dug a grave as the bedrock was only an inch or two down. Eventually I came up with the idea of building a low wall around his body as there were plenty of rocks lying around. Then we managed to find some larger slabs which we laid across the top of the wall and finally covered his head. Once we were finished, Topsy produced a small Catholic prayer book from his pocket and said a few words while I bowed my head in respect to the fallen. Incidentally, the two deceased Argie SF soldiers were later decorated by their country, both receiving the Argentine Nation Valour in Combat Medal. This is the second highest military decoration given by the president of Argentina. There were only thirteen army recipients during the Falklands War, including First Lieutenant Marquez and First Sergeant Blas. Several of our troop commented that the Argies had tried to take the fight to us and First Sergeant Blas in particular went down fighting after giving a good account of himself. They died fighting for what they believed in, which can only be respected.

SHQ requested a CASEVAC for Dan and Connor from Air Troop together with Don from Boat Troop. There followed a long wait of about ten hours as no helicopters were available. It was late evening and quite dark before they were flown to 42 Commando's Regimental Aid Post on San Carlos Water. The next day, they were transferred via another helicopter flight to the Ajax Bay Field Hospital. Their wounds were by now more than twenty-four hours old. Several times during the day, D Squadron fired off mortar and GPMG fire as distant targets presented themselves.

Diary Entry Monday 31 May 1982

Several British helicopters landed not far from us during the night 30/31 May dropping off advance elements of 42 Royal Marine Commando. More marines from 42 Commando were due to arrive by helicopter after daybreak. Meanwhile, Boat Troop were ordered to RV with Mountain Troop an hour before first light to follow up along the escape route of the enemy patrol they had been in contact with the evening before. We started moving forward before first light, advancing cautiously along the ridgeline. The combined troops, totalling about twenty-five men, checked out all the nooks and crannies as we cleared the ridge. Mountain Troop took one Argie prisoner who was wounded and willingly surrendered. Boat Troop took the next tactical bound. We moved forward and continued to check potential ambush positions meaning it was a slow process. After an hour or so of this we spotted an enemy patrol of four men out to our right moving parallel to the ridge and took up positions to fire on them. Mountain Troop quietly caught up with us and fanned out in firing positions alongside Boat Troop. When the enemy patrol was about 300m from the ridge, we realized this was as close as they were going to get to our location so we opened up. I fired one long burst and then several shorter bursts at the four men. The man I was firing at went down and I changed my magazine to continue firing. This only took me a second or two, but now I was trying to hit a limb or other body part poking out from the rocks where the enemy had taken cover. We eased up our firing and were just discussing what to do next when one of the Argies started waving a white vest tied to his rifle. They had surrendered! Then they all stood up and raised their hands as soon as we stopped firing. We moved forward cautiously to take them prisoner and discovered two were wounded and all very nervous about their fate. I put a field dressing on one of them who was shot in the ankle, while the other was being treated for a bullet wound to the buttocks.

Mountain Troop took the first bound and came across the wounded Argie soldier. He appeared to have been abandoned by his colleagues. Perhaps they had gone back to a bergen cache to recover a radio to request a CASEVAC for him? Our four prisoners were from an Argie marine SF patrol, i.e., a different unit to 602 Commando Company who were an army SF unit. We took our prisoners back to our Forming Up Point (FUP) at the end of the ridge which by now had become a scene of intense activity. Several Sea King helicopters and the Chinook, callsign Bravo November, were dropping off soldiers and guns from 29 (Commando) Artillery Regiment. A half battery of three 105mm howitzers were quickly set up with more to follow. One of the commando gunners told me that their guns were within range of Stanley. Meanwhile our CO, Lieutenant Colonel Mike Rose, turned up with Max Hastings, the *London Evening Standard* war correspondent. Several other senior officers arrived, including General Moore, Commander British Land Forces Falkland Islands. Max Hastings produced some cigarettes and seemed surprised that everyone he spoke to in Boat Troop were non-smokers. The Argie prisoners were happy to take a few cigarettes though! Incidentally, our CO went on to become General Sir Michael Rose KCB CBE DSO QGM and served as Commander UNPROFOR Bosnia in 1994 before retiring in 1997.

Soon after this there was another firefight at long range as a few more members of 602 Commando Company broke cover and tried to make a run for it. Boat Troop's 60mm lightweight mortar was used to stomp them and help them on their way. They were running in the general direction of Stanley. We sent a fighting patrol to clear their positions and found abandoned bergens and other equipment scattered about. We then took a party of Kilo Company, 42 Commando, who were going to relieve us, back to our position on Bluff Cove Peak. Kilo Company had arrived during the short firefight between elements of D Squadron and the 602 Commando Company rearguard. We then spent another night on Bluff Cove Peak to show Kilo Company the position and brief them on arcs of fire and other defensive arrangements. More members of Kilo Company arrived later.

It is worth noting that D Squadron were on Mount Kent as the eyes and ears of 3 Commando Brigade, commanded by Brigadier Julian Thompson. This Brigade normally had 40, 42 and 45 Commandos in its organization, plus 29 Commando Regiment Royal Artillery, the Commando Logistics Regiment, and various other units including the Brigade Signal Squadron and the Brigade Aviation Squadron. The brigade was hastily reinforced by 2 PARA and 3 PARA for the Falklands War. Even this number of troops were considered insufficient, therefore 5 Infantry Brigade was deployed soon after to complete the British Land Forces element. However, since both 2 PARA and 3 PARA were used to reinforce 3 Commando Brigade they were 'back-filled' in 5 Infantry Brigade by 2nd Battalion Scots Guards and 1st Battalion Welsh Guards, who joined 7th Gurkha Rifles and the other 5 Infantry Brigade troops, including artillery, engineers, aviation and logistics.

Diary Entry Tuesday 1 June 1982
We have reinforcements now: a battery of guns and a company of Royal Marines with more to follow. The Argies appear to have withdrawn to a feature known as Two Sisters to the east. Our guns have already started bombarding the Argie positions. We have finished handing over our positions to Kilo Company and are waiting for a helicopter lift back to HMS *Intrepid*.

Our recce party had been on Mount Kent for ten days and the remainder of D Squadron had been up there for five or six days. During this time, D Squadron had killed several Argies and wounded about ten more. By dominating the high ground on the Mount Kent feature we probably cut the length of the war by two weeks. It also gave General Moore and Brigadier Thompson the impetus to push forward with the Royal Marines and Paras who made an epic journey across East Falkland on foot. It had been a long, hard march for them over difficult terrain.

We also had a grudging respect for the Argie SF who more than once had stayed to fight it out with us. We were now sharing our position with Kilo Company, 42 Commando, and we jointly observed the remainder of 42 Commando moving below us in impressive numbers. Days later, on 4 June, it was the turn of 45 Commando to arrive in the Mount Kent area, having yomped all the way from San Carlos via Douglas Settlement and Teal Inlet. In a similar manner, 3 PARA were approaching Estancia House having tabbed all the way following a different route, but again passing through Teal Inlet, which by now had become a Forward

Brigade Maintenance Area. This provided a refuelling capability for our helicopters.

Major Cedric Delves, the D Squadron commander, was subsequently awarded the DSO for the Mount Kent action.

Meanwhile 2 PARA were on their way, having fought a difficult battle at Goose Green against superior numbers. It was only awesome courage and bravery that won the day for 2 PARA. Advance forces from 2 PARA moved up and occupied Fitzroy ready to receive 5 Infantry Brigade. This extra brigade gave General Moore the additional troops required for the forthcoming battles. Most of 5 Infantry Brigade arrived by sea via Fitzroy and Bluff Cove. It was there that RFA *Sir Galahad* and *Sir Tristram*, both 'Landing Ship Logistics', were bombed by Argentine aircraft on 8 June. Fifty-six men were killed and many more were seriously wounded or suffered extensive burns to their bodies.

Diary Entry Thursday 3 June 1982

We finally got on board a ship. It was HMS *Fearless*, the sister ship of HMS *Intrepid* where my bag of dry clothes was waiting for me. At least I knew my way around the ship as they were laid out identically. We all grabbed a hot meal, had a shower and I managed to cadge some kit off the storeman as all my clothes are soaking wet and stink to high heaven. The storeman gave me a combat jacket, combat trousers and a towel. He also gave me a rather old-fashioned, but brand new, Royal Marines rucksack with grey and green canvas, leather straps and brass buckles! I used the rucksack to stuff full with all my war booty which by now was becoming quite a pile.

I didn't have a sleeping bag or a blanket, but still managed to sleep for a few hours lying on the deck alongside the landing-craft dock at the stern of the ship.

Diary Entry Friday 4 June 1982

This was a day of indecision as to what to do with D Squadron. Where would we stay and what would we do next? Our squadron bulk stores and all our personal kit was still on HMS *Intrepid*. The ships were sailing in and out of San Carlos anchorage each

night and were seldom side by side for more than an hour or two. Eventually, after much negotiation, it was decided to move us lock, stock and barrel to RFA *Sir Lancelot* on the next day. This inactivity was really frustrating as we wanted nothing more than to get ashore and get on with the war. It didn't help that we were subjected to many air raids and even more false alarms.

It was quite cold and miserable sitting about with nothing to do on *Fearless*. I would have been happy if I'd had a good book, a sleeping bag, a bar of chocolate and a mug of coffee, but I had none of these items. Food was rationed and we were more likely to be given powdered soup rather than a mug of coffee. It seemed the Royal Navy weren't coffee addicts like most of the British Army!

Diary Entry Saturday 5 June 1982
D Squadron flew to HMS *Intrepid* where we had lunch and collected all our squadron stores and personal kit before flying on to RFA *Sir Lancelot*. This 'Landing Ship Logistics' vessel was to be our new home. *Sir Lancelot* was quite comfortable except for the bomb damage near the galley. We are having a rest, being held back in reserve. Other than taking a turn on fatigue duty in the galley, I spent my time in getting my clothes washed, fitness training and weapon cleaning. G Squadron had a REME armourer, Cpl J Newton, attached to their squadron who had been killed in the SAS Sea King helicopter crash. This meant we had a couple of transit cases full of specialist armourer tools and weapon spare parts, but no specialist armourer. The sights on my AR-15 assault rifle had worked loose, but with the help of one of the guys from another troop and the armourer's tools we managed to fix the problem. All we had to do now was wonder what our next mission would be?

One of the crew told me how *Sir Lancelot*, part of the Amphibious Task Group, had entered San Carlos Water on 21 May and uniquely remained there for the duration of the war. The ship was hit by a 1,000lb bomb on 24 May. The bomb failed to detonate, having been dropped by one of four A-4 Skyhawks. The bomb penetrated the starboard side of the ship and most of the crew were temporarily evacuated. Many of the crew were British Hong Kong seamen who were put on one of the beaches where they had a long wait in poor weather conditions, wearing only their navy uniforms and lifejackets. After the bomb was removed, *Sir Lancelot* became a floating base with accommodation for D and G Squadrons, 22 SAS. This happened after our CO, Lieutenant Colonel Mike Rose, had discovered that *Lancelot* was available as troop accommodation and had tipped off Cedric, our squadron commander.

My mission for 5 June saw me assigned to galley fatigue duties. Except for a short break for lunch and evening meal, I spent nine hours washing pots, pans, trays and cutlery. The entire galley staff were Hong Kong Chinese. They were a surly bunch who served up food without a smile. At the end of my shift I asked the head chef if I could make a mug of tea to take with me. 'No way! You go now!' was the curt reply, without a word of thanks for my efforts. To get revenge, I discreetly undid the bolts of the serving hatch and walked off in disgust. Late that evening, when the Chinese galley staff had gone to their cabins, I opened the hatch and together with others we cooked up a meal of egg and chips for D Squadron's supper. None of the crew dared to interfere! The next day the head chef got his head chewed off from the purser for leaving the hatch unlocked. They never did find out who the culprit was!

Diary Entry Monday 7 June 1982

It was now time for D Squadron to consider the enemy threat from West Falkland. This meant that each troop was given a new mission. Mountain Troop were allocated recce tasks at Port Howard and Fox Bay. The other prime recce task fell to Mobility Troop. Boat Troop were held in reserve but were soon deployed a day later with yet another separate tasking for Air Troop.

Boat Troop flew by night to West Falkland to mount an ambush on a track between Port Howard and Fox Bay that the enemy were supposed to be using to carry out vehicle patrols. We settled in to several sheep scrapes with a 'basha sheet' (groundsheet) in the bottom and one stretched tightly overhead at ground level with some grass and vegetation scattered over the top. The sheep scrapes were spread out in an arc less than 100m from the track junction, making this an ideal location for watching the tracks. We also had an OP on slightly higher ground behind us to ensure we could see anything approaching from a distance. We remained under the sheets by day, with one man observing and the other resting or cooking. There was no movement by day and we pissed in a spare water bottle when we felt the need. We had a designated sheep scrape 50m further away from the track for our night-time need to defecate. This was our only movement while at this location. No lights were permitted by night and this of course meant no cooking. I listened to the BBC World Service on my HF manpack radio and hear that British troops are advancing towards Stanley. Every morning began with mist, and then throughout the day an almost constant drizzle of rain, sleet and snow.

Meanwhile, as a result of a SIGINT radio interception, we knew that Argie C130 transport planes were supposedly going to use an area known as Rat Castle Shanty as a likely drop zone (DZ). The intelligence picture was that the Argentine Air Force were finding it increasingly difficult to fly C130 transport planes into the airport at Stanley due to the British force's bombardment at this time. Instead, the Argies were planning to drop supplies and reinforcements onto the West Falkland DZ by parachute. Air Troop's mission was to ambush the DZ party who were expected to turn up in a couple of jeeps and maybe a truck. The C130 para drop would then most likely be aborted, but, if necessary, Air Troop were to be prepared to take on any parachutists that landed.

On the fourth morning we received an alert from Robbie and Pete in the OP on the high ground behind us that they could see a military jeep or Land Rover in the distance. After a while one of the guys thought that he may have heard a vehicle and then nothing. We immediately sent out our cut-off groups and I clicked off my safety catch and waited for the shooting to commence. We were ready to initiate the ambush when one of the guys came over the VHF radio to inform us that there were possibly two vehicles obscured by mist close to the track junction. Then this was corrected and we were advised that they were in fact dark brown Aberdeen Angus cattle! I strained my eyes and, sure enough, I saw two square shapes that looked like military jeeps to me. After what seemed like an age, but was only a minute or two, the mist suddenly lifted and we found ourselves looking at the square backsides of about five Angus cows that were munching contentedly on the grass with their heads down. The cattle were totally oblivious to our presence and didn't know just how close they had been to imminent death. The final radio sked on 11 June instructed us to make our way to a helicopter pick-up a few kilometres away. We moved an hour before last light and walked past a crashed Argie plane with clear indications that the pilot had ejected. The aircraft was a 'Dagger', which was a refurbished Israeli aircraft based on the same design as the French Mirage. There was a lot of damage to the aircraft and the live ammunition from its cannon was scattered about from the impact of the crash. The helicopter arrived on time an hour or so after dusk. After a short flight we were back on board *Sir Lancelot*. A couple of hours later we were enjoying a hot meal as the time approached midnight.

While we were 'a-moo-sing' ourselves on West Falklands, the other troops from D Squadron were having more success in reporting enemy dispositions. At least we were able to receive the BBC World Service news bulletins on my PRC 320 radio. More than once we were a little disturbed that the BBC was predicting the future intentions of the British Land Forces, the most glaring example being what 2 PARA had been about to do at Goose Green the week before.

Diary Entry Saturday 12 June 1982
After the hot meal, Cedric our Squadron Commander informed us that two members of Mountain Troop were missing. Captain John Hamilton was believed killed in action and Corporal Roy Fonseka was assumed to have been taken prisoner. This was later confirmed by a separate source. At 0400 hours we finally got to bed knowing that we were going back on land that same evening to cover 2 PARA's northern flank. We took off at 1600 hours calling in on Estancia House on the way. 3 PARA had their echelon headquarters there. It was at Estancia House where I met my first Falkland Islanders. There were about twenty islanders, half of them forcibly displaced from Stanley by the occupying forces. 3 PARA had a big peat fire going with a large cooking vessel containing several gallons of boiling water. This gave us an opportunity to put the makings of a brew into our pint-sized mugs with sachets taken from our arctic

rations. A couple of moments later and I was enjoying a hot mug of coffee. One of life's simple pleasures! Within an hour we took off again and flew to our designated tactical area of responsibility.

Captain John Hamilton was a popular officer in D Squadron. I had worked with him and his troop (Mountain Troop) in Kenya in February 1982. John had commanded Mountain Troop all the way from Fortuna Glacier in South Georgia, through their very creditable results on Pebble Island and Mount Kent and finally on West Falkland. He was killed during a skirmish behind enemy lines at Many Branch Point near Port Howard. He had established an OP on 5 June to observe and report enemy activity at Port Howard. Shortly after dawn on 10 June, John and the patrol signaller, Corporal Roy Fonseka, both together in the OP, were discovered by a patrol from 601 Commando Company. Roy and John both engaged the enemy. As the small arms fire and grenade throwing continued, John was shot in the arm. He decided that the two of them should attempt to fight their way out. He ordered Roy to go first while he gave covering fire. Roy came out firing like a man demented. Their only chance was to match the enemy's firepower. John then attempted to follow and was shot several more times and tragically killed, but not before he had fought a furious rearguard action. The enemy force then followed up and Roy was taken prisoner. John's body was buried by the Argentinians with full military honours and the grave is situated in the small cemetery at Port Howard. When the Argentinian military commander at Port Howard was eventually interrogated after the Argentine surrender, he strongly recommended that Hamilton be given a gallantry award for his heroic actions during the firefight. Captain John Hamilton was posthumously awarded the Military Cross. He was aged 29 years. RIP Boss.

During our brief respite on board RFA *Sir Lancelot*, I learnt that HMS *Plymouth* had been hit by four bombs from enemy aircraft on 8 June. All of the bombs failed to explode but one hit a depth charge starting a huge fire. Five men were injured in the attack. This was a frigate on board which many members of D Squadron had spent time during the liberation of South Georgia. *Plymouth*'s wardroom was also where the surrender of the Leith marine contingent was signed by Lieutenant Commander Astiz.

Diary Entry Sunday 13 June 1982

We stayed the night 12/13 June on a small hill north of Beagle ridge. D Squadron SHQ stayed a little distance from us with a stores cache that included a few pallets of mortar bombs, small arms ammunition, rations, jerrycans of water and so on. On arrival we met up with an SBS patrol that augmented Boat Troop. At first light we patrolled towards Twelve O'clock Mountain. We were now only 7km north of Stanley. Air Troop spotted enemy positions and Boat Troop followed up to provide support. The Argies were actually packing up when we spotted them and they started to walk out away from us. Air Troop initiated at 900m with GPMG. I crouched down and ran forward to give the Air Troop GPMG machine gunner the extra belt ammunition that I was carrying. I could then see for myself that the Argies were outside rifle range and only our GPMGs and mortars could reach them. We had a few members of 23 (Boat) Troop from G Squadron with us as reinforcements and they had a 60mm light mortar. We also had a D Squadron 81mm mortar team to our rear. Both mortar teams were soon putting bombs down. We probably wounded a couple before the Argies disappeared over the next ridge in the direction of Stanley. We continued harassing fire with the mortars for a few minutes, but we didn't have a clear target so eventually had to concede that the enemy had got away. We advanced to the Argie positions that had just been vacated, being very careful to skirt around to the rear of the trenches in case there were trip wires or mines in front of their defensive positions. The place was in a complete mess with human shit everywhere and there wasn't a field latrine in sight. There were also several sheep carcasses and a half-eaten cow. These carcasses were just dumped immediately behind the trenches close to a cooking fire fuelled with peat. We sent a patrol to the top of the ridge to ensure the Argies didn't turn around to try and ambush us, but they were already over 2,000m away running downhill as fast as their legs could carry them. We cleared the trenches very carefully because nobody likes to be on the receiving end of a booby trap. Finally, the trenches were clear, although we spotted evidence of mines and booby traps immediately in front of the position. We had a good look around the trenches and at one end we found a couple of suitcases and kitbags. On carefully opening the suitcases we discovered they contained much-sought-after items, including tubes of toothpaste, soap, boot polish, chocolate and cigarettes. The kitbags contained cans of corned beef, steak chunks, ravioli, canned fruit and cooking oil. I also recovered some military stationery, Argentine magazines and newspapers. We moved back to our SHQ position and were briefed for a diversionary attack on Cortley Hill. The intention was to carry out a diversionary raid, by boat, to give 2 PARA a chance to attack Wireless Ridge while the enemy were distracted by us. We had a few hours to prepare so I made a nice meal of steak chunks and ravioli, followed by a can of pineapples and a bar of chocolate. Delicious! Thank you, Argies!

At the time I thought our diversionary attack was a bit ambitious. We were going to put Boat Troop ashore with our numbers made up by the SBS patrol. Our own Geminis were without reliable outboard motors so we were given the use of four rigid raiders together with coxswains from the Raiding Squadron, Royal Marines. These Rigid Raiders are made of fibreglass with a top speed of 33 knots. Capable of carrying eight fully equipped troops they were exceptionally well suited for this type of work.

The plan called for D Squadron to move off at 2100 hours, Boat Troop and the six-man SBS patrol leading, with all members of the squadron carrying two 81mm mortar bombs. We dropped our mortar bombs off at the mortar firing line, where everyone except for Boat Troop and the SBS patrol set up their fire support positions, comprising an 81mm mortar and several GPMGs in the sustained fire role. The 60mm mortar team from 23 Troop covered our right arc of fire to counter any threat from the direction of Weir Creek. Finally, we had a MILAN missile launcher. The MILAN is a light anti-tank wire-guided missile with a night-firing capability. Boat Troop and the SBS patrol finally arrived at the beach after a hard slog of more than two hours, although my load was a bit lighter for the last ten minutes as I was no longer carrying the two 81mm mortar bombs. We waited on the water's edge for an hour and were feeling the cold as we had all worked up a sweat. Now the wind had a biting edge to it with the occasional snow flurry. While we were waiting, an Argentine hospital ship, the *Bahia Paraiso*, steamed into the bay and dropped anchor 1,000m from us with all lights blazing. It was now after midnight and a decision needed to be taken soon whether to abort or go ahead with the mission.

Diary Entry Monday 14 June 1982

Deciding we could still get away with it, Ted, our troop boss, told me to radio the four rigid raider boats to come and pick us up. The boats arrived within ten minutes as they had been loitering waiting for our call. Leaving three men from Boat Troop on this 'safe beach', we now had three patrols, one of these from the SBS. Each rigid raider also had its Royal Marine coxswain who all proved to be great guys who you could rely upon in a difficult situation as we were soon to find out. Our mission was to create a diversion at the eastern end of Wireless Ridge in an area known as Cortley Hill. This was at the far end of Wireless Ridge and looked directly onto Stanley Harbour. There were two large, diesel fuel storage tanks there at a distance of about 600m from where we intended to land. If we didn't encounter enemy forces, we were to blow these tanks to create the diversion. This meant some members of Boat Troop were carrying demolition charges. As always, I was part of callsign 17 Alpha and we were on the Squadron VHF radio net. We started our journey via a circuitous route to avoid the hospital ship. When we were halfway across Hearndon Water with Blanco Bay to the east, Ted gave the signal for our 81mm and 60mm mortars to begin firing. They fell short at first and then exploded harmlessly in the peat above our selected landing point. With 300m to go our MILAN team from 23 Troop, G Squadron, fired a missile to our right at a target that they had identified with their night sights. It was actually an Argie gun position and they scored a direct hit. As we were making our final run in to the beach the remainder of D Squadron opened up with our GPMG machine guns in the sustained fire role. Immediately, several enemy machine guns and anti-aircraft guns firing on a horizontal trajectory returned fire and the sky lit up with tracer, some of it passing directly over our heads. Gradually the fire eased off as neither side had a clear target to fire on. Incredibly we still hadn't been spotted in the boats and were able to land unopposed a short distance away from the nest of enemy machine guns that had been firing away.

We formed up in three patrols with a slight gap between each patrol. I was lead scout and took up point position with Tommy immediately behind me and then Ted, the Boat Troop Boss. I started advancing cautiously up the hill with most of the firing

200m to our right, meaning we still hadn't been seen. I came across a wire, stretched taut at knee-height, and beckoned Tommy to come and check it out with me. We agreed it marked the edge of a minefield, probably immediately in front of the Argie defensive positions. We turned right and followed the wire for about 50m, before it made a sharp turn uphill. Again, we followed the wire hoping to make our way around the edge. The wire turned right again and was going directly in front of the enemy machine guns which were still firing sporadically across the bay at the remainder of D Squadron. Ted came up to me and Tommy and suggested we might like to cross over the wire and the rest of Boat Troop would follow in our footsteps through the mined area. Now this was not what I wanted to hear, but if that's what the Boss wanted, who was I to argue?

At that moment several Argies popped up from a sangar immediately to our front and started firing away at us in short bursts. We were now in a firefight and caught out in the open. We all dropped to the prone position to present less of a target, but not before the SBS marine to my left shouted that he was hit in the hand. Miraculously for him, it was just a deep graze from a bullet. We then withdrew about 20m and got into scant cover to decide what to do next. Like it or not, we were pinned down and the enemy fire was effective and we were heavily out-gunned. Ted crawled up next to me and ordered me to get back to the boats and instruct Colin, the Troop Sergeant, to get the engines started and the remainder of Boat Troop would return about two minutes after me. Ted was obviously satisfied that we had created enough of a diversion. There were many Argies shooting at us so I had to agree!

I took a deep breath and ran downhill in a zigzag fashion as I moved to try to avoid becoming a target. Due to the convex slope, the bullets were soon passing overhead and the Troop Sergeant and Royal Marine coxswains were quite safe waiting on the rocky shore. It didn't take me very long to reach the boats and I quickly updated Colin on the situation. I held on to one boat and started to turn it around as Colin and the coxswain got the engine going. Unfortunately for me I slipped on a submerged rock and found myself immersed in seawater up to my neck! Within two minutes the remainder of the guys arrived and quickly boarded the rigid raiders. My boat started moving off while two of the guys dragged me on board and I lay on top of everyone else as we slowly went out to sea. I eventually ended up half underneath Colin with his arm draped over me. I think Colin was trying to warm me with his body heat as I was shivering uncontrollably from my dip in the freezing cold seawater. There was a lot of tracer fire passing over our heads as we were still protected for the first 100m by the convex shape of the slope. I noticed that all three boats were leaving a purple-coloured luminescent trail behind them which I can only assume was something to do with disturbing the kelp or algae near to the coastline?

As we came out from the protection of the convex slope the enemy spotted the boats and let rip with their machine guns and anti-aircraft guns which can be fired horizontally. While the cannon and heavy machine gun fire continued, the three boats zigzagged their way across the bay. It was a journey that I never want to repeat. I felt the boat judder again and again as the boat took hits right along the top of the gunwale which was only an inch or so above us as we crouched in the bottom of the boat. Colin was shot through the shoulder and wrist and his blood flowed freely over me. I lifted my head once and it was like putting my head in a hornet's nest of tracer bullets. I remember thinking how many seconds before we are all killed? My rifle jumped in my hand as a bullet hit the barrel.

To make matters worse the *Bahia Paraiso* shone a searchlight on us, so we pointed the boats directly at the hospital ship. At least this desperate manoeuvre eventually forced the enemy gunfire to stop or they would be in danger of hitting their own ship. As we rounded the hospital ship, an Argie enemy force appeared close to our 'safe beach' and started firing their machine guns at us which forced us to swerve away by 400m and land a bit further along the coast. Up until this time, two Boat Troop members had been signalling from the 'safe beach' with a red filtered flashlight. The signal, in Morse, was being shone to guide us in safely. They had been steadily flashing the agreed 'dah-di-dah' (Morse code for the phonetic letter kilo) signal to guide our safe return. Unfortunately, upon discovery they had to run for their lives and made the sensible decision to head

towards our new landing point in the hope of joining forces. The enemy force then opened up with mortars on our new landing point before abruptly stopping, perhaps to conserve ammunition?

The Rigid Raider craft were manned by coxswains from 1 Raiding Squadron, Royal Marines, who were truly awesome. Just as well or we would have all died. While we began our withdrawal by boat, the remainder of D Squadron and a few members of G Squadron's 23 (Boat) Troop gave us supporting fire. The enemy fire was probably ten times heavier than what D Squadron were able to offer in return, but then we didn't possess heavy machine guns or anti-aircraft guns! As we got closer to the *Bahia Paraiso* hospital ship a searchlight was turned on us which only added to our problems. Finally, we rounded the hospital ship and made for our hastily revised landing point. After landing we got moving as soon as possible as our two other Boat Troop colleagues guiding us in by flashlight had already taken cover due to incoming mortar fire. Meanwhile, the combined D Squadron and 23 Troop covering force withdrew separately from us as it was too dangerous to regroup. Their withdrawal was not without being fired on by at least one machine gun from an enemy force near them. Then an artillery barrage landed nearby before they eventually managed to extricate themselves safely. They later found relative calm in dead ground at the squadron RV and waited for Boat Troop to catch up. Meanwhile, Boat Troop received further incoming mortar fire as we moved towards the RV point and this is when Brummie was wounded by flying shrapnel from the mortar bombs. We moved off again after administering first aid to Brummie who had received quite a serious wound. We had previously bandaged up Colin's wounds and we continued walking towards the squadron RV. After another thirty minutes, with the two 'walking wounded' among our number, we finally caught up at the squadron RV. As we met up with the remainder of D Squadron, heavy 155mm artillery fire was falling all around us. Luckily the enemy's aim was slightly off and the artillery rounds narrowly missed. Geordie, the D Squadron 'pronto', had already called for a CASEVAC helicopter and we were told it was on its way. Finally, the helicopter, a Gazelle, arrived to fly our wounded to Ajax Bay Field Hospital. It started snowing while we were lying prone in our defensive fire positions. As I was soaking wet after my dunking, I was having difficulty controlling my shivering and in danger of going down with hypothermia.

As soon as the helicopter departed, we commenced our tab uphill towards Beagle Ridge, while all the time the British naval bombardment continued directly overhead. Most of the shells seemed to be passing quite close above our heads in a fairly low trajectory as they cleared the spur that we were walking up. I remember someone once telling me that a small percentage of shells fall short and I was half expecting one of the shells to come crashing into the ground among us. Not a nice thought. At least the Argie 155mm artillery were no longer firing in our direction. The cacophony of sound was tremendous and to our left the night sky was filled with tracer from dozens of machine guns as 2 PARA advanced on Wireless Ridge and the Scots Guards did the same on Tumbledown Mountain. I later found out that the Ghurkhas were also in position over on Mount William waiting for the Scots Guards to take Tumbledown. I distinctly remember noticing the colour of tracer that the Argies were firing was different to the British tracer ammunition.

After another two hours hard slog up the hill, we finally reached our Tactical Headquarters (TAC HQ) on Beagle Ridge. I climbed into my sleeping bag in soaking wet clothes and tried to stop shivering. An hour later I was woken up with a hot mug of coffee and informed that I was on stag!

We had abandoned our four badly damaged boats once we reached shore and the boats drifted back out into the bay. I was told that the Argies fired on the empty boats all night long! Our diversionary attack had at least caught the Argies off balance. If we had achieved nothing else that night, we surely assisted 2 PARA as the enemy now had less ammunition to respond to their attack along the length of Wireless Ridge. I was secretly pleased we hadn't managed to blow up the diesel storage tanks as I felt sure they would be needed by the British Forces in support of the Falkland Islanders very soon. The intense barrage of friendly artillery and naval gunfire continued throughout the night. At dawn the fire eased off and then ceased. We were monitoring the 3 Commando Brigade radio net, while I sat close by our TAC HQ sangar. Suddenly, we heard a radio transmission over the Brigade Net reporting that a white flag was flying over Stanley and the enemy were retreating towards the airport!

The Argies surrendered on 14 June 1982. With nothing else to do we continued to sit alongside TAC HQ on Beagle Ridge. That was when Geordie, the D Squadron 'pronto', was called to the tacsat to answer a call from JHQ Northwood. Geordie started talking as if he was briefing someone. It turned out that a government minister was at JHQ Northwood and wanted to speak to Cedric, our squadron commander. Geordie explained that the squadron commander was unavailable so the minister decided to get an update from Geordie instead. This didn't faze Geordie in the slightest – had he been making his maiden speech in the House of Commons he couldn't have done a better job. Cedric turned up a few minutes later and didn't seem too bothered that he had just missed a government minister requesting an update on the situation. Geordie was beaming with pride and later told me that the SAS satellite network linked our TAC HQ with HMS *Hermes*, JHQ Northwood and also our Hereford base. Nowadays we have learnt that satellite comms can bypass the chain of command and thereby cause problems of direct interference to the troops on the ground in the midst of battle, but this was a lesson for the future. At the time it seemed absolutely bloody marvellous to have this new piece of kit. In an instant, Morse became obsolete.

While we were all talking about this, our CO, Lieutenant Colonel Mike Rose, arrived in a Gazelle helicopter. The helicopter was trailing a concrete block suspended from a rope on which a white flag was tied. The CO had his signaller with him who I knew. Ben was a corporal from G Troop (Signals) and was looking rather distinctive in a blue, quilted Gore-Tex jacket. There were only enough olive-green jackets for the SAS troops when these civilian jackets arrived a few weeks before and the 'scaleys' had to make do with blue jackets. Ben was carrying a tacsat for the CO's personal use so that he could contact HMS *Hermes* and also call direct to JHQ Northwood to keep them appraised of the situation. Soon after arrival at Government House in Stanley, the CO hauled down the Argie flag and raised the Union flag. This was taken down several hours later and replaced with a larger Union flag and this second event was used as a photo opportunity by the Royal Marines. This was fine by me as it was the Royal Marines who had defended the Falkland Islands for many years and we were just there to give them a helping hand to liberate the islands from the Argies.

We were then told there weren't any helicopters available to take us back to RFA *Sir Lancelot*. I wasn't too bothered as I had set up my basha next to a pile of ration packs and was able to grab a couple to dig out the hot chocolate drink sachets and a couple of oatmeal blocks which I crushed and mixed with milk powder and sugar to make hot porridge which helped warm me up. We still had to stag on through the night though as there could well have been some Argie stragglers in the hills around us who did not know of the ceasefire.

Diary Entry Tuesday 15 June 1982
Sea King helicopters finally arrived the next morning, i.e., Tuesday 15 June, to take us back to RFA *Sir Lancelot*. When I climbed aboard one of the helicopters, I was amazed to see the co-pilot and aircrewman smoking. I think they were celebrating the ceasefire while also under a bit of stress! I was even more surprised to find myself sat on one of several jerrycans full of petrol that were already on board, the seats having been removed to get more cargo and passengers inside the fuselage!

My war had come to an end and I lost no time in getting some sleep on board *Sir Lancelot*. However, after an hour or so I was awakened by a living legend of 22 SAS. This was not a man you said no to when he wanted you to get up. He whispered in my ear, 'Get up Tony, it's Fred. B Squadron has arrived and the fucking war is over! Don't worry, I have three bottles of whisky, let's drink to success and absent comrades.' B Squadron had been held in reserve and had trained relentlessly for whatever was required of them. This eventually turned out to be their arrival off the Falkland Islands in the closing stages of the war. B Squadron had parachuted into the South Atlantic Ocean over several days, all arriving in theatre by 13 June to assist with the final push on Stanley.

Things, however, quickly changed with the spectacular success of 3 Commando Brigade and 5 Infantry Brigade. This meant that some of B Squadron were now surplus to requirements and were kicking their heels on board *Sir Lancelot*. Kauaata Marafono, or 'Fred' as he was affectionately known by all in SAS circles, was a great warrior and one of several Fijian soldiers who had achieved a highly successful career in 22 SAS. I had a great chat with Fred while drinking the generous measure of whisky that he poured into my pint mug. Fred was philosophical that the option of offensive operations on mainland airbases had been cancelled and he said that decision had definitely saved many lives in B Squadron. I am sure that our chat over a couple of drinks put the whole Falklands War into perspective and prevented me from ever suffering PTSD. Fred had a most positive attitude and could laugh loud enough to buckle the deck-plates of any ship!

To keep myself occupied, I made a couple of trips ashore and also visited other ships in San Carlos Water. One of the most interesting was the MSV *Seaspread*, which was a diving and maintenance vessel requisitioned by the MOD and used as a floating workshop for the warships. I learnt that the *Seaspread* carried out essential repairs to more than fifty ships, including ten warships and four captured vessels during the period of hostilities. I also managed to visit one of the Royal Navy submarines, HMS *Onyx*, that had arrived in San Carlos Water and was moored beside the *Seaspread*. One of my mates from the SBS was on board and a few of us were given permission to visit the submarine. We went down to their cramped accommodation area and had a 'wet' (what a stupid name for a mug of coffee!) with them. HMS *Onyx* was a diesel submarine, and the only non-nuclear submarine of the Royal Navy to deploy to the Falklands War. *Onyx*, with her smaller displacement compared to the nuclear submarines, made her perfect for landing parties of SBS ashore on the islands in shallow water.

My brother Mike told me that when he was an apprentice engineer at Cammell Laird he worked on HMS *Onyx*. Mike was on board for diesel trials in the wet basin at the shipyard. He spent twelve hours wedged between the outer casing and the port diesel with all hatches closed while the engines were using air from the snorkel and he operated the exhaust valves. A very hot, noisy and unpleasant experience, yet definitely character building for a teenager. The submarine was not allowed to submerge with apprentices on board due to the HMS *Thetis* 'no apprentice' rule. To explain, *Thetis* was built and launched by Cammell Laird in 1938. The submarine dived on her trials in Liverpool Bay, but never regained the surface. Ninety-nine lives were lost in the incident, including twenty-six Cammell Laird employees. The incident was a devastating blow for both the Royal Navy and Birkenhead.

We were informed that, as we were soon to deploy for our delayed operational tour of Northern Ireland, Boat Troop would be given priority to be flown back to the UK. This still took another eleven days before we were able to fly back to the UK. I used this time to sort through all my kit. I had two Argie Browning 9mm handguns which I knew could cause me problems if I was caught smuggling them into the UK. In the end I decided it wasn't worth the risk and I swapped the nearly new one for a bottle of whisky. The second one was old and worn-out so I threw it over the side in San Carlos Water.

I still had about twice the amount of kit that I could realistically take home to the UK. I traded a few more war souvenirs for bottles of whisky. I then swapped a bottle of whisky to book some space in one of the D Troop transit cases that had come out full of radio batteries but were now empty. I put the Royal Marines bergen that I had acquired from HMS *Fearless* into the transit case and managed to get most of my surplus kit home in this way.

We eventually received news that a C130 would be landing at Stanley Airport on the evening of 25 June and for the following three evenings, making four flights in total. Boat Troop were to be on the second flight departing on Saturday 26 June.

Early on that morning Boat Troop flew to Stanley Airport in the only surviving British Chinook. When we landed at the airport we were informed that the plane would land and immediately take off later that evening, probably about 1900 hours, and we were to be there waiting. We were also told that there was unexploded ordnance everywhere and not to touch anything, including the Pucara aircraft, some of which still had live missiles fitted on underwing pods. We had about seven hours to kill so my mate Topsy and I asked if we could have a driver to take us into Stanley. The response was there were no drivers, but we could have a captured Argie jeep for the rest of the day if we promised to refuel it before we brought it back.

As we drove towards Stanley, hundreds of Argie prisoners were shuffling in a long line towards the airport. Many had a blanket draped over their shoulders and a dejected expression. I believe they were going to the airport to take a helicopter flight out to a hospital ship and eventually be repatriated to Argentina? This had been going on for about ten days and I was probably looking at the last few hundred to be repatriated.

The land-based Exocet launcher mounted on a trailer that had scored a missile strike on HMS *Glamorgan* was abandoned at the side of the airport road. Apparently, *Glamorgan* spotted the missile on its radar and did a sharp turn. That was just enough for the missile to strike at an angle and it caused much less damage because of this emergency manoeuvre. Even so thirteen men were tragically killed and the helicopter hangar and a Wessex helicopter inside were virtually destroyed. As we drove into town, I noticed huge piles of FN rifles and other weapons lying at the side of the road where prisoners had been disarmed on previous days.

This was my first time in town, and it was a special moment for all of us. The general clean-up was still underway, but everywhere there were signs of war damage. We had a walk around town and then knocked on the Petterssons' front door at their house on Ross Road. Topsy had met one of the family at Estancia House. The family made us very welcome and when we offered them some bars of Argentine chocolate they laughed. They told us that the houses at their end of Ross Road had been used by the Argie 'commissariat' to store bulk items, including bottles of brandy, cigarettes, chocolate, cans of meat and cases of wine. These items were ostensibly for the Argie troops, but in reality most of it went to their officers. Luckily for us there was plenty left and we ended up having a roast mutton dinner washed down with Argentine red wine. A meal for deserving conquerors! We spent all afternoon with the Pettersson family and, as a non-smoker, I even smoked an Argie cigar! After saying our goodbyes, we drove back to the airport more than a little tipsy and got a bollocking for forgetting to refuel the jeep. Not to worry, we managed to get on board the C130 when it arrived. It unloaded in about two minutes and we had another two minutes to get ourselves and one bergen each on board. Half of the fuselage interior was taken up with a temporary fuel tank that contained thousands of litres of aviation fuel. The C130 immediately taxied to the end of the runway and the loadmaster shouted to us that because of the heavy weight of the fuel tank we all had to stand on the tailgate with our arms draped over each other's shoulders a bit like a rugby scrum to alter the centre of gravity so the plane could take off. We thought he was joking at first, but he soon made it clear that if we ever wanted to take off, we should do as he said. It was a strange position to adopt for a take-off, but it worked and we were soon airborne!

Diary Entry Sunday 27 June 1982

Departed Stanley Airport on the evening of 26 June. We arrived in Ascension Island after an exhausting flight on board a C130 transport plane that was fitted with special long-range fuel tanks. Arrived home in the UK after almost thirty hours of travel.

After an exhausting flight of about ten hours, we landed at Ascension Island. Our flight crew went to get their heads down after their very tiring return trip to the Falkland Islands. They would be doing another flight to the Falklands either that same day or the next so needed their sleep. There was a VC-10 aircraft of RAF Transport Command parked next to us on the apron and we assumed we would fly home in this. How wrong we were! Pretty soon it was loaded up with RAF personnel who had been serving on Ascension Island. They were apparently going home for a week's R&R and looked very happy sporting suntans and wearing shorts and sunglasses! Taff, the regimental quartermaster sergeant major and a former SSM of 22 SAS Training Wing, welcomed us and showed us where to get a hot meal and, even more importantly, a hot shower. We had to wait about six hours until another C130 arrived from the UK to take us home. Taff kept us entertained with all the gossip about what else had been going on, so it didn't feel like time wasted, although we were understandably anxious to continue with our onward journey. Finally we took off on the second leg of our trip back to the UK. This was a standard C130 without the long-range fuel tank, meaning more passengers could be added to the flight manifest. This time we flew to Dakar in Senegal on the west coast of Africa. We landed at night and were told to sit on the grass beside the C130 well away from the terminal building. We sat there for about two hours, all the time being bitten by mosquitoes. How I cursed the RAF for not putting us on the VC-10 which would already have landed in the UK by now. We then completed our journey home after another long flight, arriving on 27 June at RAF Lyneham. As was usual for the SAS, there was nobody to meet us other than a couple of civilian drivers from Stirling Lines with one of our nondescript civilian buses, an army truck for our baggage and a few boxes of freight. Two hours later we arrived back in Hereford and were told to take two weeks leave before reporting for Northern Ireland training.

What more is there to say about the Falklands War? Many lives on both sides had been sacrificed, but at least I believe it was a just fight. I have no regrets and have only respect for the Argentinian people who I feel were grossly misled by the military junta that was then in power. The young Argentinian military conscripts suffered greatly while their Air Force and Special Forces on the ground fought with honour and distinction. God Bless the Falkland Islanders. 'From the Sea, Freedom!' We should never forget the motto of the Falkland Islands: 'Desire the Right'!

Chapter 9

SAS Service Continues

On return from the Falklands War, I took a one-week vacation on the island of Corfu. My Greek language skills weren't too rusty, so chatting to the locals over a glass of wine added to my enjoyment. I remember walking on the beach in bare feet and everyone looking at me strangely. When I sat down on my beach towel it dawned on me what the problem was. Everyone who tried to walk bare-footed could only manage a few steps as the sand was scorching hot. As the blisters started to appear all over the bottom of my feet, I realized that I still had 'frost-nip'. This was something I suffered from on South Georgia due to the poor quality of the issued boots. It took another couple of months before all feeling returned to my toes. I read up on frost-nip as I was worried that I may have caused permanent damage. I was relieved to read that there are two types of cold-weather-related injuries and frost-nip falls into the first category: conditions that occur without the freezing of body tissue.

On return from Corfu, I copied my war diary into a scrap book together with photos and printed memorabilia. I also had time to reflect on our collective performance as SAS troops and what we could have done differently. Much of this was wishful thinking as any plan only works perfectly until you cross the start line. The USMC slogan 'improvise, adapt, overcome' summed up SAS operations in the Falklands War.

It was time to carry out work-up training before returning to Northern Ireland. While B, D and G Squadrons had been in the South Atlantic, A Squadron had stagged on for additional months looking after both the SP team and our commitments in Northern Ireland. On arrival, we shared our hangar with a special duties unit and we often worked together.

On 8 October 1982, we had been in NI for two months when the Honours and Awards for Operation Corporate (the recovery of the Falkland Islands) appeared in *The London Gazette*. D Squadron's commander, Cedric, was awarded the Distinguished Service Order

(DSO) and there were two Military Crosses (MC) awarded to the Troop Commanders of Boat Troop and Mountain Troop, the latter being a posthumous award to Captain John Hamilton. There were also eight D Squadron NCOs and Troopers Mentioned in Dispatches (MID), including Colin, Chippy and Don from Boat Troop. G Squadron also gained a sizeable haul of medals. I was pleased for those honoured and we had a great party that night in the bar. Less than two weeks later I was promoted twice in the same week! The SAS promoted me to lance corporal and the next day Royal Signals promoted me to sergeant in my shadow rank. To explain, shadow rank is a means for your parent regiment/corps to keep account of you and consider you for promotion in your absence. This meant my personal records were kept at the Infantry Manning & Records Office and a copy was kept at the Royal Signals Manning & Records Office. This ensured that SAS troopers were not forgotten about or disadvantaged by their parent corps or regiment. As a footnote to the Honours and Awards, Mr Shik-Ming Kang, the senior Chinese laundryman on *HMS Brilliant* and also in charge of several other Chinese laundrymen deployed on other warships, was awarded the British Empire Medal (BEM) for helping to sustain hygiene and morale on board several warships deployed on Operation Corporate. As soon as this was read out in our briefing room, we all shouted out in unison, in a terrible Chinese accent, 'What your fucking number?'

While I was in NI, I was advised that I was nominated to attend the Yeoman of Signals (YofS) selection board in March 1983. Now, I was enjoying life in the SAS, but realistically my chances of being promoted beyond staff sergeant were slim. I would also have to retire after twenty-two years regular army service when I reached the age of 40. However, if I returned to Royal Signals and successfully completed the Yeomans' course then there was every chance of me rising to warrant officer rank quite quickly. There was also the possibility of being considered for a late entry commission and thereby serve until 55 years of age. The thing that tipped it for me was when Geordie, our 'pronto', told me that he was due to leave D Squadron in April 1984. Geordie went on to say that, as the Yeomans' course was due to finish in June 1984, the position would be held open for me to take over D Troop. Geordie had a word with OC D Squadron, and also with OC 264. Both squadron commanders were happy for me to follow this career path and offered their full support.

There were other attractions to this opportunity, not least the right to continue to wear my SAS beret as a 'badged' member of 264, and the additional pay that remaining a member of the SAS attracted.

I had already passed the 'YofS Qualifying Exam' in trade skills in 1979. I had also passed the 'YofS Entrance Exam' in 1981, a further three days of written exams. There were high attrition rates in these exams and I was fortunate to pass, given that ninety-nine per cent of my time was devoted to my work in the SAS. I was permitted to leave Northern Ireland for fifteen days to attend a 'Yeoman of Signals Maths' course in Bovington, Dorset. The first day on the course I looked a bit strange, with long hair in uniform, but apart from a few funny looks, nobody said anything as I was wearing my SAS beret. On the Friday I was working undercover in Northern Ireland, but by Monday I was in an Army Education Centre in Dorset trying to get my head around logarithms! Much of the course was spent studying amplitude gains and attenuation losses in antenna systems and co-axial cables measured in decibels. With a great deal of study and hard work I passed the course, but others found it too much and failed, thereby ending their dreams of becoming a Royal Signals comms manager.

The fifteen days went quickly, and on the final day I passed the exam. With just one day off in Hereford, it was soon time to return to NI. My work in the SAS continued without further interruption. When Christmas arrived, as many as could be spared went home for a week's R&R. Meanwhile I soldiered on as I had chosen to attend the maths course and therefore had to forsake any R&R. We were kept busy over the holiday period working in Fermanagh and South Armagh. The work was difficult and dangerous and we were often cold and wet. The only respite was when we returned to our base for a few days' rest. This included a lie-in on Christmas Day when our troop boss served us mugs of 'gunfire' (hot tea and rum) in bed. Giving the troops gunfire before going into battle is a form of Dutch courage. It is also served to soldiers in their beds on Christmas Day and is a long-standing British Army tradition. We stagged on and the weather finally started to improve as the months passed by.

‹The next few pages describing actual operations in Northern Ireland have been redacted›

...such were the difficult 'rules of engagement' (ROE) we operated under in Northern Ireland. The ROE was printed on a yellow card, and therefore we were operating under 'yellow card' rules. This meant there was no such thing as a 'shoot to kill' policy in operation in NI and we were directed to use minimum force at all times. This of course gave the terrorists a huge advantage. The yellow card provided us with rules and directives that we, as members of the British Army, must follow or be liable to criminal procedures against us. The yellow card defined the circumstances, conditions, degree, and manner in which the use of force may be applied.

<The following few paragraphs, describing Tactics, Techniques and Procedures (TTPs) used by the SAS in Northern Ireland have been redacted>

...After spending a couple of weeks working in Fermanagh and South Armagh, aka 'bandit country', it wasn't long before I had a week of working in Belfast in plain clothes. This was a total contrast, but did enable us to have a drink in Bangor at the weekend. Bangor is a large town and seaside resort on the southern side of Belfast Lough. We were always careful when having a drink in a pub or nightclub, but at least we all had long hair which helped us blend in with the locals. The pubs that we drank in were all staunch loyalist (Protestant) areas where even if people knew that we were members of the security forces most would be happy enough to see us anyway. We still had an agreed cover story that all were briefed on before we went out socially. The cover story I recall using was that we were North Sea divers on a short-term contract refurbishing a gas pipeline under Belfast Lough. That seemed to satisfy the curiosity of most people. The operational tour continued with a few further successes by Boat Troop and the others working alongside us. Whenever we had quiet periods, which wasn't very often, Boat Troop would drive to a range and fire thousands of rounds to keep our shooting skills honed.

On my return to Hereford from NI in February 1983, SAS Selection was in progress and they deployed to Belize on jungle training in March 1983. None of this concerned me as I went about my own duties. However, Dick the D Squadron sergeant major, sent for me a few weeks later. Dick wanted me to do a favour for him. One of the Selection candidates had been killed in a shooting accident in Belize and was to be buried at Aldershot military cemetery the next day with full military honours. Dick informed me that there would be an SAS trooper from each squadron travelling to Aldershot to pay their respects on behalf of the regiment. Dick wanted me to represent D Squadron. When I told Dick that I didn't own a black tie he told me to just wear my regimental 'winged dagger' tie. Anyway, we set off early the next day. My colleagues, from A and B Squadrons, both former Paras were looking forward to visiting Aldershot and perhaps seeing some of their mates there. At that time Aldershot was the main base for the Parachute Regiment. The trooper from G Squadron was a former Guards soldier so perhaps had closer affinities to the deceased who was a lance sergeant in the Grenadier Guards. I suddenly realized the other three guys were wearing black ties and I was the only one with a regimental tie. Anyway, we managed an hour in Aldershot drinking beer in a pub frequented by the Parachute Regiment. It was there that we said hello to a couple of Paras who were mates of my friends from A and B Squadrons. Soon it was time to attend the funeral at the Royal Garrison Church, followed by interment at Aldershot Military Cemetery. One of the family members approached me when he saw my SAS tie and invited the four of us back to the wake. Eventually we made our farewells and drove back to Hereford. A sad task, but somebody had to do it, as the sergeant major had said to me the day before.

One weekend in early April saw me travelling up to the Wirral to watch Tranmere Rovers play. It was the first game I had been to for a couple of years. Steve Mungall had a good game, but there was no sign of Dave Higgins who could normally be relied on to give everything he had. We played against Blackpool and drew 1–1. The crowd was quite small which was a sign of the times as Tranmere weren't doing as well as in previous seasons.

The Yeomans' selection board was full of surprises. I knew it would be tough and my preparation was meticulous. For example, they even asked what newspaper you read and why. I had pressed all my uniforms, cleaned my boots and had a haircut to create a good impression.

Three days of aptitude tests began when we were herded into a lecture theatre, where we sat facing the dais. The major, himself a former Yeoman of Signals, stood in front of us and gave us an insight into what to expect. He turned to me and announced that my situation was invidious. What he meant was, anyone in the SAS was expected to excel in any situation and therefore I must pass this selection board. Failure was simply not an option for me. This despite the pass rate being less than twenty per cent. I listened while he rambled on about me having to excel at everything that I did for the rest of my army career.

The selection board began with command tasks in a nearby wooded area where we were given bits of rope and planks of wood. Sometimes a leader would be nominated and sometimes we would have leaderless tasks. Either way, while we were trying to make a bridge to cross an imaginary ravine, several officers observed our every move while taking copious notes. We eventually finished our team-building tasks none the wiser how well we had done. We were then summoned to drink cups of coffee while each of us was allocated to a group of officers. I think our capacity for 'small talk' was being tested, as well as our general confidence being the junior person amongst a group of officers who were evaluating us the whole time. The other tasks included chairing a debate and problem solving on paper. The problems were along the lines of 'There has been a hurricane on a remote island which is sparsely populated. The storm has now subsided. You have several people to rescue, some of them seriously injured and immobile. There is only one person with basic first-aid training and limited medical supplies. One of the casualties has badly cut his hand on a broken mirror. There are no working communications, but you know that there will be a Royal Navy warship passing the far tip of the island, which is three miles away, in exactly one hour. What will you do to ensure everyone is safely rescued while caring for the casualties in the meantime?' I immediately spotted that the reference to a mirror rather than normal glass must have been a clue as to how to solve the problem. I think my solution called for the nominated first-aider to stay with the casualties while I ran the three miles clutching a piece of the broken mirror. I would then light a signal fire on arrival and use the mirror to signal to the ship in Morse and request a helicopter evacuation. All quite ludicrous, but seemingly they wanted to check out my logic and radical action thought processes.

Eventually it was my turn to be interviewed. First of all, they read out my results from the qualifying exams in trade skills and also the Yeoman of Signals maths course that I had passed the previous year. I had done well in these tests and knew I had nothing to worry about. Soon they began firing questions at me, for example: 'You are obviously a rebel, why should we give you a position of authority in Royal Signals? Won't you find the role of comms manager boring after the SAS? Most Royal Signals personnel are serving in the British Army of the Rhine, you have only served there for two years, how could you possibly understand what is required in terms of communications planning for Brigade, Division and even Corps contingency plans for a possible nuclear war?' I must have responded well to all this bullshit, because I was informed that I was one of fifteen sergeants who were selected to attend the next course starting at the Army School of Signals in September.

Before the Yeoman of Signals course began, we first had to attend a six-week Royal Signals Staff Sergeants Course (RSSSC) at 11 Signal Regiment in Catterick. Passing the course was a prerequisite before attendance on the Yeomans' course. The RSSSC covered drill, weapon training, marksmanship, stores accounting, leadership and infantry minor tactics up to platoon level. We also had to learn how to conduct a military funeral, complete with carrying the coffin and firing a fusillade of shots over the grave. Scouse, one of my mates from 264, was also on the RSSSC and had annoyed the RSM at 11 Signal Regiment. As a punishment he was selected to be the corpse in the coffin during the funeral drill. We started with an inspection of our best uniform and boots. After the inspection Scouse climbed into the coffin and was placed in the back of a hearse. We meanwhile waited for the hearse at the makeshift grave. After the civilian pall-bearers handed over the coffin, we carried the coffin on our shoulders while marching in slow-time. The *Last Post* was played after we lowered Scouse into the grave, at which point Scouse got the giggles which infuriated the RSM. As was customary, a wake followed in the Sergeants' Mess. Scouse was made to stay inside the coffin at the wake, although it was propped against a wall in a vertical position so he could at least have a drink!

I had three mates from 264 on the RSSSC. We enjoyed going out for a drink together every weekend while at Catterick Garrison. Jim (Staff Sergeant James Drummond) was SAS-badged and went on to become the staff sergeant (YofS) in command of A Troop embedded in A Squadron, 22 SAS. Sadly Jim died in June 1986 in a free-fall parachuting accident on Salisbury Plain. RIP Jim.

I was awarded the prize of top student on the RSSSC. This award came with the dubious honour of giving a speech at our dinner later that evening in the Sergeants' Mess. I greeted the RSM at the entrance to the Mess holding a silver tray with schooners of sherry as briefed to me by the Mess Manager. The drinks were supposed to be for the CO, due to arrive in a few minutes, the RSM and one for me. Tom, the RSM, was already pissed when he arrived and promptly drank all three schooners of sherry and ordered me to get refills! I spoke to the Mess barman, but he shook his head and told me there wasn't any more sherry. I managed to prise a couple of half-empty schooners off my colleagues and filled my own glass with port which was a similar colour. Tom was none the wiser and fortunately the CO arrived at that moment and the evening went off without a hitch. I chose the topic of the 'grey man' for my speech, i.e., keep out of the limelight and do a good job and it could be you who becomes top student. I also had the added bonus of being presented with a shield for my marksmanship, on which was engraved 'Best Battle Shot – RSSSC 203 – Oct 83'.

I had a week to sort out everything that I would need for a full academic year at the Army School of Signals. It was explained to me that the training was divided into three divisions. The first division was known as 'Traffic Division', to be followed by 'Radio Division', and finally 'Systems Division'.

The 'Traffic Division' included a one-week introduction to computer programming using the School's Hewlett Packard mainframe computer, which was housed in several rooms such was its size and complexity. To interface with the beast, you had to sit in a separate room and enter lines of programming into a keyboard and receive output via paper on a tractor feed. This was all new to me but eventually I mastered the basics. One of the highlights of the 'Traffic Division' was that we all took turns to be the shift supervisor in a commcen mock-up. I eventually finished 'Traffic Division' in third place before moving on to 'Radio Division' where I finished in first place, which raised me to second place overall.

We moved on to 'Systems Division', which was completely new to me. The British Army of the Rhine (BAOR) had fielded the BRUIN area communications networks in Germany for more than twenty years. It was now obsolescent and was due to be phased out in two years. Even so I was still required to learn the intricacies of the system. To exacerbate my problems, we also had to learn the new area network system known as PTARMIGAN which was due to replace BRUIN. It was at this time that I received a phone call informing me that I was to fly to Northern Ireland as a witness <details redacted>. I was met by an SAS team at the airport who were my escort for the week. On arrival I met my three fellow witnesses from our patrol of <details redacted>. At the end of the week the judge adjourned proceedings for two weeks and I was recalled again. I finally gave my evidence during this second period at Crumlin Road court. In his summing up, the judge commented that the evidence we gave had made his job easier to find the terrorist guilty. In those days there were no juries at these courts due to the threat of witness intimidation. The judge made the decision of who was guilty or innocent based solely on the evidence put before him. That may have been fitting justice in this case, but my involvement meant that I had missed two weeks of the YofS course. Despite this, I still managed to pass the 'Systems Division' section of the course. We were all promoted to staff sergeant on the final day of the course and my posting to 264 (SAS) Signal Squadron was confirmed. I was to command D Troop (Signals) in D Squadron, 22 SAS.

Despite an eventual ceasefire in Northern Ireland, it continues to be a place where the return to violence can happen at any time. The Good Friday Agreement was a major development in the Northern Ireland peace process. It was signed on Good Friday, 10 April 1998. At the present time, it appears that there will be no lasting peace, only a simmering cessation of hostilities.

My handover/takeover started the following Monday and included a week in Italy to understand the SAS wartime comms plan in the NATO AFSOUTH region. Geordie, the previous D Troop 'pronto', returned for the handover and showed me around the NATO headquarters in Naples and Verona. We discussed the difficulties of installing our heavy radio equipment for the rear link and communicating from an underground NATO war headquarters as we drank more than one carafe containing 'un mezzo litro di vino rosso'. On completion of the handover, Geordie told me that he was leaving D Troop in good hands. Two weeks later I deployed on a squadron training exercise to Jamaica.

I flew to Jamaica with the advance party and we had four days to set up and establish a rear link back to Hereford before the main party arrived. We were to be based in a Jamaican Defence Force (JDF) camp about 20km from Ocho Rios. As always, putting up the sloping vee wire antenna on its 15m high telescopic mast was the most difficult job, but we achieved it after a hard day's work. The sloping vee antenna covered a large area about the size of a football pitch. Fortunately for me, Geordie had carried out a recce before his posting and had left me a technical survey report. Comms were established the following day, and I heaved a huge sigh of relief.

I already knew most of the signallers in D Troop. In total there were twelve radio telegraphists deployed, including three sergeants. We also had a radio technician and a cypher clerk.

Mobility Troop were out training on their high-powered motorbikes alongside their JDF counterparts. The JDF guys were keen to impress, but sadly lacking in expertise. A JDF sergeant tried to copy Mobility Troop who were riding up a grass ramp at the end of the football pitch and leaving the ground for a few metres. The JDF sergeant was going too fast and ended up flying through the air for about 20 metres before hitting the side of a building with a sickening crunch. He had serious facial injuries, broken ribs and was unconscious with a collapsed lung, internal bleeding and concussion. He would most likely die if he wasn't airlifted to Kingston where the medical facilities were available to save his life. Luckily we had a medical officer (MO) with us from Hereford and he asked me to organize a helicopter MEDEVAC. I ran over to the JDF ops room and asked their duty officer to radio for a helicopter. He was very helpful at first, but when he discovered that the casualty was JDF and not SAS he lost interest and said the sergeant would have to be taken to Kingston by truck, a journey of about three hours over potholed roads. I told him the sergeant would die without a MEDEVAC. He just shrugged and told me I was welcome to make the call to Kingston myself, but he wouldn't intervene. I snatched the microphone and after confirming callsigns demanded a helicopter. The response came back that all the helicopters were taking part in the Independence Day celebrations and there would be no MEDEVAC. This incensed me as a man was dying close by. I insisted that they write my words down in their radio log and then read them back to me. I said, 'The British Medical Officer strongly requests an immediate helicopter MEDEVAC or the JDF sergeant will almost certainly die. The soldier will not be able to survive without immediate specialist medical treatment in Kingston.'

The helicopter arrived thirty minutes later and our MO accompanied the casualty to assist keeping him alive. The JDF duty officer told me I had big balls to make that call.

On return from Jamaica, I attended a range management course at Catterick Camp to supervise live firing. After the course, I continued providing comms support for the SP team and was heavily involved in trialling new equipment. We now had secure fax over satellite, a big improvement as we were able to send sketches and photos to and from the Hereford base. We also had a new secure VHF/UHF radio for the team members which was a game changer and stopped any eavesdropping on our radio nets.

Soon it was 1985 and time for D Squadron to deploy to Malaysia for jungle training in the Cameron Highlands. The HF rear link allowed us to communicate direct to Hereford. While in Malaysia, I took D Troop into the jungle for a few nights' familiarization training. This included live firing with the M16 assault rifle.

Next up was an Italian colloquial course. Several training exercises followed over the next couple of years, including two winter deployments to Norway, each of a couple of months duration. This gave me the opportunity to improve my downhill skiing and also, on my first deployment, I attended a cross-country ski course. We were soon able to ski competently across mountainous and wooded countryside. Trying to ski with a large bergen and then communicating with patrol radios at temperatures that went down to minus 30 degrees Celsius was challenging, but we coped.

In January 1986, just days before my first deployment to Norway, I was summoned to an urgent briefing. Within the hour we collected our weapons and personal equipment and flew to RAF Lyneham in a couple of SAS Augusta 109 helicopters. I discovered that a civil war had broken out in Yemen in the vicinity of Aden. We were kitted out with green flight suits and I was instructed by OC D Squadron to wear RAF flight lieutenant rank, plus a flight engineer's half wing brevet. We had with us a composite troop from D Squadron plus the WO1 Yeoman and two sergeants from 264. We all masqueraded as relief flight crew and were soon airborne in our C130, destination RAF Akrotiri. We had tacsats with us and installed one of these in the cockpit. It was surreal seeing OC D Squadron, the WO1 Yeoman of Signals and me sitting behind the pilots in the cockpit sending and receiving flash and immediate signals. After a brief refuelling stop in Cyprus we flew on to Djibouti, located in the Horn of Africa on the Red Sea.

The international airport at Djibouti was also a French air force base. Our RAF C130 was parked beside a Russian military aircraft and several French Air Force transport planes. We soon formulated a plan to fly into Aden and rescue as many British nationals as possible, while the Russians and French planned to do the same for their nationals. For the time being it was considered too dangerous to land at Aden as there was fighting in and around the airport. We were therefore instructed to sit tight and await developments. OC D Squadron held an 'Orders Group' and the plan was for the WO1 (SAS 'badged') YofS and the two SAS Signals sergeants to remain on the aircraft when we landed at Aden while I would stick close to the squadron commander carrying the second tacsat as we followed the troop rounding up the British nationals awaiting evacuation. We rehearsed the infiltration phase by running down the ramp of the C130 holding our assault rifles and doing a 100m sprint before going to ground and then practising different scenarios. The Russian and French SF were carrying out similar rehearsals alongside us, although there was no significant collaboration.

The RAF flight crew and the SAS troop went to get some sleep. Meanwhile I assisted the WO1 YofS, Connor, and the two sergeants to stag on with the tacsat connected up in the cockpit. We managed to get some sandwiches from the French Air Force who also gave us several cartons of cheap wine. We didn't have much to do other than hourly radio checks, so started to drink the wine. After a while, Connor told us that he held a private pilot's licence and he was going to start up the C130. Now I didn't like the sound of this and tried to dissuade him, but he was having none of it. He started moving the various knobs and switches on the flight panel and announced that he would start the inner port engine first. Sure enough, with a bang, the inner port engine started up and the propeller started to rotate faster and faster. Just as I thought he would be court-martialled for stealing a transport plane, Connor started laughing fit to burst. He explained that the inner port engine is also a generator and the pilot had shown him how to start this up to keep the aircraft batteries charged to power the tacsat and internal lighting. Now that's what I call a good wind-up!

On the second day we received a flash signal to advise us that HMY *Britannia*, together with Royal Navy warships and a Royal Fleet Auxiliary ship, had evacuated several hundred British and foreign nationals from beaches near to Aden. It had been a coordinated rescue with Soviet (Russian) merchant vessels and a French ship. We were also informed that our services were no longer required and we were to return to the UK via Cyprus. Luckily for all concerned HMY *Britannia* was in the right place at the right time to evacuate 1,000 refugees from Aden during the civil war of 1986.

I was promoted to warrant officer class 2 (WO2) in March 1986 and continued to command D Troop. I also managed to fit in two NATO exercises to Italy, in 1986 and again in 1987, where my Italian language skills proved useful.

I continued to support Tranmere as a long-distance supporter during those difficult years, although the club was beginning to show signs of improvement. Some of the players at this time who were playing well included Ian Muir, who was later to feature on a large mural alongside Ray Mathias (another legend of the mid-1980s) painted on the side of a house directly opposite Prenton Park. In those days I often had to make do with reading the results on the BBC Ceefax teletext news service and then the match report in the Sunday newspapers. There was no Internet all those years ago!

The summer of 1986 saw D Squadron on a short exercise to Italy. We began the exercise by boarding a US warship at Naples dockyard. It was there that we met up with our counterparts from the embarked US Navy SEAL team. Scott, the SEAL lieutenant commanding the team, told me that I was to bunk on a folding bed in his cabin. He seemed surprised when I told him that a British warrant officer was not a commissioned officer, and with a gung-ho attitude told me not to worry. This arrangement worked fine for a couple of days until my unwanted presence in the officers' quarters was discovered. I was moved to a mess-deck full of African-American sailors who were distinctly unimpressed with having a white foreigner among them. I was allocated a top bunk in a three-tier-high layout. Eventually one of the sailors came up to me and started asking questions while sharpening his combat knife. He looked at my name and unit written on a card next to my allocated bunk and asked me what SAS meant. At that point one of his friends shouted out,

'Hey man. I'm reading a book about the SAS. You guys are heroes and true friends of America.' After that they gave me a bandana to wear and I became an honorary 'bro' for the rest of the voyage! Later, Scott came to find me and told me that my presence was urgently required in the Main Communications Office (MCO). When I arrived at the MCO, an officer asked me if I knew Morse code as the Italian navy were trying to communicate to the ship using Morse. Within seconds I was banging away on the key. The Italian radio operator was good, and I received the message, in Italian, at 20wpm. Once I had finished writing it down, I quickly translated the message into English and then turned around to see all the US navy communicators watching my handiwork. The exercise culminated in a beach assault in an isolated area of Sardinia. There were about ten warships involved. I flew ashore in the second wave aboard a twin-rotor CH46 Sea Knight.

The remainder of 1986 saw me on the SP team once again. This included two operational call-outs within the UK and abroad. Eventually both incidents were resolved without needing the SAS, and the news of our involvement was kept out of the public eye.

In April 1987 I received a posting order to 7 Signal Regiment in Germany. I still had five months before the posting so was able to attend an Arabic course and deploy to Jordan for a major training exercise with the Jordanian SF.

Arabic is a difficult language to master, but I gave it my best effort and achieved a good result at the end of the course. I knew the key to getting anywhere was to perfect my pronunciation. We learnt Arabic using 'transliteration'. In other words, the words were written using the English alphabet rather than Arabic script. This made it far easier for us to quickly learn lots of vocabulary.

It wasn't long before we flew to Jordan for the exercise. We were based at an air base near the town of Al Jafr, where the Jordanian air force kept a squadron of Dassault Mirage F1 jets. The routine was the same as any major squadron deployment. First I set up the antenna field for our HF radio rear link to Hereford, and after that I concentrated on setting up the forward radio nets.

When D Squadron deployed to Jordan, we borrowed a WO1 to carry out the duties of Operations WO. Bronco Lane was the WO1 who accompanied us. Bronco was famous, not only within the SAS, but throughout the Army and mountain climbing fraternities for scaling Mount Everest in 1976. He had lost all of his toes and some of his fingertips to frostbite on the descent. Bronco eventually made a full recovery and returned to the SAS, although he had to learn to run and walk without toes and his boot size was now a couple of sizes smaller. Bronco was great fun and as mad as a box of frogs! I shared the ops room with him and he had some great stories to tell. We often drove around the airbase in an SAS Land Rover 'pinkie'. Bronco would drive straight across the 10,000ft operational runway with total disregard for the fighter jets which would take off and land without warning. One day we had just crossed the runway and a military jeep with a blue flashing light caught up with us and waved us down. A Jordanian Air Force officer jumped out livid with rage. He shouted at Bronco that we were not allowed to drive across the runway and should take the longer route by driving to the end of the runway and then go across. Bronco looked the officer up and down and said, 'Don't worry. I use the Green Cross Code.' The officer looked puzzled and Bronco elaborated, 'I look to the left, I look to the right, and then I look to the left again. If nothing is coming, I drive straight across!' The officer still couldn't grasp that Bronco was having a bit of fun at his expense. Bronco then turned to me and asked me what the Arabic word for green was and I told him it was *'akhdar'*. Bronco then repeated his explanation to the officer in broken Arabic: *'Maa fee mushkila*, Cross Code *Akhdar!'* (No problem, Green Cross Code!). The officer eventually drove off still muttering about the crazy British! A few months later, Bronco was commissioned as a captain and served with the SAS for a few more years, retiring in the rank of major. He had passed Selection in 1967 and had fought in the Aden Emergency, Oman and Northern Ireland where he was awarded the Military Medal.

I deployed to our Forward Operating Base (FOB) at Wadi Rum. We had a few large tents erected there and the FOB was occupied for several weeks while we all managed to fit in a few parachute jumps. Mobility Troop was also there carrying out training with pinkies and motor bikes. I managed a parachute jump on my second day and then the following day our RAF C130 practised 'strip landings' on the mud flats to the east of Wadi Rum. I really enjoyed this, especially when I was given the opportunity to sit in the cockpit as we landed on the rock-hard mud. As soon as we took off, we circled and then approached for another landing. I was also given the opportunity to join Mobility Troop in riding motorbikes off the ramp while the C130 turned and took off again after only a few seconds on the ground. When it was my turn, I shot off the ramp, which wasn't quite touching the ground and roared off and tried to catch up with Mobility Troop.

We had a final exercise before our departure. The plan called for D Squadron and the Jordanian SF squadron to advance to contact, supported by troop-carrying helicopters and a couple of Dassault Mirage F1 jets. The 'exercise' enemy was a group of *jihadis* holed up in a cave at the top of the huge *wadi* (dry river bed) that the exercise was scheduled to take place in. This was to be no ordinary live firing exercise, as King Hussein, ruler of the Hashemite Kingdom of Jordan, would be observing from a vantage point high up on a cliff. Colin the SQMS, ex-Boat Troop, was given the task of preparing the vantage point to literally make it fit for a king. We cleared the ground and cut steps in the rock-hard clay up to the plateau above where King Hussein was scheduled to land. Carpets were flown in and coffee pots set up. A handrail was fitted and red carpet rolled out. My role was to act as the forward air controller and assist the squadron commander in briefing the king. The day of the joint attack was very hot as the two squadrons advanced up the wadi. When contact with the enemy was made the RAF Chinook was used to position a couple of machine gun teams on high ground overlooking the *jihadis*. Finally, I received a request from D Squadron for the fast jets. I called the two aircraft that were loitering a few miles away and out of earshot. Within two minutes they flew along the wadi directly opposite us at eye-level before firing missiles and then dropping their bombs bang on target. King Hussein was passionate about all that was going on and asked many questions. After the attack concluded, the RAF Chinook landed above us on the plateau. We now had four helicopters on the landing pad: the king's helicopter, two UH-1 'Hueys' carrying his CP team, and the RAF Chinook. We had an RAF squadron leader with us as an LO, who briefed the king on how many days it had taken to fly the Chinook out to Jordan from the UK. The RAF LO had been briefed that under no circumstances was the king to fly in the Chinook as it would have international repercussions if the helicopter were to crash. Suddenly King Hussein stood up, shook everyone's hand, thanked everyone and announced he would like a ride in the RAF Chinook! Now there was no way anybody could possibly say no to the king. We all looked at the RAF officer to hear his reply. The RAF LO looked aghast and after a pregnant pause said, 'Certainly Sir, but I must accompany you to explain the technical specifications of the helicopter.' Later I asked the RAF officer why he had accompanied the king and his reply was classic. He said: 'Can you imagine me being court-martialled for allowing King Hussein to die in a helicopter crash? I would much rather die with him than fill in the accident report and then be court-martialled for disobeying orders.' Later I reflected on our two months in Jordan. I had met several members of the Jordanian Royal Family, including King Hussein and his brother Crown Prince Hassan, who was Commander Special Forces. As a footnote to this story, I was on board the same Chinook helicopter a few days later when the main gearbox failed and we made a forced landing out in the desert. It was one of those 'we all thought we were going to die moments!' Fortunately the RAF SF pilot put us down safely.

Before we left Jordan, one of the SF officers confided in me that he was immediately deploying to Iraq for attachment to the Iraqi SF. There was a bloody war going on at that time between Iraq and Iran and I asked him if he was deploying as an observer or combatant. The officer gave me a wry smile, tapped the side of his nose and said, 'Pray for me.' The Iran-Iraq war continued from 1980 until 1988, following a long history of border disputes. It was motivated by a fear that the Iranian Revolution would inspire a similar revolt by Iraq's Shi'ite majority. The Iran-Iraq war involved large-scale trench warfare and bayonet charges. The Iraqis used chemical weapons and deliberately targeted civilians. One million Iraqi and Iranian soldiers and civilians are believed to have died in the war, with many more suffering life-changing injuries.

My time with D Squadron had come to an end. The only consolation was I was promised that I would return to Hereford as the 264 (SAS) Signal Squadron 'Ops Warrant Officer' once I was promoted to WO1.

Chapter 10

Commissioned from the Ranks

It was the height of the Cold War, and Germany was divided into East and West. My new regiment, 7 Signal Regiment, was based in Herford, Nordrhein-Westfalen. I was the WO2 Yeoman of Signals in 6 Squadron, the only squadron in the regiment equipped with combat net radio rather than the PTARMIGAN comms system which the other squadrons were equipped with. PTARMIGAN was a mobile, digital battlefield wide area network comms system designed for use in BAOR, West Germany. The system consisted of a network of trunk nodes providing multi-channel voice, data and facsimile communications.

My first task in 6 Squadron was to train all the radio telegraphists on the new Clansman VRC 322 radios which had just arrived. After that I deployed to the inner-German border on a major exercise demonstrating that the British forces were determined to keep the autobahn to West Berlin open during periods of tension. Helmstedt was a small Royal Military Police (RMP) barracks on the inner-German border located at the side of the autobahn. I was accommodated in the NAAFI motel inside the barracks, which consisted of a restaurant and several hotel-style bedrooms. I deployed on the exercise with Alpha Three Troop and their AFV-432 tracked vehicles for their role providing comms for the 'Corps Recce Force', a light armoured brigade. The role of the Corps Recce Force was to provide 1st British Corps' (1 BR CORPS) first line of defence in their light tanks and tracked vehicles in the event of a Soviet invasion.

The following Friday evening, 'Active Edge' was called and we all returned to barracks without delay. Now 'Active Edge' could mean World War 3 had just commenced and hordes of Soviet troops were massing on the border, but it was just another exercise. We drove off in vehicle convoys to our 'war hide' locations. This was to prevent the regiment being annihilated in our barracks by Warsaw Pact forces. We endured a cold and miserable night on a forest track several hours drive from our barracks. We weren't allowed to start up our generators, to reduce our 'electronic and thermal signatures'. This is where we would wait for our deployment orders from HQ 1 BR Corps. Fortunately, the exercise was declared a success and we soon returned to barracks.

Six months later while on exercise, OC 6 Squadron and I received a summons from the CO. On went our combat helmets and we picked up our weapons for the 300m walk to the CO's Command Post. OC 6 Squadron went inside while I waited outside in the dark. Eventually they came out and informed me that the Regimental WO1 Yeoman of Signals had returned to the UK due to a long-term illness and wouldn't be returning. The CO had therefore decided to promote me with immediate effect and I was now the WO1 Regimental Yeoman of Signals.

My first task in the Regimental Ops Cell was to draft a Communications Electronic Instruction. This is a type of 'signals plan' detailing the situation, mission, execution, callsigns, frequencies, network diagrams, routing tables and equipment scaling. It took me a while to understand the functionality and equipment scaling of our PTARMIGAN assets. Eventually I learnt that 1, 2 and 3 Squadrons were Trunk Node squadrons, whereas 4 and 5 Squadrons were Major Access Nodes (MAN). The MAN squadrons would take turns supporting HQ 1 BR CORPS Main Headquarters (1 BR CORPS MAIN) and the step-up HQ (1 BR CORPS STEP-UP) which would become the next 'MAIN' when the General commanding 1 BR CORPS and his staff swung across.

All the best rugby players in the corps were posted to and from 7 Signal Regiment. The RSM was the team manager and one day he asked me to take the squad on a tough 'hill rep' session on Bismarck Ridge. Soon after this the Regiment won the Army Cup. The RSM held a regimental dinner to celebrate this achievement. Pride of place went to the solid silver cup displayed on the top table. There had been a rumour that the RSM was planning some entertainment and we were not to be disappointed. A zookeeper from the nearby *Tierpark* came barging in with a baby elephant! Soon the elephant was towing the zookeeper around the room and then the shit started coming out of the elephant's backside which ended up getting smeared all over the new mess carpet!

The year started with a busy exercise season, leading up to Exercise Summer Sales, a major 1 BR CORPS exercise with all HQ staff cells manned. On exercise, I deployed with Systems Executive Plans, which controlled all the PTARMIGAN assets deployed across northern

Germany. When in barracks, I continued to work in the Regimental Ops Cell. After one year, the regimental traffic officer approached me with a proposition. He was keen to get himself noticed for promotion to major. His current role was senior crypto custodian controlling crypto distribution for all units in 1 BR CORPS. What he proposed was a job swap. He wanted to work as the assistant ops officer, a job I was fulfilling in all but name, while I took on the role of 1 BR CORPS crypto custodian. I readily agreed to this as I wanted to gain a better understanding of the secret world of crypto key generation, distribution, accounting and destruction of expired keying material. We jointly approached the ops officer and CO and they agreed to the proposal. This meant that I now commanded Z Troop, which consisted of six NCOs working for me as crypto accountants. I fulfilled this role for the next year before receiving a posting order to 264 (SAS) Signal Squadron as the WO1 Ops Warrant Officer.

It felt good to be back in Hereford and I soon settled in to life in the ops cell at 264. The ops officer was SAS-badged. We also had a senior Technical Officer Telecommunications (TOT), who, although not SAS-badged, had spent over six years in the squadron and was para-trained.

Meanwhile, I had a new language to learn. Spanish was not a difficult language for me, as I already spoke Italian. Soon after the course started, my participation was interrupted to take a week out of the country for an urgent operational assignment.

The export of illegal drugs from Colombia needed an alliance of nations to unite in '*la Guerra contra las drogas*'. The UK offered their services alongside others, most significantly the United States, in combating the illegal drugs trade. In October 1989 I was sent to Bogota, the capital of Colombia, as part of a recce team to identify how the SAS could support the Colombian authorities in their fight against the drug cartels. On arrival I was introduced to a '*coronel*' (colonel) in the Administrative Department of Security (DAS), which was a sort of special police department with a para-military capability. *El coronel* told me of their requirements for a secure radio. During the meeting the whole building suddenly started trembling violently. I looked at the colonel who just said one word, '*Terramoto!*' (earthquake) which was a relief as the building had been targeted in the past. Soon my week in Bogota was over and all I had to do was write a classified recce report with my conclusions and recommendations for the comms support that the UK government should offer to DAS. Six weeks later, the DAS Building was subjected to a truck bomb attack. The bomb, consisting of approximately 1,000lbs of explosive, killed 52 people and injured about 1,000. It was widely believed that the Medellin Cartel was responsible.

Meanwhile, my liaison work continued with the regiment's 'Ops Research Cell'. They had an urgent operational requirement for a device that would identify a man down when out training on the mountains. This was especially important for SAS Selection as several soldiers had died over the years. Ops Research finally came up with a prototype device after collaborating with several companies. Unfortunately, although the device went into production, it was not particularly successful and the situation remained that way until the Global Positioning System (GPS) revolutionized location-finding devices.

All this equipment testing out on the mountains gave me an opportunity to keep fit and got me out of the office. I also acted as DS on several 264 (SAS) Signal Squadron probationary courses where I walked behind a four-man patrol as they navigated across the Brecon Beacons during their final exercise.

My involvement in comms equipment development brought me into regular contact with Ops Research. I was regularly asked to give my opinion on various items including covert cameras, eavesdropping devices and 'active ear defenders'. This last item sounds mundane, but actually significantly enhanced our operational capability. The ear defenders were electronic and powered by a small battery. They enabled you to hear a whisper while protecting your hearing from gunshots and explosions.

The Signal Squadron also provided comms support to the regiment's counter revolutionary warfare (CRW) cell and revolutionary warfare wing (RWW), much of the work being highly classified. My role kept me in fairly regular contact with these characters and they often perplexed me with their urgent requests, for example fitting radios onto powered-microlight aircraft '…by 1700 hours today'.

New equipment trials continued with several roll-outs, including a new tacsat to replace the URC101 and at only a quarter the weight of the older equipment. We also fielded a new HF area network with computerized switches which meant all the signallers had to be trained in operating the digital switches. I took part in the trials and then we introduced the

PRC 319 into the mix. This was the Special Force's new HF patrol radio with an electronic messaging unit capable of burst transmissions.

The 264 squadron commander, Harry, called me into his office one day. He was bursting with excitement and told me to shut the door and sit down. He showed me a letter that listed the names selected by the Royal Signals Commissioning Board. The letter stated that I had been selected to be commissioned as a 'late-entry' officer in the Royal Corps of Signals.

My final year in Hereford was to be as busy as every other year that I spent there. I had sold my house at a decent profit which enabled me to go upmarket and buy a four-bedroomed detached house that had just been built near Hereford Racecourse. I took golf lessons as I had been advised that I was likely to be posted back to BAOR in Germany, where most officers played golf. I also qualified as a Joint Services Mountain Expedition Leader.

I was summoned to RHQ one day for a counter-terrorism planning conference. We were informed there was to be a joint exercise with the French national gendarmerie unit, GIGN. This tactical unit was responsible for counter-terrorism and hostage rescue. GIGN had already been involved in over 1,700 missions and had rescued more than 800 hostages, making them one of the most experienced counter-terrorism units in the world. The exercise was to take place in the western approaches to the English Channel with a Forward Mounting Base on the Brittany peninsula. The SBS would also be involved and the French navy were to provide a couple of warships dedicated to the exercise. I was selected to go on the recce with the regimental second-in-command, together with a member of CRW and one of the SP team commanders. A few days later an RAF Chinook helicopter from the SF Flight flew us to Brittany. On arrival, we were accommodated overnight in a French air force base. The next morning, our French LO instructed our pilot to fly to a nearby civilian airport. We landed alongside a white-coloured 'Super-Puma' helicopter belonging to the Ministry of Interior, who jointly controlled GIGN along with the French armed forces. The Puma flew us to a warship steaming several miles off shore. After landing on the small flight deck, we were met by the captain. The discussion centred on whether the RAF could possibly land a Chinook on such a small flight deck. The RAF crew were then flown back to their helicopter and an hour later they returned in the Chinook. I was spellbound watching the huge Chinook trying to land on the ship in such a choppy sea. It was a windy day which didn't help matters, but with a concentrated effort they managed to put the aircraft down on the deck. The helicopter had landed diagonally with the front and back of the aircraft hanging over the side and stern of the ship such was the lack of space. It was an excellent piece of flying and the RAF crew were pleased with their handiwork. I visited the Main Communications Office to confirm what radio frequencies were compatible with the ship to communicate directly with the vessel during the exercise. There was just time to enjoy the captain's *bonhomie*, when we sat down to an excellent lunch with a glass of wine in the wardroom, before we bid *adieu*. We flew back to the airbase to refuel and then onwards to Hereford. A few days later things were happening in the Middle East that caused the exercise to be shelved.

I was awarded the 'Licentiateship of City and Guilds' in electronic communications in 1990, which was added to my CV. I was still concentrating on learning Spanish, but as we moved into the second half of 1990 there was fresh impetus for our Arabic speaking skills. Saddam Hussein, the President of Iraq, had invaded Kuwait on 2 August 1990. This was to be the start of a seven-month long occupation and culminated in the First Gulf War.

A recce party from 22 SAS deployed to the Middle East to identify a place where a sabre squadron could be accommodated and train in desert warfare while being available for a no-notice deployment to the war zone. On their return I was informed that I was likely to deploy within a month to Saudi Arabia. Meanwhile Harry, the 264 squadron commander, was trying to get my commissioning date put back by six months so that I could take part in the likely hostilities. Unfortunately Royal Signals was hell-bent on sending me to the Falkland Islands as an acting captain and would not postpone this. It was therefore decided that it would make more sense for the 264 ops officer to go on the recce, leaving me in Hereford to run the Squadron Ops Cell. On 17 January 1991 the air campaign of the First Gulf War began, followed by the coalition invasion of Kuwait.

In late January 1991, I found myself at Headquarters Mess, Royal Corps of Signals, at Blandford Camp, for my one day 'commissioning course'. This course was known in the corps as the 'knife and fork' course. There were only two of us on the course and we were welcomed by the mess manager, a retired Royal Signals major. After a cup of coffee in a gold-rimmed cup and saucer, we were given a slide presentation showing the organization of the corps. The presentation included the names of all senior Royal Signals officers. We progressed to the 'knife and fork' part of the course when we closely inspected the table layout for a formal dinner that evening. The two of us were advised that we were to be seated close to the top table. This was so we would be within earshot of the commandant of the School of Signals and also the Signals-Officer-in-Chief (SOinC) who was a major general and the senior guest. I was advised that I should develop the art of speaking knowledgably on a variety of subjects while being able to eat my food in the correct manner without dawdling. I like to think that I conducted myself well at my first Officers' Mess dinner, I certainly had plenty to say and finished my food before the commandant and SOinC! On my return to Hereford, most of the regiment had already deployed to the Middle East while awaiting the Coalition's advance into Kuwait. This meant that I couldn't be dined out. Instead I bought a barrel of beer in the Sergeants' Mess and invited everyone in Stirling Lines to come and have a drink with me. I made a short farewell speech and that was the end of my thirteen years in Hereford.

Now that I was commissioned, my time with the SAS was over. A couple of days later I travelled to RAF Brize Norton for the flight to the Falkland Islands. The 'South Atlantic Airbridge', as the route was known, took about seventeen hours flying time with a refuelling stop at Ascension Island.

The landing at RAF Mount Pleasant was bumpy as there was a strong crosswind blowing. We had to remain in the arrivals lounge while we were given a briefing on unexploded ordnance, including information about the thousands of anti-personnel mines scattered around East Falkland. I realized just how far my army career had progressed when I awoke the next morning. My boots, that I had left outside the door as instructed, had been polished and a cup of tea handed to me in bed by a female mess orderly. The orderly was one of several females hired on twelve-month contracts from St Helena. Once I left for work the orderly would return to make the bed and vacuum the carpet. St Helena is a volcanic island in the South Atlantic and a British Overseas Territory.

RAF Mount Pleasant is located over thirty miles from the capital, Stanley, and was constructed after the 1982 war. I was now OC B Troop, Joint Communications Unit Falkland Islands (JCUFI). I had the commcen and the Crypto Distribution Agency under my command. B Troop consisted of my second-in-command, a Royal Navy fleet chief petty officer, and forty-five personnel, comprising fifteen each from the RN, Army and RAF.

There was a drinking culture at RAF Mount Pleasant. We worked Monday to Friday and Saturday mornings. Friday afternoon at 4 pm was when everything stopped for 'Happy-Hour'. I would normally have a beer in the JCUFI Bar, followed by a few more in the Officers' Mess. At my first mess meeting, we were informed that the Mess had made an embarrassing amount of money from the sale of alcoholic drinks. Therefore, with immediate effect, the price of wines and spirits was to be reduced by ten per cent and all beer was to be *gratis* until the end of the month. Free beer? Happy days!

My six-month tour of duty in the Falkland Islands gave me an opportunity to tour my old battlefields. I found Brummie's Argie frying pan with folding handle in the cleft of a rock at Bluff Cove Peak which he had mislaid in 1982. I marvelled at my find and then returned it to its hideaway.

I was in the commcen one day when one of the young sailors shouted across to me. I knew he was from Birkenhead and supported Tranmere Rovers, but I was still surprised to hear that Tranmere had signed John Aldridge. 'Aldo' was a former Liverpool legend and had signed for Real Sociedad in Spain two years earlier. Tranmere paid the comparatively low price of £250,000 for Aldo when they signed him on 11 July 1991. Aldo scored forty goals in his first season at Prenton Park, a club record. He eventually scored a total 174 goals in 294 appearances for Tranmere Rovers.

I took four days R&R in May 1991. On the first day I flew to Port Howard on West Falkland and stayed overnight at the farmhouse. The flight was in a Britten Norman Islander aircraft which took off from Stanley airport. On arrival at Port Howard, we landed in a field using the lights of a Land Rover to guide us in through the mist. The next morning I walked to John Hamilton's grave. It was an honour to have served with John and I was pleased to be able to pay my respects. I spent the remainder of my R&R walking the 1982 battlefields.

I sailed to South Georgia about halfway through my tour to carry out the annual crypto inspection of the JCUFI detachment. The voyage took three days aboard HMS *Dumbarton Castle*, an offshore patrol vessel acting as the Falkland Islands guard ship. She was quite a small ship and the weather wasn't kind to us. Most of the crew and the few embarked passengers were soon seasick and took to their bunks if they possibly could.

On arrival at Grytviken, we handed over the mail and were given cans of beer to drink while they caught up with the news from home. There was a Royal Engineer officer stationed at Grytviken with the secondary appointment of harbour master. He collected the harbour dues from visiting deep-sea trawlers and the occasional cruise ship. There was a flourishing trade exchanging fish for venison from the wild reindeer herd on South Georgia. The dinner menu that first evening reflected this, as the main course was a choice of either roast venison or icefish curry. Incidentally, the icefish is only found in southern waters. The fish has a body that is almost completely transparent, meaning you can see its veins and internal body organs, giving it the appearance of being made out of ice.

The crypto inspection didn't take long. That left me with time to explore, including a steep scramble to the summit of Brown Mountain. The mountain was covered in snow with tantalising views from the summit towards Mount Paget, the highest peak on South Georgia at 2,935m. Soon it was time to descend and walk across a frozen lake towards Grytviken. The trek took me past Shackleton's grave, which is a tribute to British endurance. Sir Ernest Henry Shackleton (1874–1922) was a polar explorer who led three British expeditions to the Antarctic. He was buried in Grytviken cemetery after a service in the nearby Lutheran church. Near the small cemetery was an area on the coastline with a group of elephant seals comprising a bull seal and his harem. Elephant bull seals typically reach a length of 16ft and weigh 6,600lb (the females are much smaller). The walk continued to Grytviken and this gave me an opportunity to look over the former whaling station. Rusting on the foreshore was a line of whale catchers. There was also a small church and a derelict ski-jump. Soon it was time to sail back to the Falklands.

OC JCUFI sent for me two weeks later and asked if I would lead a team in a 'march and shoot' competition. I agreed, of course, especially when I discovered the route would take us over some of the summits that the British Forces had fought battles on during the Falklands War. The competition was hosted by the Falkland Islands Defence Force (FIDF). I took the JCUFI squad out training for several sessions before selecting our team. The competition consisted of a 20km march in the mountains surrounding Stanley followed by a 'falling-plate' shooting competition. The route was from a starting point on the Mount Pleasant Road to the west of Stanley and over Mount Harriet, Tumbledown and Sapper Hill before dropping down to the road just outside Stanley and following it to the rifle range. My team consisted of twelve JCUFI personnel. They were the fittest men in the unit and we trained hard.

The week before the march and shoot competition I heard the football scores on the BBC World Service. Tranmere Rovers had won the League One play-off final at Wembley. This was part of the 'Rocket Ride to the Moon' during Johnny King's years as manager. Chris Malkin scored the winner in extra time. I was over the moon myself as I celebrated that evening.

On the day of the competition, the teams set off at staggered intervals. We soon started to overtake the other teams as we went steeply uphill. As we approached the rifle ranges, OC JCUFI shouted to me from the roadside that we were currently in first place. We were given five minutes on arrival to load and then take our turn at shooting down the 'falling-plates'. We hadn't been given an opportunity to practise our shooting skills in the previous weeks, so I wasn't surprised when the results came out. FIDF came first in the shooting and second in the march making them first overall. We were awarded third place overall.

My next posting was to 16 Signal Regiment in Krefeld, near the Dutch border. I commanded the Crypto Distribution Agency, responsible for all crypto keying material for British units in BAOR with the exception of 1 BR CORPS. Meanwhile, most of the regiment had just returned from Kuwait after the First Gulf War. Things were quiet so I volunteered to manage the regimental cross-country team and was pleased to discover that we had some good runners in the team.

I attended the 'top rope and abseiling instructor' course at the Silberhütte British Forces adventure training centre in the Harz Mountains. The course qualified me to take small groups on single-pitch climbing and then abseil back down the rock face. The Harz Mountains straddled the former inner-German border. Early one evening, four of us drove to East Germany now that the Cold War had ended. As we approached the border, there was about 1,000m of newly-laid asphalt that crossed the border corridor. We saw an abandoned East German sentry post and stopped to inspect it. It was constructed of plywood and painted a drab olive green. Downstairs was a built-in bed, alongside a small table and two chairs. We climbed up the ladder to the lookout post and contemplated how grim it must have been to have manned this post. We continued driving into East Germany and the roads became very dilapidated. The nearby town looked like it was trapped in the 1930s. There was even a broken-down steam train at the railway sidings. The reinforced concrete street lamps were all broken and rusting away. There was nowhere to buy a coffee so we turned around and drove back to prosperous West Germany. If anyone needed a lesson that communism didn't work, it was demonstrated right there in stark relief.

My friend Tom was OC HQ Squadron, previously RSM of 11 Signal Regiment, where he had made my life hell on the promotion course eight years before. By now Tom had mellowed and offered to teach me how to play golf. Most Saturday mornings we would drive to the eighteen-hole course at RAF Wildenrath. I remember my first visit when on returning to the club house Tom asked me to buy him a pint while he changed his shoes. As soon as Tom disappeared, a very attractive lady golfer in a plaid mini-skirt started to give me the eye. Then she walked over and handed me a glass of whisky and said cheers. When Tom returned I told him I had scored with the pretty girl in the corner, who saw us looking and raised her glass to us. Tom laughed his head off and told me she had just achieved a 'hole-in-one' and it was tradition to buy everyone a whisky if this happened. Oh well, that burst my balloon!

There was a major restructuring of the British Army in 1992, called 'Options for Change'. With the collapse of the Warsaw Pact in 1989, a Soviet invasion of Western Europe seemed unlikely. As part of Options for Change, troop strength in Germany was to be halved by replacing BAOR with a much smaller organization to be designated British Forces Germany (BFG). The plan called for 16 Signal Regiment to reduce in size and relocate to Rheindahlen. The regiment's new role was to provide close support to a new NATO organization named Headquarters Allied Rapid Reaction Corps (ARRC). Rheindahlen was already the base for HQ BAOR and many of the staff transferred to HQ BFG. These major changes affected me directly as I was to take on the roles previously held by three officers. I was now the Operations Officer, but also took on the role of Regimental Training Officer and continued as the Regimental Traffic Officer. Slowly my workload increased. This gave me a busy final eighteen-month period in the regiment.

In 1993 I attended an 'Alpine Trekking Leader (*Klettersteig*)' instructor's course. *Klettersteig* is a style of protected climbing. A fixed steel cable runs along the rock face. The cable is used as a climbing aid by clipping onto it using a couple of karabiners. Iron rungs, narrow ladders and footbridges are provided to climb vertical sections or to bridge chasms. A good head for heights is essential, together with a rope and other climbing aids. My adventure training qualifications meant that I had the knowledge and experience to organize a really challenging Regimental Summer Camp the following year in Bavaria. I personally led the *Klettersteig* routes and five soldiers had the opportunity to sample some of the most challenging protected climbing that the Bavarian Alps had to offer.

In summer 1993, 16 Signal Regiment deployed to Vogelsang Military Training Area for our annual battle camp. The training area lies in the German North Eifel hills. It was established by the British after the Second World War before the Belgian army took over in the 1950s. I ran a three-day combat survival course in the nearby forest. We also practised 'fighting-in-built-up-areas'. Most of my training wing staff were 'field-firing' instructors, meaning they could supervise live firing on designated military training areas. This meant all the troops participated in section attacks and other minor tactics using live ammunition. Fitness played a key part in our training and every morning started with a run. We also swam in a large indoor swimming pool which, like everything else in the original buildings, had 'Nazi' artwork displayed everywhere, often depicting the Aryan warrior.

HQ 1 Signals Brigade tasked me to travel to Palmanova in northern Italy. I met up with Commander Armoured, who was a British full colonel, and his chief of staff, a cavalry major, before we boarded a sleeper train. Commander Armoured was the officer ultimately responsible to the corps commander for all armoured assets within 1st British Corps. Once on board, we had a couple of drinks and got to know each other before a good night's sleep. They briefed me on the *'Pozzuolo del Friuli'* Mechanized Cavalry Brigade, to whom we were to make a presentation on the ARRC capability. It transpired that they had both been trying to learn Italian for the last couple of weeks and had a few useful phrases. They were surprised to learn that not only could I speak passable Italian, but having been in the SAS I knew a bit more about the sharp end of soldiering than they at first realized. We got on very well and I enjoyed the trip.

During my part of the presentation, I explained that 16 Signal Regiment would provide the Italian Brigade with a PTARMIGAN 'communications gateway' and 'satellite-bridge' to link their communications into the other deployed ARRC formations. We were invited to a formal dinner in the Officers' Mess hosted by the brigade commander. I was surprised to see pewter platters, bowls and wine goblets on the tables. One of the brigade officers saw me inspecting the battered and bashed pewterware and told me that most items were over two hundred years old and quite valuable.

My technical report on the communications capability of the *Pozzuolo del Friuli* Brigade and how the whole network would be integrated into HQ ARRC's PTARMIGAN system was widely circulated at senior officer level, including Commander 1 Signal Brigade. The report had shown that I was capable of taking on high profile tasks within Royal Signals at short notice. My reward was to be promotion to the rank of major and take on the appointment of training major in a TA signals regiment.

The manager of Tranmere Rovers, Johnny King, was a former Everton player who had gone on to play for Tranmere. He is widely recognized as being the most successful manager in the history of the club. I only managed to attend a few games at Prenton Park during this period, but I avidly followed the team from afar and was delighted with all the players being signed up to the cause, including Pat Nevin and Liam O'Brien. During this time (1993–95) Tranmere narrowly missed out on promotion to the Premier League three times. I managed to attend a couple of games in early 1994 and the team was on fire. It had been assembled with significant investment from the club's owner, Peter Johnson, who had a personal fortune at that time of over £150 million.

My posting order arrived in February 1994, stating that I was to be posted to 37 Signal Regiment (Volunteers) in Redditch, Worcestershire. In July I completed my handover and then had two weeks leave to move from Germany. I decided to sell my house in Hereford, which had been rented out, to finance buying a house over the border in Wales.

RHQ and HQ Squadron were housed in a modern TA centre on the outskirts of Redditch, not far from Birmingham. Tom, the training major who I was to take over from, showed me around. There were only a few permanent staff, i.e., the CO, QM, adjutant, RSM, a few SNCOs and civilian staff.

The CO, John, was a regular army lieutenant colonel and we got on well. John was a great mentor and explained that he would be posted in five months. His replacement would be a TA volunteer who would have to rely heavily on me to run the operational and training side of the regiment. There was a lot for me to take in and I also had to visit various headquarters, not to mention the regiment's outlying squadrons which were based at Coventry, Cardiff, Blackburn and Stratford-upon-Avon. I had two weeks on the road with my predecessor before he was 'dined out' of the regiment and I was 'dined in'.

After six weeks we deployed on annual camp to Altcar Training Camp near Liverpool. What impressed me about the TA, nowadays known as the Army Reserve, was the positive attitude that so many volunteers created by their enthusiasm to learn everything possible about their role with limited training time. The regiment had to conduct their own recruit cadres and then progress to trade-training, culminating in an exercise during annual camp where their skills could be fully tested in a realistic training environment. The TA soldiers qualified for a 'tax-free' cash bounty if they attended annual camp as part of a twenty-seven day minimum commitment and successfully passed their mandatory military tests.

The Commander of 2 (National Communications) Signal Brigade, our parent HQ, visited us every few months. Our squadrons were spread across three different regional brigades, meaning I was required to attend meetings at their separate headquarters. I attended drill nights and regularly worked weekends. Drill nights always finished with a drink in the Officers' Mess. Later, those sleeping over in their offices, including me, would have last orders in the Sergeants' Mess after a personal invitation by the RSM. The next morning the RSM would always bring me a cup of tea to my office. Once I had washed and shaved, it was time for the two of us to drive to a nearby café for breakfast.

I had been in role for one year when the CO, Stamford, announced that he was going to France on a long business trip, followed by a family vacation, and I was to command the regiment in his absence for six weeks. While this didn't faze me, it did mean that I got invited to a CO's conference at HQ 2 Signal Brigade. This was an eye-opener for me as I observed all the COs jostling for pecking-order and their petty moaning.

On the CO's return, Stamford asked me to take him on a confirmatory recce to Penally Camp in Wales, the location for annual camp in August. We looked around and Stamford declared himself satisfied with the facilities and my draft training programme. There was just one thing he wanted to change and that was to hold our regimental dinner in a castle! Stamford explained that he had been in the TA for over twenty years and Penally Camp was where he had deployed on his first annual camp as a subaltern. The yeomanry squadron he was in at the time had held their squadron dinner at Pembroke Castle. We drove there the next morning and the owner, a retired army major, quickly agreed to the request. The logistics of holding a regimental dinner at the castle were significant. All the food had to be cooked in a field kitchen set up in the grounds for the day. Several generators supplied the electrical power and the power cables had to be laid a distance of 120m up the spiral stone staircases and across the ramparts. Hard work perhaps, but it was a moment to remember when we were led by a piper into our banqueting hall.

In February 1996, HQ 2 Signal Brigade contacted me. They wanted to know if I could still speak Greek. They explained that the annual FINABEL conference was due to take place in Edinburgh and there was a requirement for an escorting officer to be able to speak conversational Greek. FINABEL was an organization promoting cooperation and interoperability between the national armies of the European Union member states. Now I thought this was a great opportunity for me and told the staff officer that my Greek language skills were a little rusty, but if I could be given some time to revise then that wouldn't be a problem. I was told only three weeks were available, did I want the job? Yes, I was your man, I told them.

Three weeks later I drove to Army Headquarters Scotland. I felt self-conscious walking into the five-star Balmoral Hotel in Number 2 Service Dress complete with Sam Browne belt. I reported to the chief of staff, the senior staff officer in the headquarters. He gave me room keys for the Greek delegation and two wrapped presents for the Greek general and his wife. He also gave me a greetings card and a message which he asked me to translate into Greek and write inside the card. Translating 'The General Officer Commanding Army Headquarters Scotland welcomes you to this beautiful country of Scotland in the United Kingdom' was pushing my translation skills a bit too far so I just wrote, 'The Army welcomes you to Scotland'. Even so, it still took me a while to write the message in Greek cursive script.

The next morning the limo driver, a lance corporal in the Royal Logistic Corps, was waiting for me outside the hotel, along with two police outriders on motorbikes. We sped through the traffic for the short drive to Edinburgh Airport. After a short wait, the passengers came through the gate. Suddenly I saw a group of four people walking towards us. The eldest man, who by his mannerisms was obviously the Greek general, was accompanied by a middle-aged woman, who I assumed was his wife. I found out later that the other two were his chief of staff and an interpreter. I saluted, then, speaking in Greek, I introduced myself and the driver to the two-star major general. We continued for several minutes talking in Greek before the general switched to English. It turned out they all spoke English – much to my relief!

We flew the Greek national flag on our black limousine as the police outriders turned on their blue lights and we sped back to the hotel. The highlight of the visit was a formal dinner at Edinburgh Castle, hosted by the Chief of the General Staff (CGS), the professional head of the British Army, who met all the escorting officers before the dinner. General Charles Guthrie welcomed us and reminded us to be on our best behaviour. He then stepped forward for each of us to be introduced to him. I knew that the CGS had served in the SAS and I spotted SAS wings on his mess dress. When he noticed my SAS wings, he asked me what squadron I had served in. When I told him D Squadron he said, 'I was G Squadron! What Troop?' I told him Boat Troop, and he replied, 'That's excellent, I was Boat Troop too!' The CGS carried on talking to me for several minutes before he shook my hand yet again and moved on. General Guthrie went on to become Chief of the Defence Staff, a five-star general, in 1997. I still have the menu card: for the main course we dined on 'Collops of Rannoch Moor Venison'. The Black Watch provided the pipes and drums looking resplendent in their regimental kilts.

Next morning, the motorcycle outriders escorted us as we quickly drove out to Edinburgh Airport. Once more I saluted the general with the limo driver standing to attention beside me. The general said a few words of thanks and presented each of us with a memento. Mission accomplished!

On my return to Army Headquarters Scotland I paid a courtesy call on the senior Royal Signals officer. I knocked on his door and walked in to find that the lieutenant colonel SO1 Comms sitting behind the desk was none other than Paddy, my former squadron commander at 264 (SAS) Signal Squadron. I couldn't stay long but it was great to see Paddy again.

In 1995, all units of 2 Signal Brigade, including 37 Signal Regiment, were issued with the National Communications Radio System (NCRS). The equipment was fitted inside an enclosed trailer towed behind a Land Rover. NCRS was an adaptive high frequency radio system, consisting of a pair of HF radios controlled by a microprocessor. NCRS was a great concept, but it simply didn't have the processing power.

To keep fit, I ran in a military orienteering league on Wednesday afternoons. I also joined a gym in Abergavenny, where I had moved to. Hereford was only thirty minutes away, so I regularly drove there to meet up with friends. I was also within spitting distance of the Brecon Beacons, which is the spiritual home of the SAS and somewhere I often went.

After much discussion with the Royal Signals Officer Manning Office, I agreed to a sideways move in January 1997 as Training Major, 39 (Skinners) Signal Regiment (Volunteers), based in Bristol. The regimental badge was a lynx, to denote affiliation with the Worshipful Company of Skinners.

My new CO, Hugh, was a regular officer, which meant that I had less work to do than if he had been an Army Reserve officer. The role and equipment were identical to my last regiment, so I soon settled in. The regiment had a squadron based in London, another in Banbury, and another regional squadron in Bristol.

Because 2 Signal Brigade had achieved full operational capability with the NCRS system the previous year, it was decided that for 1997 the regiments would be allowed to plan their own training programme for annual camp. This meant that 39 Signal Regiment were planning to carry out annual 'bounty' tests, communications training, and an ambitious escape and evasion exercise. My task was to find a suitable location and write the training programme.

In the meantime I visited Headquarters London District to discuss our Uxbridge squadron. While in London I took the opportunity to visit the

Worshipful Company of Skinners, to which the regiment was affiliated. There I met David Hart Dyke, who was the Clerk and Chief Executive there. David was the former captain of HMS *Coventry* which was attacked and sank in May 1982 in the Falklands War. We briefly discussed the sinking and David remarked that he could remember it like it was yesterday. We quickly moved on to the present day to discuss a planned visit of senior members of the Skinners' Company to annual camp.

In June 1997 I read a signal message requesting an officer to volunteer for two months with G2 (Intelligence) Branch, at Headquarters Multi-National Division South-West (MND (SW)) in Bosnia-Herzegovina. I duly circulated the request, but there were no takers. I suggested that perhaps they would consider me? Luckily, the regular CO was remaining in post until January 1998 and he agreed that I could volunteer. My proposal was accepted and I was given orders to fly out from RAF Brize Norton a couple of weeks after annual camp.

Annual camp took place at Stanford Training Camp, near Thetford in Norfolk. The CO's priority was the escape and evasion exercise that I had put together. The first week was dedicated to the exercise and we had the huge training area to ourselves. The exercise commenced with a training phase. One important aspect of the training was a river crossing. With a safety boat in the water, as well as a rope for the non-swimmers to haul themselves across, we started at first light. The crossing was carried out wearing combat trousers, olive-green T-shirts and training shoes. The only thing which wasn't expected was that all the female soldiers, and there were many, had removed their bras. The cold water meant we had the best impromptu wet T-shirt contest you could imagine.

The officers' annual camp regimental dinner was a great success and our guests included half a dozen stalwarts from the Skinners' Company. I had to smile when one of the old 'buffers' told me about his arrival at the railway station. We had sent a rather attractive female driver in a minibus to pick him up. While making polite conversation on the way to the training area he asked the driver what her civilian job was. Her reply completely dumbfounded him when she told him she was an exotic dancer at a top London club. She even gave him a card with the name and address of the club should he ever wish to see her in action? Yes, we had all sorts of people in the TA! After ticking off annual camp as a job well done it was soon time for me to deploy to Bosnia.

Before I did so, I attended a pre-deployment course on Salisbury Plain. We were divided into eight-man sections for our training. We went for a run each morning before spending hours on the training area practising various training scenarios, including foreign weapons, IEDs, booby traps and anti-personnel mines.

We had several Bosnian interpreters who helped make the training scenarios realistic. We took turns as section commander. Everyone learned how to react when simulated explosions and gunfire were raining down on us and an urgent CASEVAC was required. The interpreters were housed in the Officers' Mess at Westdown Camp. One evening, I asked some of the interpreters to teach me a few words in Serbo-Croat. The first thing they taught me was how to say hello (*zdravo*) and goodbye (*do videnja*). All of the female interpreters were absolute stunners. One of the girls brought me back to earth when she told me that she was an asylum seeker from Sarajevo. She went on to tell me that she had been forced to live in a cellar with her family for over a year as they were under siege by the Bosnian Serb militia. Daily the militia indiscriminately fired artillery shells down into the city. Almost no food could be brought in and the only way out was via a tunnel dug for hundreds of metres to the airport perimeter where an occasional plane landed with medical supplies and took out the most seriously wounded. Sarajevo was blockaded for 1,425 days and 13,952 people were killed during the siege, including 5,434 civilians. What was heartbreaking was, because the interpreters had worked for the British Army in Bosnia, they had all received death threats. They therefore had no choice but to accept the British government's offer and seek asylum in the UK.

The following week saw me fly in a chartered aircraft from RAF Brize Norton to Split Airport in Croatia. The airport was deserted when we arrived there. We were bussed to a reception centre housed in a large villa on the coast. The villa was originally the summer residence of President Tito, the former leader of Yugoslavia. Once we were processed, beds were allocated to us in a large dormitory.

The next morning, I flew by RAF Chinook helicopter to Headquarters Multi Division South-West (MND (SW)) in Banja Luka. We were based in a former metal factory. I was allocated a bed in a two-man sleeping pod. The G2 intelligence branch was led by an Intelligence Corps lieutenant colonel, together with two majors as operational staff officers. It was one of these staff officer appointments that I was to fill for the next two months. MND (SW) was formed as part of the Implementation Force (IFOR), a multi-national peacekeeping force led by NATO, in Bosnia-Herzegovina. In December 1996, IFOR became the Stabilization Force (SFOR), continuing in this role for more than eight years.

I arrived just as the results for the Bosnian municipal elections were being announced and, as a consequence, I had to play 'catch-up'. My role was to cover the '*Republika Srpska*' National Assembly elections and the implementation of the municipal elections results.

My first task every morning was to scan the Bosnian newspapers, armed with a highlighter pen. All of the papers were in Cyrillic script, similar to the Greek script which I already knew. I quickly learnt that there were three main ethnic groupings: Serbs, Croats and Bosniaks. Once I had identified interesting stories, I would mark up the names of the main protagonists and get one of the NCOs to cut the articles out. Then the press cuttings would be sent to the interpreter's office to be translated by late morning. Once the translations were returned to me, I would write a draft analysis of the day's regional news for the SO1 to edit and then brief the divisional commander at the evening briefing. Before the commander's briefing I would set up the 'G2 Conference Call', and then hand over to the SO1. Each battle group's intelligence officer would provide their local intelligence update to the SO1.

I was soon trusted with more interesting work, including visiting opposing forces to gather information or to personally brief senior visitors. Whenever I had the opportunity, before the weather got too bad, two or three of us would book out at the guardroom and go for a run along the roads and tracks. Almost every house in the surrounding countryside had a plum tree orchard and the fruit was made into a plum brandy known as *slivovitz*. I drank it several times while I was in Bosnia and it certainly had a kick to it!

Soon after my arrival, I sent a 'bluey' (military airmail letter) to my brother Tom. I wrote, 'My job is to assess the forthcoming Serbian Republic (of Bosnia) National Assembly Elections which take place on 23 November. I am trying to identify likely flash-points, for example displaced persons returning to their former homes in order to vote. Their homes are by now either destroyed or occupied by people from another ethnic group. This is where my work comes in, to try and prevent further bloodshed.'

The only time I ventured into Banja Luka was when an RMP captain took me on a foot patrol through the old town. We drank coffee on a terrace outside an old restaurant beside the Vrbas River which runs through the town. I smiled and said hello (*Zdravo!*) to everyone as we walked around. Another highlight of working in the G2 (Intelligence) Branch was the opportunity given to me to visit the Malay, Dutch and Czech battle groups in various parts of Bosnia.

The weather quickly deteriorated and soon we had heavy snow. One day I was sent, with an Australian captain, to Sarajevo for a G2 (Intelligence) meeting. We flew to Sarajevo in a Mi-8 Hip helicopter from the Czech armed forces with the return trip in an AAC Lynx helicopter. A snow blizzard caused the return trip to be postponed by twenty-four hours. We were allocated a portable cabin for the night, which unfortunately didn't have any heating, meaning at minus 8 degrees Celsius it was too cold to sleep. Fortunately the Americans had a mess hall operating twenty-four hours a day and as long as you were eating you could stay there all night. We managed to get a table next to the hot-plate and ate very slowly for the next eight hours!

Once the snow settled, the only place to run was around the perimeter road of the metal factory, a distance of about 800 metres. The run was soul-destroying, made worse as there were trucks belching diesel fumes with snow and mud forming an ankle-deep slush. I was out on my daily run when I spotted a senior officer rolling a cigarette. Now you don't see many officers 'rolling their own', and sure enough it was Cedric, my former squadron commander from D Squadron, 22 SAS. Cedric recognized me immediately and nodded, still rolling his cigarette. I spotted him again at 'prayers' that evening in the headquarters where he sat next to the commander to listen to the briefing. It turned out that Cedric was in Banja Luka for a brief visit before taking over in January 1998. He had been appointed GOC 3rd (UK) Division and promoted to major general in July 1996. In December 2000 he was promoted again as Lieutenant General Sir Cedric Delves KBE DSO.

Before my tour ended, I briefed the UK Secretary of State for Defence, the Right Honourable George Robertson (Labour), when he visited HQ MND (SW) at Banja Luka metal factory. Mr Robertson had recently taken over the appointment and seemed genuinely interested in what the intelligence branch had to say about the current situation between the former warring factions. The peace process was proceeding slowly, but I was able to tell him the progress that had been made. Soon it was time to pack and start on the journey home. Unfortunately the weather had grounded all helicopters so it was a trip by bus. This was a long, uncomfortable ride lasting several hours with a brief stop for lunch at a MND (SW) base established in a former bus depot at Mrkonjic Grad. We eventually crossed the border into Croatia and drove to Split. We were once again accommodated overnight at Tito's summer residence. The next morning, we caught a flight from Split airport to the UK.

Returning to work in Bristol was an anti-climax. I had a training area to book once again for annual camp 1998. The planning for this and various weekend exercises kept me occupied.

The Lanyard Trophy was an annual march for Royal Signals units, organized by 216 (Parachute) Signal Squadron with regular army and TA categories. I acted as team manager, with the RSM assisting me. The competition took place along the South Downs Way in May 1998. I led the team and set the pace, assisted by the RSM. Unfortunately he twisted his ankle after six miles and was forced to drop out at the next official checkpoint. This meant we were going very slowly for those four miles. Meanwhile 63 (SAS) Signal Squadron were surging ahead. Slowly, but surely, we reduced the deficit. It was a close call, but 63 (SAS) Signal Squadron held on to their lead and 39 Signal Regiment came in second. My certificate states that the team 'Completed the 40-mile Lanyard Trophy March, carrying 40lb of equipment in a time of 11 Hrs 0 Mins, finishing in second place.'

Royal Signals were having personnel retention issues. The internet revolution was booming, as were the new mobile phone networks springing up across Europe. Finding telecommunications engineers was proving difficult for the various system integrators. Their response was to entice Royal Signals personnel by offering higher salaries than they could achieve by staying in the army. The corps' response was to interview all soldiers who applied for premature voluntary release and persuade them that they would be losing a long-term career for a short-term gain in an uncertain economic climate.

The first person to be interviewed by me under this initiative, Sergeant P, was a radio technician who had already received a job offer. We sat in my office and I drew up a table. First I wrote his current salary in the left-hand column, then I put the new job's salary in the right-hand column, and so on. When we were finished adding details of transport costs, number of days leave, allowances and so on I was gob-smacked. Sergeant P was just an average sergeant to be honest. He had already failed his promotion course and was going nowhere fast in his army career. He also had a partner, but they were unmarried and with a young child. In those days unmarried couples weren't entitled to a subsidized married quarter. His situation was plain to see. Leaving the army would give him a significant increase in basic salary, plus overtime, a company car, and no weekend working. It was a 'no-brainer' for me to sign his release forms and he was overjoyed that he would be able to accept the job offer.

I wiped the board clean and did my own calculations. Next I made a phone call to a former colleague who was working as a telecommunications manager. He told me there was work immediately available and quoted typical salaries for someone of my ability and experience. I thought it over and resigned the next morning.

When the Royal Signals Officer Manning Office asked me why I wanted to leave, I stated truthfully that I would have to wait a minimum of five more years before being considered for promotion to lieutenant colonel. This was too long for me to hang around being posted sideways because there was no career progression path to offer me. It was agreed I would leave in twelve months after completing resettlement training.

Resettlement training is a support system before leaving the armed forces. The Career Transition Partnership (CTP) was set up by the Ministry of Defence to provide free, comprehensive guidance and information for eligible service leavers. CTP helps with free education, retraining and job opportunities, as well as advice on finance, pensions and training grants.

In early 1998, Headquarters 43 (Wessex) Brigade tasked the regiment to host an Exercise Executive Stretch in June 1998. I was quite excited about this as it meant I would be meeting people from local industry. I produced a set of joining instructions which explained that the exercise was designed to enable participants to test themselves through team-building tasks. This would involve leadership, problem solving and decision making under pressure. It further explained that the exercise scenario placed them at a partisan training camp and would simulate training for paramilitary operations in a hostile, fictitious country.

To plan the exercise, I used all my previous knowledge running combat survival and leadership training. Once the exercise commenced, the first twenty-four hours were more or less non-stop. The various training activities included weapon training, tunnel obstacles, night movement, mine clearance, observation, fly-past, drive-past, close-target recce (CTR), and assault course.

Once they had learnt these skills, we moved into the final exercise phase which took most of Sunday morning. The 'executives' were transported in a convoy of trucks and we deliberately drove them into an ambush. Then they made a fighting withdrawal firing blank ammunition and made for a predetermined ERV. Once they arrived at the ERV, they were instructed to make a dash for freedom over the border, which involved a 5km run along the training roads and through the woods until they reached the start of the assault course simulating the border. This was where we included a river crossing to ensure that they finished the exercise soaking wet! The fastest team was presented with a prize and everyone received a finishing certificate.

Straight after Executive Stretch, we deployed for annual camp at Swynnerton Training Camp. Located in Staffordshire, it consists of a camp and large training area. My plan called for the regiment to separate into comms detachments deployed all over southern England, gradually getting closer to Swynnerton each night. They all arrived in Swynnerton Camp after four days, which then gave us ten days for a regimental battle camp. On our last day, we held a cross-country race around the training area, followed by a regimental BBQ where much beer was consumed.

Soon it was 1999 and my final six months in the army. I enrolled on a part-time course in business management at the University of Hereford. After passing the course with distinction, I was accepted to study for a Master of Business (MBA) degree at the University of Gloucestershire. I was also allocated a place on a Higher National Diploma (HND) in telecommunications engineering with Blackburn University, which offered a part-time course for service leavers. Several modules required me to attend short courses at Blackburn University. The most challenging courses for me were the advanced 'Maths 1' and 'Maths 2' modules. The standard of maths was higher than GCE 'A' Level, so I needed all my brain cells for it!

I started applying for jobs during my last three months in the army. This led to Cable & Wireless inviting me for an interview. This went well and I was offered a management position. In the mid-1980s, Cable & Wireless became the first UK company to offer an alternative to British Telecom's monopoly. After checking with Royal Signals Officer Manning Office, a start-date was agreed.

I decided that it would be a good safety net for me to join the TA on leaving the regular army. I approached HQ 2 Signal Brigade and was offered a staff officer's appointment in the role of SO2 G3 Operations and Training. The advantages of being part of the headquarters meant we only trained one weekend each month without having to attend a weekly drill night. For my farewell party, I invited all the permanent staff from Horfield Common TA Centre to join me on a pub crawl along Whiteladies Road in Bristol. The next morning, I said farewell to all the staff. I had served thirty years in the regular army, including thirteen years at Hereford.

Chapter 11

Civilian Life – Bracknell to Baghdad

I started work at Cable & Wireless in July 1999. Based in Bracknell, I managed a team of engineers ensuring the digital trunk network was used to best advantage. We would carry out system modelling using bespoke computer software to 'stress test' the network. Cable & Wireless paid me well and gave me a very good relocation package. I had no intention of moving house, so instead purchased a second-hand caravan and rented a pitch not far from Bracknell. I normally worked ten-hour days, driving home at the weekends. Late each evening I studied for my MBA. While the salary and perks were excellent, I hated the job. As soon as I got a job offer which allowed me to live at home, I moved on. I also spent one weekend every month with HQ 2 Signal Brigade in my role as an Army Reserve officer.

I moved to Chronos Technology in May 2000 as an Account Manager. Chronos was a forty-five-minute commute from my home near Abergavenny. The perks included a company car with unlimited mileage. My clients were mainly mobile phone companies in the UK and Europe and I earned sales commission. My first trip to the Republic of Ireland was interesting. For personal security, I never mentioned my military background. Initially, I flew direct to Dublin, but as my client base started to expand and include companies in Belfast it wasn't long before I started flying into Belfast City Airport. I would rent a car in Belfast and later the same day drive across the border. It seemed surreal driving through South Armagh, passing road signs for Newry, Bessbrook, Warrenpoint and Crossmaglen. These were all former places that I had travelled to when operating undercover all those years before in the SAS. The route continued past Dundalk to Dublin.

In November 2001, I attended the graduation ceremony at the University of Gloucestershire to accept an MBA degree. The following year I was awarded an HND in telecommunications engineering from

Blackburn University. I surprised myself by passing the maths modules without scrambling my brains!

I received generous commission during my first two years at Chronos and easily surpassed my sales target, including the largest single order received by the company up to that date. Chronos Technology was a great place to work and I liked all the overseas travel involved, including Europe and the United States.

At this time Tranmere were doing fine in League Two, but when I went to watch them at Cheltenham on 4 February 2003 they lost by three goals to one. One of our players at this time was Iain Hume, a Canadian forward who we sold in 2005 for £500,000.

In February 2003 I was attending a 2 Signal Brigade study weekend, when the Signals-Officer-in-Chief (SOinC) informed us that the invasion of Iraq by coalition troops was imminent. One month later, a combined force from the United States, Great Britain and other coalition countries invaded Iraq and toppled the brutal regime of Saddam Hussein. The euphoria of victory was followed by a period of great instability. Soon the first security companies started to operate in Iraq, offering protection for clients trying to do business in the chaotic situation left behind after the invasion.

While all this was going on, the UK was suffering from a recession. It started to bite in my sector in mid-2003 and sales dried up overnight. It soon became obvious that we had too many account managers chasing non-existent sales. My salary took a nosedive as I was surviving on basic pay without commission. In February 2004 I took the redundancy package on offer.

I soon found a job via the SAS 'old boy network'. The job was working in Iraq as a watchkeeper for a private security company (PSC). Many former SAS officers and soldiers were on the 'The Circuit' providing close protection (CP). Soon after the invasion of Iraq, there was a huge surge in demand for CP operatives to provide support to the Coalition Provisional Authority (CPA) and international companies who were setting up shop. These companies all required security to enable them to do their jobs. The security teams, in turn, required radio and satellite communications. This was my speciality, working as a watchkeeper for Control Risks Group (CRG). The CP operatives deployed in Iraq needed a highly specialized skills set and carried a variety of personal weapons.

As instructed, I reported to the CRG office in London. Once all had arrived, we completed our induction session. The person in charge, Dave, ex-SAS, recognized me and came over to say hello. Immediately after the form-filling we boarded a waiting bus which took us to RAF Brize Norton. The CRG group soon bonded in the bar at Gateway House transit accommodation. One by one we introduced ourselves and I quickly learnt that six of us were to travel to Basra and the remainder were flying on to Baghdad. We were flying out on an RAF flight as it was a Foreign & Commonwealth Office (FCO) contract.

We were woken early the next morning and met up for breakfast. Several hours later we took off in a VC-10 air trooping aircraft to RAF Akrotiri. After landing we were driven to a transit building, where we rested on bunk beds with 'piss-proof' mattress covers. We were kept waiting, with only lunch and dinner to relieve the monotony. Eventually we were taken under cover of darkness to a C130. The RAF pilot announced before take-off that we were flying first to Basra Airport and those travelling on to Baghdad International Airport (BIAP) were to remain seated as the aircraft would remain on the ground for just a few minutes. We were also instructed to wear one set of the body armour provided and sit on a second set once we entered Iraqi airspace. All interior and exterior lights were switched off thirty minutes before landing. Without warning, far above Basra Airport, the pilot put the plane into an alarming corkscrew dive and then banged off the chaff dispensers and flares which offer some protection against any surface-to-air missile threat. Once on the ground, we were escorted into the empty passenger terminal and told to get some sleep on the camp beds provided.

The next morning, a CP team arrived to take us to Basra Palace. I recognized the team leader, Scottie, who was formerly in D Squadron, 22 SAS. We were issued with body armour and instructed to put it on. I discovered that I was in Scottie's vehicle. Scottie told me that he had seen my name on the flight manifest and handed me a loaded Browning Hi-Power 9mm handgun for my personal protection. We drove hard and fast in a three-vehicle convoy to Basra Palace.

Basra Palace is a large complex containing several palaces and many other grandiose buildings. The entire area was surrounded on three sides by 12ft high concrete walls extending around the perimeter for almost four kilometres. The concrete walls had built-in sangars every hundred metres. The complex was fronted by an artificial marina resembling saltwater lagoons with direct access to the Shatt al-Arab waterway which fronts the palace complex. The Shatt-al-Arab is formed by the confluence of the Euphrates and the Tigris and discharges into the Arabian Gulf. There was plenty to keep the British troops occupied as 1 Mechanised Brigade were busy taking over from 20 Armoured Brigade heading up Multi-National Division South-East (MND (SE)).

The CRG personnel were accommodated in portable containers with two men sharing each room. We ate in a prefabricated dining hall, where the daily menu included several choices of well-prepared food, including steaks, fresh fruit and salads. We also had a fully equipped gym with air-conditioning.

My first three days in the country were spent on an induction course. I was issued a Browning Hi-Power pistol and an AK-47 assault rifle and, after refresher training, we went to the improvised range where I test-fired both weapons. We also had lessons in battlefield trauma, contact drills and IEDs. In the evenings I learnt my job in the ops room, where I discovered that we had good VHF coverage around Basra city, but very little beyond the city in the VHF band. This made it necessary to use HF radios for travelling between Basra and our outposts at Al Amarah and Nasiriyah. While the HF radios extended our range, they were prone to interference. CRG's task was to escort members of the Coalition Provisional Authority (CPA) to various locations to identify projects where they could assist the Iraqis to rebuild their nation. The CPA staff included UK members from the Department for International Development (DFID). The CPA acted as the transitional government of Iraq and was created and funded by the US Department of Defense. The CPA was divided into four regions including CPA Central (Baghdad) and CPA South (Basra). The CPA awarded contracts for reconstruction projects, but the coalition military were overstretched and unable to provide security.

I would unlock the CRG ops room at 6 am and phone the HQ MND (SE) ops room for a SITREP covering any terrorist activity that had occurred overnight. I would then copy this SITREP onto a whiteboard for all callsigns to read before deploying on their tasks. I would also mark up the ops room maps with 'no-go' areas. I was introduced to the army ops room staff and was pleased to recognize some of them as this would simplify liaison. They were very supportive, and when I spotted their data terminals giving them the ability to send emails via this secure 'intranet', I asked if we could have one of the terminals for our ops room. I do love operational environments, as decisions are made quickly without any of the bullshit that occurs in a peacetime scenario. The next morning, I was on the roof assembling a telescopic mast to support the antenna that would give us 'line-of-sight' to HQ MND (SE). The Royal Signals installation team soon arrived with the antenna and data terminal. Within the hour we had a secure means of communicating with HQ MND (SE) without the need for phone calls.

A typical day with CRG would see our armoured Toyota Landcruisers, normally operating as a three-vehicle callsign, deploy with several CPA clients on board either to a construction site or a meeting with Iraqi officials anywhere in south-east Iraq. I was soon to discover that Iraq was a dysfunctional country. By the end of my first month, I had already visited Al Amarah and Nasiriyah. The CPA building at Nasiriyah was inside a British Army FOB on the banks of the Euphrates River about 370km southeast of Baghdad. Al Amarah is situated on the Tigris River about 50km from the Iranian border. These two towns each had a small CPA staff and their CRG security team co-located with the coalition military.

My first leave came around quickly. We were driven to the Kuwaiti border. From there one of our 'fixers' was waiting to drive us to Kuwait City. It felt very strange to be in a luxury hotel. Once inside the hotel room, I stared at myself in the mirror, noticing the dried salt on my shirt from where I had been wearing body armour on the journey to the border. My hair and clothes were covered in fine dust. Kuwait has a total ban on alcohol, so for something to do we walked across the road to a beach café. There was a small group of rich Kuwaitis on jet skis trying to impress the few girls in bikinis brave enough to sit on the beach. Anyway, it was nice to relax and eat ice-cream in an air-conditioned café.

My leave was quite surreal as I had rather a lot of money in the bank and no real aim. The obvious choice was to hit the gym and I went every day plus a walk over the Brecon Beacons. While I was on leave, I received an email from CRG advising me that I had been promoted to TL (Comms). Soon it was time for my flight back to Kuwait via Dubai. The CRG 'fixer' met me at the airport and took me to the hotel. Early the next morning, the fixer drove me to the Iraq border. It was good to see the CRG guys waiting for me.

My new role included providing comms training to all new arrivals as part of their induction training. One of my priorities was to improve VHF communications as we had to rely on the unreliable and noisy HF frequency band as soon as we moved away from the city. I partly solved the problem by installing a VHF repeater station at Az Zubayr base. The base had a British infantry company located there to provide protection to a small team of British civilian police instructors who were training members of the new Iraqi police force. At midday a British army warrant officer came over for a chat and invited us into the army cook-tent for some lunch. It was great fun to be sitting amongst the soldiers. We were all sweating our bollocks off, while eating steak and kidney pie, instant mashed potato and mushy peas, washed down with a pint mug of tea. The next day I drove around carrying out the comms tests with a second vehicle providing close protection. I was pleased that we had much better comms towards the Kuwaiti border and all the dodgy areas now had workable comms. This was another plus for me and I was thanked for my efforts by the CRG country manager. Soon he flew down from Baghdad to visit us in Basra, and although I didn't know it at the time, he was sizing me up for another promotion.

I was manning the CRG Ops Room in Basra Palace a week later when I received an urgent call over the radio from the British civilian police instructor at Az Zubayr who I had provided with a radio in case they ever needed anything from us. He informed me that they had just had a suicide bomber blow himself up at the front gate and they required urgent medical assistance to deal with the casualties. I immediately contacted the ops room at HQ MND (SE), but they had already tasked a helicopter Medical Emergency Response Team to evacuate the casualties.

CRG were informed that the CPA was to be dissolved on 28 June and we would continue to work with the FCO and DFID. A British embassy was to be established inside the Green Zone and British consulates inside the Basra Palace site and Kirkuk in northern Iraq. Soon afterwards, CRG were tasked to assist the CPA officials at the Pink Palace in Al Amarah to withdraw back to Basra Palace and recover the comms equipment. As the TL (Comms), I had to prioritize what comms equipment was to be retrieved and what would be destroyed in-situ. I had a three-vehicle CP team to assist me in the task. First of all, we reported to 1 PWRR Battle Group at Camp Abu Naji, a few kilometres from the Pink Palace. We were told to complete our task before last light as sniping by Mahdi militia often took place at dusk. On arrival at the Pink Palace, I organised the CP team in removing antennas and stowing radio equipment and desktop computers in the vehicles. I knew we would be short of space so the CP team had been reduced by one man per vehicle to give us additional loading capacity and this shortfall was taken up by incorporating me and the other comms guy into the CP team. Within a couple of hours, all the high value items were on board the three vehicles. We burnt all the paperwork and destroyed everything else remaining. I gave the office furniture to the soldiers from 1 PWRR in case it might be of use to them. 1 PWRR were manning the nearby CIMIC House and providing the perimeter defence for the whole compound. The trip back was uneventful and I was pleased that we had managed to recover all the valuable items. The location had been the former office complex and residence of the Ba'ath Party governor of Maysan province. The Pink Palace became the seat of local government from August 2004, after the dissolution of the CPA. Al Amarah was manned by fewer than ninety soldiers of 1 PWRR. During the 'CIMIC House Siege' these soldiers faced approximately 500 'Mahdi Army' militia who mounted eighty-six assaults on the compound over a period of twenty-three days in August 2004. In defending the compound, the British faced incoming fire from RPG and 107mm rockets and replied with 33,000 rounds and countless 81mm mortar bombs.

During my second spell of leave I received an email from the country manager. He had promoted me to the post of Comms Manager (Iraq) and I was to move to Baghdad after spending one week in Basra handing over to the new TL (Comms). I had a busy week in Basra as the CPA had ceased operations and a British consulate was being established nearby. CRG were given space in the basement of the new building to set up an ops room. Meanwhile, it was time for me to leave and start my new job in Baghdad.

I was escorted by a CP team to the front doors of the departure lounge at Basra Airport. The 'sniffer' dogs checked my bags for explosives and my name was checked against the flight manifest. The passenger terminal had seen better days, but I managed to get a cup of coffee. The one-hour flight up to Baghdad was in a C130. It was the same procedure as the landing at Basra four months earlier. We arrived over BIAP at high altitude, and then after a violent, gut-wrenching, corkscrew manoeuvre, landed far below us two minutes later. Once inside the passenger terminal we met up with the CRG team leader waiting for us. He handed me an MP5 and body armour. Once the CRG callsign had loaded up its passengers, namely two clients and me, our three Landcruisers were ready to drive the 12km from BIAP to the Green Zone along the military Main Supply Route, designated Route Irish. There were frequent roadside bombs, suicide bombers driving into manned checkpoints, and drive-by shootings to contend with on Route Irish.

The Green Zone is the most commonly used term for the International Zone in Baghdad. It was taken over by the Americans in 2003 as the governmental centre of the CPA. There are a number of palaces, military barracks, government ministries, hotels and residences. The first thing I noticed on arriving at the Green Zone was an enormous M1 Abrams main battle tank facing the ongoing line of traffic waiting to enter the zone. The Americans were clearly taking no chances. There were also machine guns set up inside concrete, sand-bagged sangars and rows of Jersey walls, Bremer walls and Hesco containers packed with sand. The high Bremer walls prevented us from being shot by snipers from most angles, which was reassuring. There were also a couple of MD530 'Little Bird' helicopters flying overhead, operated by Blackwater Security Consulting, a private military company contracted by the US government. Soon we arrived at the CRG compound, which was also surrounded by Bremer walls to provide a simple and effective perimeter. The compound contained fairly basic accommodation. Each portable building had two rooms raised on top of concrete blocks and a roof covered in two layers of sandbags filled with sand to provide protection from mortars and rockets fired by insurgents into the Green Zone. The area of the Green Zone is roughly ten square kilometres and there are only a few entry points, including the July 14 Bridge over the River Tigris. The American and British Embassies are also inside the Green Zone.

Within an hour of my arrival in the Green Zone, I had signed for my MP5 and Glock 17 handgun. I was allocated a bed-space in the signals basha next to the window. Now the problem with that particular bed-space was that there were no sandbags in front of the glass window whereas the outside walls had sandbags up to a height of 4ft. This meant that if a mortar landed next to the basha while we were sleeping, in all probability the double row of sandbags on the roof and outside the walls would protect us, but only if we kept away from the window. Luckily I was able to get a bed-space well away from the window after a few days.

I was taking over from Andy, the other comms manager, and my 'back-to-back', meaning one of us was always in country able to make executive decisions, due to the practice of job-sharing. Andy had four days to hand over to me before he departed. The plan was he would return after four weeks to relieve me. Andy introduced me to the comms team. I already knew Andy and three others, all ex-264, and good guys to be around. Then I met our ex-RAF radio technician, who was doing a great job in difficult conditions. The final member was Faisal, a computer technician maintaining all our IT equipment. Faisal had been born in Dubai to Pakistani parents. Andy also took me through the recruiting process as we had two vacancies that needed filling. Then it was a visit to the ops room where I met the ops manager, ex-SAS of course. The watchkeeper showed me the wall maps covering our area of operations and I listened to the radio nets as the CP teams went about their business of escorting clients around Baghdad and further afield.

The next day I signed for all the radios and computers as I was now responsible for their distribution, repair and maintenance. Afterwards we visited CRG locations in the city and near the airport. We had several locations in other towns, but the plan was that I would visit these with the country manager. Soon it was time to shake Andy's hand and wish him a safe journey home. The first thing Andy did on his arrival back in the UK was to resign, as he had another job lined up! Fortunately, Danny stepped up to the mark and was promoted as my back-to-back. There was a lot of this poaching between private security companies (PSC). CRG were reluctant to lose any more comms managers so Danny and I were given a pay-rise to persuade us to stay!

I was now responsible for providing comms and IT support at country level for 400 private security contractors. Additionally, I had direct responsibility for recruiting and on-the-job training of sixty watch-keepers, communications and IT specialists spread across six contracts and fourteen locations. My role included the manning of all ops rooms, technical surveys, comms and IT equipment procurement, installation and maintenance. I also had several comms and IT-related projects to manage at different locations in Iraq. Every time I left the Green Zone I 'tooled up' with my MP5 and Glock 17.

It soon became apparent that the MP5 had limited range due to its 9mm calibre. Eventually I was able to replace it with a SIG 551 Assault Rifle with folding stock. This was a much better weapon for the situation, as it was small, lightweight, and with high-velocity 5.56mm calibre. I was also trained on the Minimi machine gun, which was carried in each vehicle as a support weapon.

It was quite eerie the first time I left the Green Zone. Sunni and Shia Muslims lived in a divided city. There would be Iraqi vehicle checkpoints everywhere. The armed militia at these roadblocks always waved us through with nothing more than a cursory glance. Despite this, as you saw people looking down at you from roof-tops you never quite knew if you were going to drive into an ambush. My first trip downtown was to visit the Netherlands embassy, which had a Dutch (all ex-special forces) CRG CP team looking after the ambassador. They had some difficulty communicating with our ops room in the Green Zone. I soon repositioned their VHF antenna on the roof and also replaced a corroded coax cable. The ambassador thanked me personally for restoring their radio comms.

I still had two watchkeepers to recruit and eventually recruited a couple of former members of 152 Signal Squadron (SASR) attached to the Australian SAS Regiment.

We lost a CRG CP operative, Mark Carman, and an oil consultant, Bob Morgan, working for the FCO to a roadside IED on 24 May 2004.

Faisal, the IT technician, came to see me one day to complain about his accommodation. He was housed in the 'transit room' crammed full with bunk beds. Most guys were only there for one night before flying home on leave. Faisal wasn't getting any sleep as the guys would keep the lights on all night and drink cans of beer sitting on the bottom bunks. To solve the problem, I moved Faisal into my basha in the bed-space by the window that I had occupied on my first night in the Green Zone. All went well for a week and then Faisal came to see me in a state of agitation. The guys had told him he would be the first to get shot if we were ever attacked as the window was next to his bed. His request was simple. He wanted a handgun to keep under his pillow! Now the last thing I needed was someone handling a loaded gun while unaccustomed to weapons. He wasn't happy when I turned him down. However, Faisal bounced back the next day when he bought a lethal looking Arabic *jambiya* dagger. Some of the guys started coaching Faisal in our makeshift gym. Soon his muscles were bulging and he was no longer the puny guy of a few months earlier. Incidentally, we had many mortar attacks on the Green Zone during this period, including some falling very close to our compound. The day after the increased mortar activity began, Faisal lined his bedsprings with a layer of sandbags, raised the bed on blocks and slept on his mattress under the bed. This was a basic but effective defence from mortar attack. Faisal slept under his bed for a several weeks until the mortar attacks abated and we all came through unscathed.

Even though the terrorist threat was assessed as very high, my first trip to Kirkuk, in Northern Iraq, was by road as no aircraft were available. We drove to Kirkuk and then onwards to Erbil. At this time the British consulate was in the US compound at Kirkuk, on the edge of the autonomous region of Kurdistan. There was no love lost between the Iraqi Arabs and the Kurds. We carried out rehearsals before leaving the Green Zone, including 'actions on' drills for IED, ambush and vehicle breakdown. The main purpose of my visit to these areas was to meet the TL (Comms) at each of the CRG locations. Our route was directly north and the only time we stopped was at an armed checkpoint manned by Iraqi Kurds who welcomed us to Kurdistan. We followed the road north before turning off the highway to reach Kirkuk Airbase. In 2004 the airbase was home to the USAF 506th Air Expeditionary Group.

After an overnight stay at the airbase, where CRG had a large presence, we drove to the US compound on the other side of Kirkuk City. Just as we arrived at the compound housing the American and British consulates, we heard the sound of a large explosion nearby and could see a huge cloud of black smoke drifting skywards. Soon we heard over the radio that a nearby church had been bombed.

The next day we drove to Erbil and discovered that most of the PSCs were located in two rows of villas that had been surrounded by Bremer walls to create a compound. There were Kurdish security men paid for by the PSCs who were armed with AK-47s and machine guns to ensure only those who were welcome got into the street. The various PSCs had a common defence plan and were able to muster about forty CP operatives between them to respond to any attack on the compound. After meeting the CRG team, I replaced some faulty communications equipment. Next I assisted the comms watchkeeper to extend the CRG intranet with a point-to-point wireless link between the two CRG villas. The work was soon completed to everyone's satisfaction and we ate a takeaway meal. During the night I heard automatic gunfire in the distance, but had no problems getting to sleep.

Early the next morning we set off back to Baghdad. The three vehicles were making good time and soon we were back on the main highway to Baghdad. With 85km still to go, one of the vehicles broke down and came to a halt just off the road. As rehearsed, we placed the three vehicles in a triangular formation and adopted all-round defence with our three Minimi machine guns and personal weapons pointing outwards. We were unable to repair the Landcruiser and so we carried out a map appreciation to locate the nearest friendly base. This was FOB Spartan, 30km to the south of us. We decided to tow the vehicle there in the middle of our three-vehicle convoy. Meanwhile, a hostile crowd of young men on motorbikes arrived. They were making shooting and throat-cutting gestures. A couple of the motorbikes raced off northwards and we assessed they were going to collect weapons. We quickly attached a tow-rope and started towing the vehicle towards FOB Spartan with me in the disabled vehicle. We had agreed that if anyone rode alongside the vehicle, we would do nothing unless they produced weapons, at which point we intended to slightly lower our bulletproof windows and spray them with automatic fire.

At first things went fine, but soon the towing vehicle started to overheat. The motorbikes caught up and we readied our weapons to fire. Luckily, a US military patrol in several armoured vehicles arrived and the motorbikes made a hasty retreat. The Americans escorted us into FOB Spartan where we had a meal and refuelled the two good vehicles. We left the broken-down vehicle behind and it was recovered a few days later. We crammed everyone into the two vehicles and safely returned to the Green Zone in Baghdad. We had a bit of luck being so close to FOB Spartan, others were not so lucky, and the number of CP operatives killed continued to rise.

I was responsible for issuing the CP operatives with a mobile phone, complete with a prepaid scratch card. I would normally visit either the Green Zone Café or the 'sooq' to buy phones and extra 'top-up' cards. I was delayed one morning when I needed to purchase more items. That was lucky for me as both locations were blown up by suicide bombers that morning in October 2004. The bombings resulted in much loss of life and many more seriously wounded. One of our guys who worked at a clients' compound next to the *sooq* summed up the devastation when he said he opened the office door to be confronted by small piles of burning debris and in the midst of all of this was a human leg with a boot still attached to the foot. Anyway, that was the end of the café and *sooq* as neither reopened. After that I used to get our camp manager, an Iraqi, to buy these items for us in the Karada district across the July 14 Bridge. This worked well until he was kidnapped and shot dead after being held in captivity. CRG used go-betweens to negotiate with the kidnappers, but unfortunately the kidnappers decided to make an example of him for collaborating with foreigners.

I was travelling home on leave on 5 November 2004 and landed at Cardiff airport. Faisal was with me to attend an IT course at the CRG head office in London. We had obtained a letter on headed notepaper from the British embassy in Baghdad stating 'To whom it may concern' that Faisal was an IT contractor working at the embassy as a member of the CRG team. The letter also stated that the British embassy needed Faisal to attend a course in London prior to new servers being installed. On account of this would the immigration services admit Faisal into the UK without a visa as he was vital to the essential services being provided by the embassy. Finally the letter said he would be escorted at all times by me. This did the trick and we cleared immigration. We travelled to my home and later that evening went to a bonfire night celebration at the village hall. We were inside the hall eating curry and drinking beer when suddenly the fireworks display started with several very loud bangs. A few eyebrows were raised when Faisal dived under a table and dragged a woman underneath with him!

I now had the job of keeping Faisal entertained before his course started. The next morning, we drove to the Big Pit National Coal Museum at Blaenavon, and I was able to show Faisal what a former working coal mine looked like. He really enjoyed the visit and asked lots of questions. After an informative tour underground, we emerged into daylight feeling ravenously hungry. We made our way into the former miners' canteen to check what was available for lunch. The choice was fairly limited, but

Faisal looked at the old-fashioned menu and chose faggots in gravy, with mashed potatoes and peas. Now a Muslim shouldn't be eating pork, but I wasn't thinking and soon we were tucking into the wholesome food. It was only when Faisal announced to me that he had just eaten the best 'minced beef' of his entire life, that I realized perhaps I should remain silent on what had been on his plate!

I had no intention of escorting Faisal for the first week of my leave until his course started, despite what it said on the letter. I made a phone call and then gave Faisal a lift halfway to London and handed him over to one of our guys who was on leave and lived near London. Faisal was dropped on the outskirts of London with instructions on how to get to the CRG head office. I was more than a bit concerned about how he might get on. Fortunately, I heard about ten days later that he had made it safely back to Baghdad. I now had my own course to attend. This was the Risk & Security Manager course held at the Royal Military College of Science at Shrivenham sponsored by Cranfield University.

It wasn't long before I had more technical problems to solve. One issue was we needed a way to track our vehicles, and I knew that a GPS system could achieve this via satnav. What we needed was an active satnav transponder that not only showed the vehicle commander exactly where they were but would also 'ping' their location so that we could track the callsigns from the ops room. Eventually we bought several of these devices and it helped keep everyone safe.

Another urgent requirement was for internet access at all CRG compounds across Iraq. We achieved this by installing VSAT satellite equipment at each location. The VSAT technology is a means of providing a broadband internet connection via satellite. Our first VSATs were installed by an American company before my arrival. I ordered additional VSATs for new locations and also upgraded existing systems to increase bandwidth. As the situation became more dangerous on the ground the American company finally shut up shop and returned home several million dollars richer. To solve the problem of how to maintain the system, I placed an order for phone support and forty-eight-hour airfreight from the United States, using FedEx who were still flying into Baghdad Airport at the time. I soon learnt how to install the satellite dishes and set up the terminal equipment to provide the broadband connection.

We must have saved CRG a small fortune on VSAT installation with this DIY approach. One example was Australia House, the CRG team house in the Green Zone that looked after the Australian embassy. The team, mostly former Australian SASR, looked after the Australian diplomatic staff whenever they ventured outside the Green Zone. Australia House was situated on a road full of large villas. One day the ops manager was making a cup of coffee in the kitchen while looking out of the window when a car bomb exploded outside. The trees along the street-front took most of the blast, but the force of the explosion still blew the window out and the pane of glass hit him full in the face. Luckily for him, CRG had recently covered the window panes with anti-blast film. This kept the glass in one piece, so rather than pierce his body with hundreds of glass fragments, the sandwiched pane hit him full in the face. This gave him a couple of black eyes and a ringing noise in his ears for the next few days. We were prompted by this to bring the team into the main CRG compound. I then recovered all the VSAT equipment, including the large satellite dish from the roof.

It was about this time that we had a visit from Sir Michael Rose, a director at CRG. Mike Rose was my former CO at 22 SAS during the Falklands War. It gave me great pleasure to brief him on the comms and electronic countermeasures available to CRG. He took great interest in all that was taking place and was a great boost to our morale in what was a particularly difficult period in Iraq.

CRG paid for a lavish meal on Christmas Day at the Al-Rashid Hotel inside the Green Zone, where over one hundred CRG staff sat down to a rather bizarre meal in which every dish was served cold, including chicken legs, steak, and lamb kebabs. At least there was plenty of beer to drink! Before Christmas lunch, we posed for a group photograph under the 'Arc of Triumph'. These are actually two triumphal arches, each consisting of a pair of hands holding cross-swords. They serve as the two entrances to the parade ground constructed to commemorate the Iran-Iraq War.

In early 2005, I accompanied the CRG country manager on a flight to Kirkuk. By this time the road journey to Kirkuk was considered too dangerous. Instead we were driven up Route Irish by a CRG callsign. On arrival at BIAP, we caught a plane chartered by CRG. It was an Antonov-24 which flew in from Dubai via Basra. The Russian crew of three didn't say much. The flight engineer, dressed in dirty overalls, pointed to a water boiler and brew-kit in the tiny galley. The coffee, cream and sugar sachets were from American military MRE ration packs, so no expense was spared! Once we were over Kirkuk airfield, we took the normal high-altitude corkscrew landing pattern before coming down to land beside a row of USAF C130s and several helicopters. I was shown around by Bruce, ex-264, who was the TL (Comms). Everything was fine and I attended 'prayers' that night in the briefing room and met all the CRG CP teams. The next day we flew back in the Antonov-24, which had returned to collect us.

We were having a beer in the open-air one evening when the Green Zone came under attack. There was an almighty bang directly above us, and then a split-second later came the sound of a huge explosion. A 'Katyusha' rocket had brushed the palm tree next to us with its tail fin bringing a few palm fronds down on us while knocking the rocket off course. The rocket crashed on some waste ground nearby and our perimeter wall absorbed most of the blast. That was a close call! Thereafter rockets fell inside the Green Zone almost every day and night for a period of several weeks.

The CPA had transferred power to the Iraqi Interim government on 28 June 2004 and this gave the impetus for the various coalition partner nations to establish embassies in Baghdad and consulates in Basra and elsewhere. The security situation in Basra was quite tense at this time. On arrival, I was pleased to meet up with Mac, ex-D Squadron, 22 SAS, who I knew well. Mac had recently been promoted to the post of Ops Manager in Basra. Meanwhile, Tony, the TL (Comms), arrived and showed me all the improvements since I had departed. Extensive renovation of the British consulate building was progressing at a fast pace. It was a former palace built during Saddam Hussein's presidency, with a large basement and a flat concrete roof with an ornate dome at one end. FCO staff had already transferred from the CPA to the new British consulate and more arrivals were imminent. We ate together in the new prefabricated dining hall behind the main building. This was located alongside the sleeping accommodation cabins, newly installed for the FCO staff and CRG team. After lunch Mac went off to deal with a query from one of our callsigns up in Nasiriyah. Meanwhile Tony and I walked around the side of the building to look at the standby generators. Suddenly, I spotted a huge pile of headstones from graves stacked up in neat piles on a piece of waste ground beside the consulate building. I immediately recognised these as headstones from a Commonwealth war cemetery. Tony told me that he had heard they had recently been brought here for safekeeping after the Basra war cemetery, which was full of British and Indian army graves, had been vandalised.

On 30 July 2005 there was an incident at Basra of a command-wire roadside improvised explosive device (IED) causing fatalities to two CRG personnel, Andrew Holloway and Ken Hull. It was a sad day for all of us.

The British consulate remained at Basra Palace, until they were forced to evacuate at the end of October 2006. This was after experiencing regular mortar attacks over the previous two months. The evacuation took place by military helicopters over a period of one week. The situation thwarted the investment efforts of DFID and delayed further progress in rebuilding regional infrastructure in the southern governorate.

The US military equipped their vehicles with electronic countermeasures (ECM) equipment to counter the radio-controlled improvised incendiary device (RCIED) threat. The ECM equipment jammed mobile phone signals in a 'bubble' around the transmitter which prevented RCIEDs from being initiated in the vicinity of the vehicle. Soon the American PSCs followed suit. CRG was forced to acquire similar equipment or be left behind. I was sent to England on a course to learn all about the new equipment. I returned to Baghdad with two civilian technicians who were only too keen to work sixteen hours a day, finish the job and get the fuck out of Iraq leaving me to keep the items running smoothly. I spent the following week training all our CP operatives on the ECM equipment, which proved highly effective in countering the RCIED threat.

To avoid the risk of driving around Baghdad, we used coalition helicopters whenever possible. I had a few rides out to BIAP on board US Blackhawk helicopters which flew below 200 feet all the way to the airport, frequently changing course to try to avoid any shoulder-launched missiles locking on to them. The RAF were also flying the same route with a couple of Puma helicopters. One day I was going on leave and we flew out to the airport in one of the RAF Pumas with the other Puma flying in tandem close behind us. We were really low, probably below a hundred feet, and it seemed at times like the pilot was pulling up ever so slightly to clear the lines of washing fluttering on the Baghdad roofs. There was also a couple of American Blackhawks to starboard flying a bit higher. The two Pumas landed at BIAP and the Blackhawks followed suit and landed beside us. At this point, the American pilots walked over to us and one of them said something like 'Damn! That was what I call fucking seriously low flying! I would like to meet the dude flying your helo so that I can shake him by the hand!' After a few moments our short, slightly overweight pilot climbed down to meet them, and pulled off her helmet. The look of astonishment on the Americans' faces when they realized our RAF pilot was a female was priceless!

We decided to have a New Year's Eve party in the CRG compound. An outdoor bar was set up and a sound system appeared from somewhere. We also set up a large BBQ grill that turned out steaks and burgers non-stop. I volunteered to work behind the bar all night long. We invited our friends from other security companies and a few influential people from around the Green Zone. There must have been about 200 people present. Later that evening, about ten US marines decided to gatecrash our party. They were subject to the US military's 'General Order No. 1' which specifically prohibited 'possessing, consuming, introducing, purchasing, selling, transferring or manufacturing any alcoholic beverage…by military personnel or civilians serving with the Armed Forces of the United States…and present for duty in Iraq.' Now the CRG duty officer told the US marines that as they were dressed in civilian clothes he would let them in and if they wanted to have a few beers that was fine but not to kick the arse out of it. Anyway, soon after midnight I witnessed a scuffle between Faisal my IT technician, all five feet six inches of him, and one of the marines. It turned out the marine was very drunk and had made adverse comments about Faisal's height, his skin colour and his religion. Faisal was no pushover, having been coached by the CRG guys in weightlifting and boxing for the last year, and he did the right thing and stuck one on the American who went down. But instead of staying down the American came up fighting and all the other marines piled in. Within seconds the CRG guys threw a few punches and surrounded the Americans until it all calmed down. The US marines were then escorted off the premises and told never to return.

In early 2006, CRG reduced the number of personnel as a cost-cutting measure. The security industry was competing for fewer contracts in Iraq and consequently the clients were demanding savings as contracts were renewed. I was working as the assistant ops manager in addition to my duties as the comms manager. Most of our new CP operatives were no longer coming from an SAS background, instead we were recruiting from right across the British Army and further afield. These new arrivals were less experienced, but willing to work for less money. The next cost-cutting initiative was to recruit former Iraqi army paratrooper officers who could speak English. These guys were recruited in batches of six men and had to undergo a two-week training course. I admired these guys for what they were doing, but at the same time you couldn't totally trust them.

The FCO contract looking after British embassy staff as they travelled outside the Green Zone was top priority for GPS tracking equipment on all the vehicles. Fortunately the US government agreed to loan CRG the Movement Tracking System (MTS) as already used by the US military. The MTS is a communications platform designed to track assets on the battlefield with encrypted text messaging and a GPS tracking system. I took on the project to install the equipment into designated CRG vehicles.

I was still trying to fit in my work as a staff officer with the Army Reserve and usually managed to fit in a weekend at HQ 2 Signal Brigade every time I went home on leave. I even managed to attend annual camp for two weeks in August 2005. Things changed when it was announced by the MOD that Army Reserve personnel could no longer work as civilian contractors in war zones if their duties required them to carry a weapon. There was no way I was going to continue working in Iraq without a personal weapon, so I resigned from the Army Reserve.

Saddam Hussein's final days were lived out at a former palace in the Green Zone. Since his capture by US forces in December 2003 he had been kept prisoner at various locations, including a former palace at Camp Victory, close to the runway at BIAP. CRG were awarded a contract in January 2006 to train an Iraqi guard force to guard the perimeter of the designated palace inside the Green Zone. I was tasked to connect up a VHF radio to enable the CRG instructor to have communications with the CRG ops room a couple of kilometres away. On arrival with the installation team, I was introduced to the Iraqi interpreter who explained that the palace was being converted into a law court with holding cells in the basement. Then a bearded American in khaki uniform introduced himself. He explained that he was a US marshal whose team were ensuring that the building contractors built the prison cells and the courtroom to the highest specifications. He took me on a tour and informed me that the former palace was being brought up to standard before the transfer of Saddam Hussein and Ali Hassan al-Majid aka 'Chemical Ali'. This character was a first cousin of Saddam Hussein, notorious for his use of chemical weapons attacks against the Kurds. The trial of President Saddam by the Iraqi interim government began in August 2006 and he was convicted on 5 November 2006. Saddam was convicted of crimes against humanity and sentenced to death by hanging. The sentence was carried out on 30 December of that year.

I was shown Saddam Hussein's cell and it looked a typical American design with a concrete sleeping platform, a mattress and lots of stainless steel. The court room upstairs was still under construction. The US marshal told me that the CRG Iraqi guard force would man the perimeter while US military police would guard the palace interior. The US marshals would collect Saddam from his cell each day and escort him into the courtroom. The tour over, I checked the newly installed radio was working fine. As I still had some time to spare, I watched the CRG instructor assemble the trainee security guards into some semblance of order. The trainer was a fluent Arabic speaker and a former colleague of mine from D Squadron, 22 SAS. Then it was time to drive back to the CRG compound. Another job well done.

In February 2006 I went to London to be dined out at the Army Reserve centre at the Inns of Court. This was the home of 68 (Inns of Court and Yeomanry) Signal Squadron. The commander of 2 Signal Brigade, Brigadier Nigel, a former OC at 264 (SAS) Signal Squadron, thanked me for my six years' service with the Army Reserve. This, together with my previous regular army service, made a total of thirty-six years' service. I was presented with a nice gift, and then, after several glasses of port, my time in the army was over. The Honourable Society of Lincoln's Inn is one of the four Inns of Court to which barristers of England and Wales belong and where they are called to 'the Bar'.

In early 2006, I attended a CP Refresher Course in Hereford. The company hosting the course was owned by a former SAS colleague. It was a prerequisite to hold a CP qualification before attendance on the course. My SAS bodyguard course provided the route onto the course. The course instructor was a retired SAS officer who I first knew as a sergeant from when he was my patrol commander in the Belize jungle.

My CP qualification meant that CRG started using me to work as a CP operative. Because I was busy every day working as the comms manager and now also assistant ops manager I could only help out in the evenings. My CP tasking was normally the airport run along Route Irish which had started up again. At this time my driver and fellow CP operative was an Iraqi and former paratrooper officer who now worked for CRG. While waiting for clients at BIAP he would teach me Arabic to pass the time.

CRG informed us that the high wages were about to be drastically cut as contracts were renegotiated. I decided to jump ship before the cuts were implemented. I left Iraq in July 2006 and set myself up in the UK as a self-employed security consultant. My parting gift was the award of the Iraq Reconstruction Service Medal. The citation read, 'I am delighted to inform you that you have been awarded the Iraq Reconstruction Service Medal for your work in support of the British government while serving with Control Risks Group (CRG) in Iraq.'

Was the participation of the coalition forces in Iraq a worthwhile venture? It is hard for me to answer that, but while I believe the intentions were good, the overthrow of Saddam Hussein did little to improve things in the long-term. Nor should we forget the sacrifices on all sides, including the deaths of many members of the coalition forces and not least the private security contractors that worked alongside me in CRG and other PSCs.

I had sent a few speculative emails seeking assignments before I left Baghdad. Sure enough, I picked up one day's work to review the comms element of the new 'in-house' CP course being run by CRG in the UK. The second task was five days' work to write a business development plan for a data communications company owned by a former member of 264 (SAS) Signal Squadron.

Then a security company based in Hereford wanted me to audit an ongoing security contract. The task was to carry out a security review of a university in southern England. They were pleased with my efforts and gave me a second task. This was to carry out a discreet anti-fraud investigation to try to detect any irregularity or misappropriation of funds on behalf of one of their clients. I spent days trawling through all the paperwork, including invoices, expense claims and receipts. Finally I was able to prove that, while there was no evidence of fraud, there were distinct signs of poor accounting. I recommended a few changes in procedures and the problem went away.

I phoned my contacts at CRG to ascertain if there was any CP or security consultancy work abroad available for me. They offered me a couple of months work in Yemen. The requirement was for a security consultant to work on the CRG Schlumberger contract. Schlumberger is the world's largest provider of oilfield services and CRG had this lucrative security contract on a worldwide basis. I accepted the contract and flew out from London Heathrow via Dubai to Sana'a, the capital of Yemen. I was now part of a four-man team headed by Phil, ex-SBS. The other team members, Graham and Chris, were both ex-SAS.

When I landed at Sana'a International Airport, there were only two passenger aircraft on the ground, both operated by *Yemenia*, the national airline of Yemen. The civilian airport's single runway was shared by a military airbase flying Soviet SU-20 fighter jets. Phil met me at the airport and drove me to the Schlumberger compound. We were not armed under the terms of our contract, and instead had to rely on our drivers who as Yemeni nationals were allowed to carry an AK-47 rifle everywhere they went. I always insisted that my driver put his AK-47 with folding stock between us in our car so that I could grab it in an emergency.

I was soon set to work carrying out security audits of villas where expat employees of the client company were living with their families. At the time there was a programme of upgrading the security facilities in all living accommodation. This work included raising the heights of perimeter walls, anti-blast film, bars on windows, installation of safe rooms and CCTV. On the first weekend, I was invited by Phil to visit the British embassy club. We enjoyed a brunch and then stayed to drink a few beers. Within a few weekends, I knew most of the expat security consultants based in Sana'a.

My driver, Mohammed, drove me everywhere in the company car as I was not permitted to drive. I was accommodated in one of two 'bachelor' villas that were separated by a couple of miles. At the time, I was the only person living in the house, with an armed Yemeni security guard. He slept at night in the gatehouse to the compound. Whenever the guard came into the kitchen to make a cup of coffee, I used the opportunity to improve my Arabic. Mohammed would collect me in the morning and take me to the office. At midday he would drive me to the larger 'bachelor' villa for lunch as it had a kitchen with a Lebanese chef. Mohammed would drop me off at my villa after work and return an hour or so later with my dinner in an insulated box.

One day I was eating lunch when the chef came out to greet me. I hadn't seen him for a while. The chef's English was fairly basic, but he said to me something like, 'I think you be very fat now, because your dinner is too much!' After a few questions it transpired that at the end of the day Mohammed would collect from the kitchen two cooked chickens and a huge dish of rice, plus salad, bread and a basket of fruit. Then he would scrounge a much smaller meal for himself. This smaller meal is what I had been receiving. The larger meal was taken home by him and went to feed Mohammed's family, comprising two wives and thirteen children!

We always had a team member deployed on security audits of the desert oil rigs. When it was my turn, I took a *Yemenia* domestic flight to Riyan Airport at Mukalla near Shabwah oilfield. I was the only expat on board the crowded Boeing 737 and it was a relief to get off the plane on landing. My instructions were to remain in the passenger terminal until Chris came to collect me. After a couple of tense hours spent sitting there without a mobile phone signal, two Landcruisers roared up to the front of the terminal in a cloud of dust. I spotted Chris who I had met in Sana'a four weeks before. He explained that the road had suffered a landslide and this had delayed their arrival. Chris updated me as we drove to Shabwah oil camp. On arrival, Chris introduced me to the 'Camp Boss', the oil industry's equivalent of an army quartermaster. Formalities over, the Camp Boss allocated me a room in a prefabricated building and a can of mosquito insecticide, which was soon put to use!

The next morning, Chris took me through a security audit of a nearby oil rig and demonstrated how to compile and upload the audit report. We did some fitness training that afternoon. After dinner, I had a chat with an Ethiopian who was very friendly. He spoke perfect English and gave me an impromptu Arabic lesson.

The following morning, my escort team assembled. I now had two Yemeni drivers with Landcruisers and a sergeant and corporal from the Yemeni army, all armed with AK-47s. None of them spoke any English. They all started chewing *qat* as soon as we got out of sight of the oil camp. *Qat* is an amphetamine-like stimulant native to the Arabian Peninsula. *Qat* chewing is a social custom in the region, going back thousands of years. The plan was to audit eight oil rigs stretching across the Shabwah oilfield and then drive to Marib before continuing all the way to Sana'a. I audited two oil rigs each day and we slept at the second rig each night. Although I followed the routes on my hand-held GPS, Ali Al-Badr, my driver, navigated by the direction of the ripples in the hard sand we were driving on, never asking me which direction to travel in. The major defence to thwart a suicide truck bomb at these desert rigs was the sand berm that completely encircled each rig platform, offices and sleeping accommodation. The buildings consisted of shipping containers and prefabricated cabins.

Early on the morning of the fourth day we continued driving across the desert until we came to a graded track which eventually became an asphalt road. After several hours, we arrived at a police road block on the outskirts of Marib. The police were from the local tribe and were immediately obstructive to the two army soldiers in our vehicles. The soldiers were from the south of Yemen and there was obviously no love lost between them and the police. They all started shouting at the top of their voices and the police gestured that I should go into the nearby small building. I refused and slapped the back of my hand repeatedly on my papers. Eventually, with a lot of bad grace, we were waved through. Instead of getting the hell out of there, the idiots parked outside a small building that served as a mosque next to the police checkpoint and went inside to pray. I was left by myself locked in the vehicle in the sweltering heat. A beggar soon turned up. I opened the vehicle window just enough to give him a coin. As he grabbed my hand to kiss it, I noticed the unsightly skin infection on his arms. Soon he went to tell his mates of my *largesse* and within minutes there was a crowd of beggars surrounding the vehicle trying to get money. Luckily, the '*qat* team' came back from the mosque at that moment and we drove off.

Just as we were leaving Marib, we took a diversion on the outskirts of town that took us to a site of antiquity. The site had a fence around it and the gate was locked. With much blaring of horns to attract his attention, the caretaker finally came out and unlocked the gate. I was amazed when he informed me in English that this was the site of the Queen of Sheba's temple. I knew that Sheba was mentioned in the Bible and many scholars believe this to be the modern-day town of Marib. I had an uncanny feeling that I wasn't safe in this place, and after some persuasion from me the *qat team* finally agreed to leave after only fifteen minutes. One year later, eight Spanish tourists and two Yemeni drivers were killed nearby, when an Al-Qaeda suicide bomber rammed an explosive-laden car into a tourist bus which killed ten people and injured a further twelve. Sadly, there has been much Al-Qaeda related activity in this region over the years.

After we left the temple, it was a long drive back to Sana'a over a high mountain pass which gave a spectacular view of the plains below. Just over the other side of the pass was a village which reputedly sold the best *qat* in Yemen. That was an excuse for my team to buy large sacks of the stuff! Later, when we arrived back at Sana'a, we were met by another police roadblock on the outskirts of the city. This time the police wanted the *qat* team to unload their weapons and place the magazines out of sight. It is the right of every male Yemeni citizen to carry arms. Probably ninety per cent of the male population carry an AK-47.

Shit always happens in the Middle East on Fridays immediately after midday prayer. It is the time to start feuds or blow people up. It was also time for Mohammed to deliver our lunch and dinner in insulated boxes as he always took Friday afternoons off. Just after Graham and I started eating lunch, we heard the sound of automatic gunfire some distance away. Soon afterwards we received a phone call from one of the expats at the larger bachelor villa to inform us of shooting outside their compound. The Schlumberger security guard, a Yemeni who was armed with an AK-47, had immediately locked the main gate and quickly ushered all the expats down into the large 'safe room'. Our role, without weapons, was merely to monitor the situation, which was extremely frustrating. It transpired that two rival families had a land-ownership dispute relating to a building plot in the street. One family had brought in builders and started construction of a villa. The other family shot one of their rivals outside the nearby mosque and then they all turned up and started shooting at each other. One member of each family was wounded before the police negotiated a ceasefire. The next day we reported to the Schlumberger ops director and he thanked the CRG team for the training that we had given the security guard. A few days later there was a photo-opportunity for the company newsletter where the ops director presented the smiling security guard with an additional month's pay as a reward for his bravery and quick thinking.

Phil B, the CRG director responsible for the provision of worldwide security consultancy services to Schlumberger, decided to pay us a visit. Phil B was also ex-SAS and was only staying one night. That evening we were all invited out by the director of G4S who had just won an order from us to upgrade the physical security at the Schlumberger villas and apartments where the senior oil workers lived with their families. G4S was a big player in Sana'a and making lots of money on security contracts. Their boss was a retired South African army colonel. The CRG security team was invited to a barbecue at his villa. The villa had impressive security measures, together with an armed guard watching the comings and goings. We were treated to an authentic South African *braai*, with lots of succulent grilled meat. Afterwards we sat around the firepit drinking beer.

The next morning, Phil B broke the news that he had to reduce the team by one member. Then he turned to me and said sorry but you will have to go on the basis of 'last-in, first-out'. As a sweetener, Phil offered me a two-month contract in Nigeria starting in January, which I readily agreed to.

While in Yemen my Arabic had improved and I had managed to keep fit, but the job had been very frustrating as I spent most of my time stuck in a bachelor villa with only one trip out to the oilfields. I was dropped off at Sana'a International Airport at the end of my two months to catch a flight home.

In early January I flew out to Nigeria from London Heathrow. The flight was uneventful and soon I landed at Lagos International Airport. I cleared immigration, located my suitcase and then plunged into the crowd in the arrivals lounge. Fortunately I had been briefed to look for a man holding a sign with the word 'Schlumberger' written on it. Finally I spotted the 'Schlumberger' sign and struggled through the crowd to reach the agent.

We stayed close together as we were jostled out to the car park. There was a driver in the minibus, which was locked as soon as I climbed aboard. The agent informed me the driver would take me to the Schlumberger compound, and to keep the door locked and window up. This all demonstrated good security procedures and I was happy with my reception, as it would have been a nightmare trying to get myself safely across the city. Lagos is the largest city in Africa with one of the busiest ports. We passed several shanty towns, some of the shacks built on stilts over salt lagoons. Eventually we reached an upmarket area of the city with large houses inside high walled compounds. The barrier was raised on arrival and we drove straight inside the Schlumberger compound. I reported to the gatehouse and was allocated a room for the night. The next morning I met several other workers who were travelling with me to Port Harcourt in the Niger Delta.

We boarded a bus parked on the street. There were two police Land Rovers with armed policemen waiting to escort us. We drove for several hours along the main road before arriving at a filling station on the outskirts of the large town of Warri. We were able to use the restroom there while the policemen guarded us with their pump-action shotguns. We continued the journey until we were delayed at a police roadblock and advised there was a shooting in progress ahead where some 'bandits' had attempted to hijack a car. After a tense wait, we drove on and finally arrived safely at Port Harcourt.

I was surprised when we drove into the Schlumberger compound to see landscaped gardens and an outdoor swimming pool. After reporting in, a Nigerian employee escorted me to the CRG villa where I met up with the security team. Later on, I was shown around the compound and my duties were explained to me. The compound was supposed to be for senior management who had been living there with their wives and families. However, due to the ongoing security situation, most of the wives and all of the children had been evacuated.

The next day, I visited the company medical clinic, where a nurse gave me a booster vaccination for yellow fever. After that it was a short walk to visit the ops room, manned by two Nigerian watchkeepers, who maintained radio comms with all company vehicles. Then I was driven to the main office one mile away to meet the Nigerian ops director who controlled the security budget. After that I was taken to two 'bachelor' compounds, a few miles distant, the larger of which also had an outdoor swimming pool, gym, dining room and bar.

My first task was to carry out a security audit on the larger 'bachelor' compound. It was all fairly straightforward stuff, returning later that evening in darkness to count how many of the perimeter security lights required replacement bulbs. The list quickly grew as I spotted more shortfalls in the physical security measures.

One day I was a passenger with my driver in a company car. Only the CRG security team were allowed out without a police escort. I pulled my baseball cap down over my face and slunk down in my seat to avoid being seen. We were not allowed weapons so there was certainly a risk involved, but the journey was short. As we drove past the police station, I noticed three bodies laid out side by side in front of the building. I asked the driver why and he told me that bodies were always left on display whenever bandits were shot by the police. The families were only allowed to take the bodies away after three days, by which time the cadavers were bloated and covered in flies.

I met Fred Marafono for the last time in February 2007. Fred and I had shared a bottle of whisky at the end of the Falklands War and he was well known to everyone who had served in the SAS. He had arrived a couple of weeks after me to join the CRG team at Port Harcourt. One day, we were teaching a group of Nigerian drivers how to change a wheel. When they still hadn't got the wheel off after ten minutes Fred called a halt. Telling them to stand back Fred showed them what to do. He jacked up the heavy 4x4 vehicle and changed the wheel by himself in about three minutes. Not bad for a 66-year-old! I loved chatting to Fred, and over a glass of whisky he told me that he was born in 1940 on the tiny island of Rotuma, north of Fiji. He went on to say he was 21 when he joined the British Army and initially served in the Light Infantry. He then passed Selection before serving twenty-one years with the regiment. Kauaata 'Fred' Marafono was awarded an MBE in the New Year's Honours List of 1983. He went on to work for David Stirling, the founder of the SAS, in his private security company. Later Fred participated in Sierra Leone's war, often known as the 'Blood Diamond War'. He initially worked for Executive Outcomes in Sierra Leone, but stayed on when that company left the country. Fred died aged 72 in March 2013.

After four weeks I was placed in charge of security at the larger 'bachelor' compound. I tried my best to raise standards and get the Nigerian guard force on side. At first all went well until there was a kidnapping down in the port area when an immediate lockdown was put in place. Early one morning, I carried out a spot check. I set my alarm, and once awake walked quickly to the guard house. When I enquired where the Nigerian guard commander was, the guards averted their eyes. I tracked him down in the TV lounge where he had locked himself in. He had stripped down to his underpants and was fast asleep on a sofa. I told him to dress and then gave him a severe reprimand. Unfortunately for him, he had been caught sleeping on duty three months earlier, so after consulting with the team leader I sacked him.

A few days later I received a phone call from the former guard commander asking me to reinstate him. When I told him that it was outside my control, he threatened to have me kidnapped if he wasn't given his old job back within one week. He didn't know that I was due to leave the country within forty-eight hours, so his threat didn't concern me.

After two days, I flew to Lagos on a charter flight as road movement had become too dangerous. After a few hours wait, I picked up my connecting flight at Lagos Airport. Incidentally, four Schlumberger employees were kidnapped from the large compound in June, four months after I departed. The gunmen entered the compound dressed in police uniforms. Attacks on oil facilities and kidnappings continued throughout 2007, forcing thousands of foreign workers to flee, and reducing oil output by one third.

The CEO of the Hereford security company asked me to take on a couple of tasks. The first was a security audit of Didcot Power Station, which brought in a week's wages. The second task required me to fly to Riyadh, the capital of Saudi Arabia. I was to assist in writing a tender for a major upgrade of the security facilities at the Ministry of Interior. A car packed with explosives had detonated just outside the building in December 2004. Two years later, the Saudis issued a tender for a major security upgrade.

Months earlier, I had submitted a speculative CV to EADS Airbus. Two weeks before flying out to Riyadh, I received a phone call from the HR manager. She enquired if I wished to be interviewed for the ops manager's role with GPT Special Project Management Ltd (GPT), an EADS Airbus subsidiary based in Riyadh. I confirmed my interest and was invited for interview in London. I mentioned at the interview that I was flying out to Riyadh the following week, so it was arranged for me to meet up with Nigel, the GPT ops director, while in country.

I phoned Nigel from my hotel and we met up later that day. Nigel and I already knew each other from our time in Germany. After retirement from Royal Signals as a lieutenant colonel, he now worked for GPT. Nigel explained that GPT was a subsidiary of Paradigm, in turn an

EADS Airbus company, and Nigel was the senior British employee in country. Nigel then came straight to the point and offered me the job with a generous salary. I accepted with a starting date one month later. Nigel collected me at the hotel when my task was complete and drove me to the airport. We sat in the airport car park while I read and signed the contract.

Four weeks later I arrived in Riyadh. GPT's sole customer was the Saudi Arabian National Guard (SANG). The SANG had over 220,000 troops with a dual role of protecting the House of Saud and guarding strategic facilities, including Mecca. The SANG is kept apart from the army, so as to guard against a military coup. We interfaced through the Saudi Arabian National Guard Communications (SANGCOM) project team from the British Army, led by a Royal Signals brigadier. The SANGCOM project supplied the SANG with military communications equipment, training and maintenance, and the contract was reputedly worth two billion pounds (£2bn). SANGCOM had a large team of military personnel and UK civil servants and Saudi Arabia reimbursed costs. The process involved SANGCOM placing orders with the UK prime contractor, GPT, on behalf of SANG.

I was accommodated in an expat compound with a fully-furnished apartment. The extensive compound was surrounded by high walls and had its own guard force. It also boasted two swimming pools and a nine-hole golf course.

I worked at the SANG garrison on the outskirts of Riyadh. To assist me in my role as ops manager, I had three regional support managers covering Western Province (Jeddah), Central Province (Riyadh) and Eastern Province (Dammam). The job was demanding and I was on call 24/7.

Nigel sent for me after twelve months. He wanted me to take a sideways move into the role of Business Development Manager. The job combined security, health & safety (H&S) and quality assurance (QA). I declared my interest, but explained I didn't hold a QA qualification. That was soon solved by sending me on a QA lead auditor's course. The course enabled me to conduct quality audits on our third-party suppliers to ISO-9000 standards while using a quality management system database.

I was now working in the main GPT office in Faisaliyah Tower, a well-known landmark in the city's business district. In my new role, I visited every location to provide QA training before the next external audit. The visits included trips to Ar-Ar and Najran. Ar-Ar is a town in north-eastern Saudi Arabia close to the Iraq border. On arrival, I was met by two SANG military policemen who provided me with an armed escort. I flew out that evening as it was considered too risky to let me stay overnight. When I told the military policemen that I had lived in Iraq for over two years they looked at me in amazement. I also flew to Najran on the Yemeni border. Security was tight as there had been a shootout with smugglers a few nights earlier as they tried to bring illegal immigrants across the border.

The role of company security manager was challenging, in particular keeping all the expats safe while trying not to interfere with their ability to travel freely around the kingdom. A few years earlier, a British GPT employee had been shot dead outside a Riyadh supermarket. The assassination was believed to be the work of 'Al-Qaeda in the Arabian Peninsula', a militant Islamist organization formerly active in Saudi Arabia and nowadays largely operating from Yemen.

Once a month I would make the four-hour drive to Dammam to stay overnight with the GPT regional support manager (eastern province). The next morning, we would drive over the causeway into Bahrain. We always stayed in Juffair, a suburb of the capital Manama, where there are many hotels and a few shopping malls. It is also the location of the Naval Support Activity Bahrain, the base for the US Fifth Fleet and their coalition partners. We normally stayed in one of the larger hotels, most of which had nightclubs with live music and dancing. A typical weekend in Bahrain would see us have a few drinks in a bar before going to one of the nightclubs catering for expats and sailors. In one nightclub, a couple of pretty girls dressed in cowgirl outfits would circle the drunks trying to get them to buy shots, and they were never short of takers. The next morning, we would meet up for a late breakfast and discreetly ask the waiter to bring us a cooked breakfast, including pork sausages and bacon. Soon it was time to check out of the hotel and begin the long drive back to Riyadh.

I was now working in Faisaliyah Tower with three staff. Together we comprised the 'QA section'. My assistants were two Pakistani citizens and a Filipino who was our QA field inspector. I had a busy workload, including QA audits on new construction projects. I had to quickly acquire specific in-depth knowledge of subjects such as quantity surveying, even witnessing the pouring of ready-mixed concrete and signing off to confirm the load met quality standards. During my tenure I rewrote all the 'codes of practice', for example handling asbestos, to the latest UK and Saudi standards. I also arranged for first-aid training and revised the security procedures. I really enjoyed the job, but nothing lasts forever, and at the start of 2010 I began to look for work outside Saudi Arabia.

As the GPT security manager, I shared security information with two other EADS subsidiary companies operating in Saudi Arabia. Once a month, all three security managers would meet for dinner at a downtown restaurant to update each other. One month they brought along the British CEO for EADS Defence & Security. The CEO mentioned that he was transferring to Abu Dhabi for a new joint-venture between EADS Defence & Security and an Emirati company. I resigned a month later and gave him a call to enquire about a possible vacancy. He asked me to visit him in Abu Dhabi for an interview, where I was offered the position of Head of Site Operations. They held the position open for me while I served my notice period with GPT.

As head of site operations, I would be responsible for security, information assurance, health & safety, and facility management. While the CEO was from EADS Defence & Security, the managing director was an Emirati. He was on leave when I arrived and, on his return, claimed he hadn't been aware that security would be part of my remit. I was therefore informed that my services were no longer required as security must be entrusted to an Emirati citizen. I eventually spent three weeks in country, writing security procedures to assist whoever was going to be appointed. The Emiratis failed to honour the contract they signed with me, although EADS eventually compensated me for my work. I arrived home to a miserable situation with my wife and quickly realized that our days as a married couple were numbered. Every day started and ended with an argument.

The following month, I received a phone call from a former colleague from Chronos Technology. Greg was now the managing director of a rival telecoms system integrator. He wanted to know if I was interested in a vacancy with their subsidiary company located in Dubai. I confirmed my interest and was invited to a job interview. On my arrival, Greg introduced me to Craig, the owner of the Dubai company. Craig questioned my commercial background to confirm if I knew how to manage a company. I obviously satisfied him with my responses as I was offered the post of general manager, and I flew out to Dubai two weeks later.

I was met at Dubai International Airport by the outgoing general manager. Within a few days we started to get into the detail. I was shocked to discover there was very little money in the bank, with several suppliers chasing overdue payments. Craig phoned me that evening and I expressed my grave concerns that the company would go under if it wasn't given an immediate injection of cash. This obviously grabbed Craig's attention and he flew into Dubai a couple of days later to check for himself. To my relief, he immediately pumped in 100,000 US dollars which at least ensured that the most pressing debts would be paid and the workforce would receive their wages.

During the following week, I visited all our clients. Some of them owed us considerable sums of money, but they complained about everything and I was given 'snag lists' to resolve before they would consider paying us. I took this on personally and ensured all the snag lists were cleared at the earliest opportunity, but still the money only trickled in. I had my first leave back in the UK and kept busy. Every day I would keep in touch with the office, hardly speaking to my wife before returning to Dubai. We had fallen out of love and soon afterwards decided to get divorced as we no longer had anything in common.

I continued to give the company my best efforts, picking up quite a few new orders, but profit margins were tight. Some of our employees were relatively inexperienced, meaning the snag lists grew longer. It was a very frustrating time for me, but I stuck it out for a year. I had spent a lot of my time trying to break into the lucrative oil and enterprise sectors, but unfortunately with very limited success despite a great deal of interest from potential clients. Try as I might the deals couldn't be closed. It seemed to me that there was a cartel of companies sharing this business and the door was kept firmly closed to newcomers.

Several months later, I was sitting in the nearby mall drinking coffee. At the next table was a beautiful Filipina girl muttering to herself. I asked her if she was alright and she replied that she couldn't speak much English. Eventually I understood that she was worried about her CV. We sat together while I studied her CV. She had been working in the Philippines as a sales supervisor in a fashion boutique. I could see that there needed to be a major revamp of the CV and suggested she let me correct it and I would meet her the next day. Irene was waiting the following day and I showed her the changes that I had made. She thanked me and I asked her if she would let me buy her dinner. We have now been happily married for almost ten years.

Before leaving Dubai, my friend Faisal from our CRG days in Baghdad contacted me. He had resigned from CRG and was working in Dubai. We agreed to meet up to watch a movie. It was good to see Faisal, who was dressed in jeans and a polo shirt with a large unruly beard. We chatted about Baghdad and our experiences there. He reminded me of the day a Humvee military vehicle drove up behind him as he was walking in the Green Zone. As the Humvee drove over a speed bump, the machine gunner negligently fired a burst of heavy-calibre bullets right in front of Faisal, tearing up the concrete paving slabs. Faisal unsurprisingly shit himself! How we laughed as he retold the story.

After the movie we had a coffee. I asked Faisal if he wanted to meet up later in the week for a few beers, but Faisal declined explaining to me that he was now married and his father-in-law was an *imam* (Muslim clergyman). Faisal had changed his ways and was clearly in love. I walked him back to his car and he asked me to wait while he went into the nearby public toilets and changed into traditional Muslim attire. That was the last time I saw Faisal, standing there in his *thobe*. We had shared a life-changing experience in Iraq, but circumstances meant we could not easily continue as friends. Farewell, Faisal my friend. *'Fee Amaanillah'* (May Allah Protect You).

Irene and I flew to the Philippines at the end of 2011 to spend Christmas with her family. Eight hours later, on landing at NAIA Airport in Manila, we were met by two of Irene's brothers who had travelled from their province to escort us home on a long-distance bus ride. We eventually arrived at Irene's *barangay* (community) in the small town of San Fabian.

Irene's father and her 4-year-old daughter Pauline both gave me a big smile on our arrival. Irene's father was able to speak a little English, but the first words that I spoke to him were in Tagalog as I wanted to show him some respect. Irene was an unmarried mother – the child's father had not accepted his responsibilities and 'done a runner'. The next day Irene and I told her father that we were engaged and she showed everyone her engagement ring. A few days after our arrival, it was Pauline's birthday and we held a karaoke party in the garden. Karaoke is the number one leisure pursuit in the Philippines and usually involves much drinking to accompany the singing. Over the years I have added a few songs in Tagalog to my repertoire! Pauline soon saw me as the father figure in her life and we quickly bonded as a family.

I spent hours every day learning Tagalog. It was quite a difficult language for me to learn, but fortunately many loanwords are from Spanish so I already had quite an extensive vocabulary. It was interesting to discover that many other loanwords originated from English, Chinese, Arabic and Malay.

I flew back to the UK for a short visit in early 2012, to collect a copy of the divorce decree from my solicitor and settle the bill. Almost as soon as I returned to the Philippines, a former colleague now working in Bahrain contacted me to see if I was interested in working as an industrial security project manager. This entailed living in Bahrain but working several days each week in Saudi Arabia. After discussing this with Irene, I accepted and started work within days.

My new job in Bahrain was at RMI (Middle East). It was necessary for me to understand the rules and regulations contained in the directives of the Saudi High Commission for Industrial Security (HCIS). The law in Saudi Arabia required all industrial projects to be approved by HCIS before an operating licence could be granted. These HCIS projects relate to the construction and operation of complex industrial facilities including oil refineries, mines, metal rolling mills, power stations and desalination plants. My job was to work with the system designers to evaluate and recommend changes to the detailed design. I had to incorporate the most recent technological solutions, systems and methodology appropriate to the need and compatible with existing and future systems.

My primary role as a project manager was to ensure compliance for integrated security systems. I phoned Irene every day, but it soon dawned on me that the only way we could be together was to marry, then she could accompany me to Bahrain. To make this happen would require me to live for several months in the Philippines to establish residency and then apply for a marriage licence. Love, as always, won the day. To solve my dilemma, I was forced to resign from RMI after three months. I left on good terms and RMI said they would welcome me back.

Once I was back in the Philippines, Irene applied for a 'Certificate of No Marriage Record' from the Philippines National Statistics Office. Then it was my turn to apply for a Certificate of No Impediment (to marriage) from the British embassy. Once this was accomplished, we visited the town hall in San Fabian to book a civil wedding. Irene and I agreed a budget and she told me to leave the wedding planning to her, because prices would rise dramatically if I was to show my face.

As the big day approached, a wedding marquee was erected in our garden, with space for fifty guests inside and a further fifty guests sat outside under the stars. We also had a 'sound system' and a makeshift dance floor. At the other end of the house, three whole pigs and twenty chickens were to be roasted over a charcoal pit. This was accompanied by huge mounds of stir-fried noodles.

On our wedding day, I travelled with Irene's family in a *jeepney*, a sort of bus, to the mayor's official residence. Irene, looking beautiful as always, arrived later in the wedding car. The Mayor of San Fabian and her husband jointly conducted the wedding. They welcomed everyone in the Pangasinan language and then switched to Tagalog and finally to flawless English. The ceremony was conducted in all three languages in a seamless manner. Irene's daughter, Pauline, was a flower girl and looked as pretty as a picture. We held a wedding lunch in a hotel, before returning for our reception in the wedding marquee. We handed out takeaway meals to over 150 neighbours at the garden gate, before one hundred guests sat down to eat. The dancing continued long into the night. The next morning, Irene and I went to Clark Airport for our honeymoon flight to Boracay.

On return to San Fabian, we applied for a UK visitor visa for Irene and spent four weeks visiting my family. During our visit, I took Irene to watch her first Tranmere Rovers game. At the time, Tranmere was top of the table. It wasn't to last however, as we lost against MK Dons 0–1 in front of a crowd of over 10,000. Injuries to key players led to a dramatic downturn in form. Irene took a while to understand the rules of football, but soon she was part of the Super White Army.

The cost of living in the Philippines was much cheaper than the UK, but even so we had to rely on my savings. I got in touch with RMI and they had a vacancy with an immediate start. They agreed that Irene could follow once she had a Bahrain spouse visa.

On arrival in Bahrain, my first project was to supervise the security aspects of an oil refinery being built in Jubail which was in the final stages of construction. When I reported for duty, the Saudi project manager I was to work alongside allocated me an office and arranged sleeping accommodation in the construction camp. After that he introduced me to the security manager who briefed me on the project scope. I was required to work two days a week in the Bahrain office and three days at the refinery.

Irene joined me after five weeks. We decided to leave Pauline behind to continue her education. We moved into an apartment at Juffair near to all the bars and restaurants. Irene really enjoyed eating out and going to nightclubs to listen to live music. We also managed two visits to the Philippines to celebrate Pauline's fifth and sixth birthdays.

The refinery started to refine oil into diesel fuel six months after my arrival. Then it was time for me to take on a similar project at an oil refinery in Yanbu in the western province. The work at Yanbu required me to take a flight from Bahrain to Jeddah. Then I would drive a rental car the four-hour journey to Yanbu.

In January 2015, I was informed that my work visa would not be renewed by RMI as I was now over 60 years old. Before we left Bahrain, Irene took and passed the International English Language Testing System exam at the British Council office.

Once back in the Philippines, we came to a joint decision to settle in the UK. This entailed applying for UK settlement visas for Irene and Pauline. The visa application, including collation of supporting documentation, took two months to complete.

Three months later, a courier delivered a package containing a covering letter and passports with the UK settlement visas affixed. Within two weeks we flew to the UK. The huge changes in downtown Birkenhead prompted me to buy a house out of town. A week later we made an offer on a small house that was accepted. While waiting to move in, we stayed with my brother Tom and his wife who looked after us as only family can. We had bought a house close to a local primary school so Pauline was enrolled there. The next priority was to start looking for work.

I assumed that I would be able to get a security-related job without any difficulty. How wrong I was! I finally found work as a food processing operative in a poultry factory. There were approximately 3,000 employees split into two shifts. My job was to trim excess fat from chicken breasts, at the rate of one every five seconds. The repetitive work was mind-numbing. Over ninety per cent of the workforce were Eastern Europeans and it was cold and noisy working on the production line. After five weeks I asked for a day off work to attend the funeral of a former army colleague. The Czech supervisor was condescending and said he would consider my request. I thought about the situation that evening and studied my contract. Realizing that I only needed to give seven-days' notice and the funeral was in nine-days' time, I resigned the next day.

Soon after the funeral, I was contacted by a friend of mine who had worked with me in Saudi Arabia. Ed was by now retired and living in Liverpool. We met for lunch and Ed explained that he had a terminal illness with only months to live. Ed asked if I would cut his lawn every week as he could no longer manage any physical exertion. I agreed to this and soon I was taking on the role of carer two days each week. Ed greatly appreciated my efforts and I felt honoured to help a friend in need.

I was adjusting to semi-retirement in the UK and becoming used to the idea that I would never get another permanent job. Then Ed died suddenly in July 2016. I met Ed's sister at his funeral and she informed me that Ed had bequeathed a sizeable cash sum to Irene and me. Thanks Ed, we shall miss you.

My next job was casual work as a match-day steward at Prenton Park, the home of Tranmere Rovers. Whenever I am inside the stadium, I think how my life has gone full-circle and here I am back in Birkenhead. I like the work as I can watch the team at close quarters. I have had a full and exciting life, but for me, nothing can beat the atmosphere at Prenton Park when Tranmere are winning and the crowd are behind the team shouting 'Super White Army!'

Epilogue

A History Lesson

Most books by former members of 22 SAS have been written by long-standing and well-known characters. My book is different. It describes the rite of passage of someone who from an early age possessed that certain something to have what it takes to become an SAS trooper. I was a very small cog in the fighting machine that is the Special Air Service. I have also tried to give you an insight to the specialized world of signalling from the age of the Morse key right up to satellite technology. Despite my signals training, I was never an out-and-out specialist, far from it. In the words of the United States Marine Corps, I have learnt how to adapt, improvise and overcome whatever has been thrown my way throughout life. I have been many things: an SAS trooper, a Royal Signals officer, a security consultant, a close protection operative and even a matchday steward at Tranmere Rovers Football Club!

Much has changed in the SAS since my day, but investing time and resources on the right man is still the reason why 22 SAS is the best SF unit in the world. I was privileged to visit Hereford in July 2016 for the 75th anniversary of the creation of the SAS. I met with numerous retired officers and soldiers that I had served with and marvelled at all the technological advances in equipment. The role of the SAS has expanded and this has meant more specialized manpower is required. This has required the creation of more SF and support units to keep the SAS operating at maximum efficiency.

Nowadays, UKSF is a tri-service organization. In addition to 22 SAS, there is the Special Reconnaissance Regiment (SRR) and also the Special Forces Support Group (SFSG).

Similarly, 264 (SAS) Signal Squadron has been absorbed into 18 (UKSF) Signal Regiment. The Signals Regiment comprises the SBS Signal Squadron, 264 (SAS) Signal Squadron, 267 (SRR) Signal Squadron, 268 (SFSG) Signal Squadron and 63 (SAS) Signal Squadron (Reserves). 63 Squadron supports the SAS Reserves, i.e., 21 SAS and 23 SAS.

One of my aims in writing this book is to pay tribute to the SAS trooper. The trooper is the bedrock of the SAS, and many go on to do good things in the defence and security of our nation.

There was another reason for writing this book and that was to tell my personal story, a story which I hope will provide you with an insight into a boy brought up on the backstreets of Birkenhead who went on to achieve much. My upbringing gave me an opportunity to see both sides of the religious divide between Catholics and Protestants. My SAS service also provided me with an opportunity to witness the futile inter-sectarian violence in Northern Ireland and later in the Middle East, both of which gave rise to a mutually destructive world of terrorism.

I have met some amazing characters along the way, including Roy Fonseka from the Seychelles. When I was writing this book, Roy told me about what happened after the skirmish behind enemy lines near Port Howard which cost the life of Captain John Hamilton. Roy told me that the sergeant major of 601 Commando Company, Sergeant Major (*Suboficial Mayor*) Francisco Altaminaro, had treated him well for the few days that he was held in captivity. Francisco had recently contacted Roy and explained that he was coming to the Seychelles on a diving expedition. Roy met up with Francisco on his arrival in the Seychelles and invited him to their Remembrance Parade. Roy said a few words at the remembrance ceremony and presented his former adversary with an SAS beret in a frame and an inscription that read 'From one warrior to another. Remembering Captain John Hamilton. Killed in Action, Port Howard, Falklands.' The presentation was screened on the local TV news and the news clip shows the pair of them embracing after Roy handed over the SAS beret. They then stood shoulder to shoulder for one minute's silence to remember fallen comrades.

When discussing this book with Mark Palios, we reminisced over some of our happy memories of Tranmere Rovers. Mark described the 2018 National League play-off final at Wembley when Tranmere faced Boreham Wood. Tranmere have a reputation for always doing things the hard way and this was to be no different. Liam Ridehalgh was sent off in the first minute leaving Tranmere only ten men to battle on for the remainder of the game. Tranmere took the lead when Andy Cook headed the first goal after six minutes, only for Boreham Wood to equalize just before half-time in the eighth minute of extra time! To add to Tranmere's worries, they had used all their substitutes through injury by this time. After 60 minutes Boreham Wood appeared to be in the ascendancy, but the Tranmere fans got behind their team and this gave them the uplift they needed to persevere. At this time, Mark turned to his wife Nicola and told her that the game was there to be had and Tranmere would ultimately win. Tranmere gamely dug in and grabbed the winner after 80 minutes when James Norwood headed home a cross from Connor Jennings. The win gave Tranmere a return to the English Football League after an absence of three years. Mark told me that this game, above all others before or since, gave him a tremendous satisfaction and he put Tranmere's success down to team bonding and a positive mental attitude that made the team strive for victory come what may.

My own circumstances have changed greatly over the years, but I still wake up every morning happy and contented. I thank God and good luck to having by my side, Irene, my beautiful wife, and of course my family would not be complete without the ever-smiling face of Pauline, our daughter. I have survived a challenging career and made some good friends along the way. As a former SAS trooper, I can truly say that I have 'beat the clock'.

The names of those members of the Regular SAS who have died on duty are inscribed on the regimental clock tower at Stirling Lines. Inscribed on the base of the clock is a verse from *The Golden Road to Samarkand* by James Elroy Flecker:

> *We are the Pilgrims, master; we shall go*
> *Always a little further: it may be*
> *Beyond that last blue mountain barred with snow,*
> *Across that angry or that glimmering sea…*

Glossary

1 BR CORPS	1st British Corps
22 SAS	22 Special Air Service Regiment
AAC	Army Apprentice College
AAC	Army Air Corps
ACE	Army Certificate of Education
ACF	Army Cadet Force
AFSOUTH	Armed Forces South (HQ AFSOUTH, Naples, Italy)
AFV	Armoured Fighting Vehicle
ARRC	ACE (Allied Command Europe) Rapid Reaction Corps
BAOR	British Army of the Rhine
BBC	British Broadcasting Corporation
BEM	British Empire Medal
BFG	British Forces Germany
BIAP	Baghdad International Airport
CAP	Combat Air Patrol
CASEVAC	Casualty evacuation
CEO	Chief Executive Officer
CGS	Chief of the General Staff
CIMIC	Civil Military Cooperation
CO	Commanding Officer
COBRA	Cabinet Office Briefing Room
Commcen	Communications Centre
CP	Close Protection
CPA	Coalition Provisional Authority
CQB	Close Quarter Battle
CRG	Control Risks Group
CRW	Counter-Revolutionary Warfare
CTP	Career Transition Partnership
CTR	Close Target Recce
DAS	*Departmento Administrativo de Seguridad* – Administrative Department of Security (Colombia)
D-Day	'D-Day' is the day when an attack or landing is scheduled to begin
DFID	Department for International Development
DIY	Do It Yourself
DSO	Distinguished Service Order

DS	Directing Staff
DZ	Drop Zone
ECM	Electronic Countermeasures
EPAW	Express Prior Authority in Writing
ERV	Emergency Rendezvous
FCO	Foreign & Commonwealth Office
FIDF	Falkland Islands Defence Force
FN	FN Rifle (from *Fabrique Nationale* – Belgian Arms Manufacturer)
FOB	Forward Operating Base
GCE	General Certificate of Education 'O' (Ordinary) level and 'A' (Advanced) level
GCSE	General Certificate of Secondary Education
GIGN	*Groupe d'intervention de la Gendarmerie Nationale* – French National Gendarmerie counter-terrorist unit
GPMG	General Purpose Machine Gun
GPS	Global Positioning System
HAZMAT	Hazardous Materials
HCIS	High Commission for Industrial Security (Saudi Arabia)
HE	High Explosive
HF	High Frequency (3–30 MHz)
HLS	Helicopter Landing Site
HMS	Her Majesty's Ship
HMY	Her Majesty's Yacht
HND	Higher National Diploma
HQ	Headquarters
HRH	His/Her Royal Highness
IA	Immediate Action (Plan)
IED	Improvised Explosive Device
IRA	Irish Republican Army – Irish terrorist organization (see also PIRA)
JCUFI	Joint Communications Unit Falkland Islands
JDF	Jamaican Defence Force
JHQ	Joint Headquarters
KIA	Killed in Action
kph	Kilometres Per Hour
LAN	Local Area Network
LAW	Light Anti-armour Weapon
Lee-Enfield	British Army .303-inch calibre bolt action rifle
LO	Liaison Officer
LUP	Lying Up Position
MAN	Major Access Node
MBA	Master of Business Administration
MC	Military Cross

MCO	Main Communications Office
MEDEVAC	Medical Evacuation
MID	Mentioned in Despatches
MM	Military Medal
MND	Multi-National Division
MO	Medical Officer
MOD	Ministry of Defence
MTS	Movement Tracking System – US military satellite-based asset tracking and communications system
NAAFI	Navy, Army and Air Force Institute
NAS	Naval Air Squadron
NCO	Non-Commissioned Officer
NCRS	National Communications Radio System
NHS	National Health Service
NI	Northern Ireland
NVG	Night Vision Goggles
OC	Officer Commanding
OP	Observation Post
OTP	One-Time Pad
PE	Plastic Explosive
PIRA	Provisional Irish Republican Army
PoW	Prisoner-of-War
Pronto	Appointment title – senior signaller
PTSD	Post-Traumatic Stress Disorder
QA	Quality Assurance
QGM	Queen's Gallantry Medal
QM	Quartermaster
QMSI	Quarter Master Sergeant Instructor
R&R	Rest and Relaxation
RAF	Royal Air Force
RAS	Resupply at Sea
RCIED	Radio-Controlled Improvised Explosive Device
RCT	Royal Corps of Transport – now part of the Royal Logistic Corps
REME	Royal Electrical and Mechanical Engineers
RFA	Royal Fleet Auxiliary
RHQ	Regimental Headquarters
RIB	Rigid Inflatable Boat
RMP	Royal Military Police
ROE	Rules of Engagement
RSM	The senior warrant officer in an army regiment or battalion
RSSSC	Royal Signals Staff Sergeants Course
RTU	Returned to Unit
RUC	Royal Ulster Constabulary

RV	Rendezvous
SANG	Saudi Arabian National Guard
SANGCOM	Saudi Arabian National Guard Communications – UK MOD project team
RN	Royal Navy
RWW	Revolutionary Warfare Wing
SAS	Special Air Service
SASR	Special Air Service Regiment – Australia
SBS	Special Boat Service
SEAL	US Navy SEAL (Sea, Air and Land) – US Navy Special Forces
SF	Special Forces
SFSG	Special Forces Support Group
SHQ	Squadron Headquarters
SIGINT	Signals Intelligence
SIM-32	Sixty-four paratroopers jumping simultaneously with thirty-two deploying from each side-door of a C130
SITREP	Situation Report
SLR	Self-Loading Rifle
SMG	Sub-Machine Gun
SO	Staff Officer – class 1 (Lt Col), class 2 (Maj), class 3 (Capt)
SOinC	Signals-Officer-in-Chief
SOP	Standard Operating Procedure
SP team	Special Projects – SAS (counter-terrorist) team
SQMS	Squadron Quartermaster Sergeant
SRR	Special Reconnaissance Regiment
SSM	Squadron Sergeant Major
STUFT	Ships Taken Up from Trade
SUV	Sport Utility Vehicle
TA	Territorial Army – now the Army Reserve.
TAB	Tactical Advance to Battle
TACBE	Tactical Beacon Equipment
TAC HQ	Tactical Headquarters
Tacsat	Tactical Satellite
TL (Comms)	Team Leader (Communications)
TOT	Technical Officer Telecommunications
TQ	Tactical Questioning
TTP	Tactics, Techniques and Procedures
UKSF	United Kingdom Special Forces
UN	United Nations
UNESCO	United Nations Educational, Scientific and Cultural Organization
UNFICYP	United Nations Forces in Cyprus
USAF	United States Air Force

USMC	United States Marine Corps
VERTREP	Vertical Replenishment (of ships by helicopter)
VSAT	Very Small Aperture Terminal – broadband satellite equipment
VVIP	Very, Very Important Person
WO	Warrant Officer (WO1 = First Class, WO2 = Second Class)
WPM	Words Per Minute
YofS	Yeoman of Signals